THANKS TO GOD
AND THE REVOLUTION

Thanks to God
and the Revolution

THE ORAL HISTORY OF
A NICARAGUAN FAMILY

DIANNE WALTA HART

The University of Wisconsin Press

The University of Wisconsin Press
114 North Murray Street
Madison, Wisconsin 53715

3 Henrietta Street
London WC2E 8LU, England

5   4   3   2   1

Printed in the United States of America

Library of Congress Cataloging-in-Publication Data
Hart, Dianne Walta, 1939–
Thanks to God and the Revolution: the oral history of a
Nicaraguan family/Dianne Walta Hart.
336 pp.   cm.
Includes bibliographical references
1. Nicaragua—History—Revolution, 1979—Personal narratives.
2. Nicaragua—History—1979– 3. Nicaragua—History—1937–1979.
4. Estelí (Nicaragua)—Biography. 5. Estelí (Nicaragua)—Social
conditions. 6. Estelí (Nicaragua)—Economic conditions. 7. Family—
Nicaragua—Estelí—History—20th century. 8. Oral history.
I. Title.
F1528.H36   1990
972.8505'3—dc20   90-50090
ISBN 0-299-12610-2   CIP

A DEDICATION TO MOTHERS

I FIRST MET Doña María in 1983. She is the mother of the children whose stories—along with hers—will follow. She was in her middle sixties then, proud of her children, and worried about getting too many wrinkles. I saw her every summer after that. Her heart weakened; diuretics and a lack of appetite made her slim; even two or three strands of her brown hair turned gray. Her good humor stayed, even though it seemed to her at times that her children had abandoned her. I last saw her in 1987. She died two weeks ago, just before I began the book on the oral history of her family. I dedicate the book to her.

I also dedicate the book to my mother, Elizabeth Kranz Walta, whose sense of justice has given courage, strength, determination, and vision to everyone who knows her, especially to her children. She paid for trips to Nicaragua when she didn't want me to go, and then prayed all the while I was gone. Years ago, she said that instead of flowers on her grave, she would prefer that a book be there. I intend for her to get the book before that.

CONTENTS

ACKNOWLEDGMENTS

I AM DEEPLY grateful to my husband Tom for going to Nicaragua with me, for carrying my luggage, for straightening out snafued plane tickets, for enduring my intensity, for taking over more than his share of the household, and for calling this *our* book. I thank my daughters Lisa, Heather, and Megan for taking such good care of themselves while I was gone that I did not have to worry and for caring about the family in Nicaragua almost as much as I do. My gratitude goes to my colleague Gloria Levine who is the most critical, and therefore the best, reader I know, to Madeleine Fischer for her excellent transcription of the tapes, to Larry Thorpe, who had no idea how much help he was going to be when he asked to read the manuscript, and to Josette Griffiths for struggling with and conquering all those important details.

I would like to thank those at Oregon State University who found money and support for me: Rod Frakes, George Keller, Bill Wilkins, Peter Copek, and Bob Frank. I also thank the Center for Humanities at Oregon State University for the grant that allowed me released time from my teaching to begin this book, the Oregon Committee for the Humanities and Dick Lewis for the Summer Research Grant that enabled me to go to Nicaragua in 1987, and the Merle and Ellen Morgan Gift Fund that generously helped finance the tape transcription. I appreciate the support I received from Oregon State University's Research Council, College of Liberal Arts, and Foundation.

I would also like to thank Cyd Perhats for being in the Estelí park when I needed someone to hug me while I cried, Laura Rice who inspired me to do this research, Ray Verzasconi for believing I could, and Harvey Williams for his advice and encouragement. I appreciate Carl and Mary Shelley for lending me their apartment on the Oregon coast so that I could write without interference, Dorice Tentchoff for finding Carl and Mary Shelley for me, Paul Farber for quickly and thoroughly reading my first grant application, Sally Malueg for reading all the others, Margaret Thomas for telling me about the

First Oregon Professional Women's Tour to Nicaragua, Marjorie
Thorpe for reading the manuscript, and Joel Garfunkel for evaluat-
ing Omar's medical history.

   I want to thank Barbara Hanrahan at the University of Wisconsin
Press for asking to "have the inside track" on this project—the sweet-
est words a writer can ever hear—and for her understanding and
support during difficult times.

   And I thank Doña María, Leticia, Marta, and Omar for sharing
their lives with me.

THE LÓPEZ FAMILY

THE NAMES ARE pseudonyms, and the dates are approximations. All of the family members were born in Nicaragua. The grandmother, *María López*, was born around 1919 and died in 1987. The names and dates of her children who survived to adulthood follow in the order of their births:

Diego was born in 1941 or 1943.

Adela was born in 1943 or 1944 and died in 1986.

Leticia was born in 1947 and married *Sergio* (born in 1949) in 1970. They have four daughters: *Marisa* (born in 1971), *Sofía* (born in 1973), *Chela* (born in 1975), and *Nora* (born in 1981).

Norma was born in 1949.

Leonardo was born in 1951 and died in 1970 in a car accident; he was nineteen.

Marta was probably born in 1960 and is one year older than Omar. Her son, *Miguel*, was born in 1976.

Omar was probably born in 1961; he is one year younger than Marta. In 1977, he married *Dora*, and she died that year. After the triumph of the revolution, he married *Irene* (born in 1961). They have two daughters, *Isabel* (born in 1980) and *Dora* (born in 1982). Irene has two children by a previous marriage.

Pedro was probably born in 1963 and died in the revolutionary struggle in 1979 at the age of sixteen.

FOREWORD: BEHIND THE REVOLUTION

WHEN IN 1972 I announced to friends that I had received a Fulbright award to teach in Nicaragua, I was surprised to find how many people had no idea where I was going. One person, knowing that I was a Latin American specialist, wanted to know why I was going to Africa. Although Nicaragua has become more visible in the years since, most North Americans still know relatively little about it.

Nicaragua has usually been in the wings of the center stage of history. It had neither the advanced native culture nor the material riches that attracted the early Spanish to Mexico and to Peru. For 300 years following the Spanish conquest, all of Central America was a relatively unimportant part of Mexico. Following the Wars of Independence that liberated Mexico from Spain in the early nineteenth century, Nicaragua and the other countries of Central America went through a fitful period of internecine struggle. Although the idea of forming a durable political union had many advocates, mutual mistrust and individual ambition kept the dream from being realized.

In the 1850s Nicaragua's visibility increased somewhat. In competition with the Panama route to the Pacific, North American capitalist Cornelius Vanderbilt developed a route across Nicaragua. It was shorter than the Panama crossing, and became even more popular. Thousands of fortune hunters crossed the country on their way to the California gold fields. In 1855 William Walker, a North American military adventurer, hired himself out to one of the Nicaraguan political factions. In short order he took power himself, engineering his own election as president of Nicaragua. He even conspired to have Nicaragua admitted to the United States as a slave-holding state. But the various Central American and Nicaraguan factions set aside their differences long enough to drive Walker from the country.

With the decision in 1903 to build the canal through Panama, interest in the Nicaraguan site decreased. However, concern about political instability, foreign influence, and threats to U.S. economic interests in Central America and the Caribbean led to changes in U.S. foreign policy. Throughout the region, military intervention became the rule. In Nicaragua U.S. military forces were present almost continually from 1912 to 1933. During this time they maintained nearly complete economic, political, and military control.

In 1927 the Liberal soldier Augusto César Sandino took exception to a U.S. proposal to supervise elections and create a "nonpartisan" national police force. He withdrew to the mountains where, for the next five years, he and his nationalist guerrilla army resisted the numerous attempts of the U.S. Marines to defeat him. Meanwhile, the U.S. diplomatic and military missions engineered the election of their supporters and organized, trained, and equipped a modern army, the Nicaraguan National Guard. When the U.S. missions withdrew in 1933 they left the Guard under the command of Anastasio Somoza García. In short order Somoza arranged the assassination of Sandino and his own election as president of Nicaragua, thus inaugurating the family dynasty that ruled for more than forty years.

During this time the Somozas—initially the father, later sons Luis and Anastasio, Jr.—expanded and reinforced their control. From the beginning they had the strong support of the U.S. government. Franklin Roosevelt was reputed to have said of the senior Somoza, "He may be a son-of-a-bitch, but he's *our* son-of-a-bitch." Professing their concern for the "communist threat" and their support for U.S. policy, the Somozas could always count on military assistance, including a permanent military training mission. As strong proponents of free enterprise and foreign investment, they were assured economic assistance. In the 1960s Nicaragua became a showcase for the Alliance for Progress.

With the assassination of the senior Somoza in 1956 the two sons took control. Luis took over as president while his brother Anastasio (a West Point graduate) headed the National Guard. Following the death of Luis in 1967, Anastasio arranged his own election as president. He was especially effective in developing the family power base. In addition to his control of the National Guard, he maintained control of the Liberal party, which dominated the political process. Even when he himself was not the president, he dictated the choice of candidates and policies of the government. Through intimidation and manipulation he acquired vast land holdings and interests in a wide range of economic activities, including mining, farming, transportation, banking, and industry. Few dictators have so completely dominated all three sectors of power: political, economic, and military. His strategy included the promotion of fear and mistrust among his opponents, and the rewarding of those who, if not loyal, at least would not compete seriously.

Although many factors led to the overthrow of the Somoza dynasty, greed was a key element. Following the earthquake of December 1972, which destroyed half of Managua, economic aid began flowing into the country in record amounts. The USAID mission became the largest in all of Latin America. In 1973 alone, the Nicaraguan government contracted loans of over $200 million from diverse sources. (I recall sitting in on a meeting of advisors to Somoza who questioned the seeming contradictions between several loan requests. "Never mind that," Somoza responded. "Just tell them whatever they want to hear. We need all the money we can get.")

If the aid had gone to economic development and social programs, Somoza might have been a hero. As it was, an astonishing level of corruption funneled much of the money into the pockets of Somoza and his supporters. Government contracts with huge profit margins went to companies which they owned or controlled. The government bought paving blocks from Somoza's cement company and trucks from his Mercedes-Benz dealership. Following an inside tip, one of Somoza's political cronies bought a large tract of land which he knew the government had selected as the site of a public housing development. He then sold it to the government (which paid for it with money borrowed from the United States) for one hundred times what he had paid for it only days before.

While the wealthy managed to get by (or even to prosper if they didn't threaten Somoza) and the small middle class struggled, the situation of the vast poor majority deteriorated. Most of the urban poor and nearly all of the rural peasants found themselves without the most fundamental necessities for a humane existence, such as basic education, health care, nutrition, and shelter. The response to this condition was the standard trickle-down policy. Those who advocate this approach believe that aid provided to those at the top will stimulate investment and provide those at the bottom with jobs, income, and an incentive to move up. Even in the best of circumstances this is a dubious strategy. In a country like Nicaragua it is doomed to failure. First, there is never enough money to satisfy the demand. Even at a high and constant rate of economic growth it would take generations for Nicaragua to catch up to the wealthier Latin American countries, to say nothing of the industrialized countries.

Second, it is unlikely that much of the money would go into the local economy and "trickle down." There is little to purchase that is locally produced, the population base is neither large nor wealthy enough to provide a significant market for new products, and the risk factors for investment are highly unpredictable and generally negative. As a result, money is more likely to flow out than down. Money is spent for imported consumer goods or for travel and investment abroad.

Third, the trickle-down approach neither addresses the immediate needs nor acknowledges the basic humanity of the poor. When I interviewed Somoza's Minister of Public Health in 1973, he proudly described to me the reduction of polio cases to what he referred to as "an acceptable number" (fewer than 20 cases per year). When I asked him when they expected to eliminate polio altogether, he replied that they didn't have sufficient resources. Later, when I posed that question to the health people at the USAID mission, they gave me essentially the same answer: an all-out campaign to eliminate polio "would not be cost-effective."

Is it any wonder that the poor should be attracted to another course? This was provided by the Sandinista Front for National Liberation (FSLN). The FSLN combined nationalist and Marxist objectives with the liberal trend within the Catholic church. By endorsing liberation theology and its objective of "a preferential option for the poor," the FSLN gained the support of liberal Christians and offset accusations of being "godless communists."

As support for the FSLN increased, support for Somoza decreased. His excesses and the brutality of his regime, which increased as his opponents became more audacious, embarrassed his former allies. The government of the United States and even other Central American dictators withdrew their overt approval. Many of Somoza's traditional Nicaraguan opponents, while not concurring in all the objectives of the FSLN, saw in it the instrument of Somoza's removal. They backed the FSLN, in the belief that the FSLN would not have the skill or the political support necessary to run the government. With almost no national or international support, Somoza was forced to flee to the United States. On July 19, 1979, jubilant crowds, led by the forces of the FSLN, triumphantly entered Managua. After years of struggle, with more than 40,000 lives lost, millions of dollars of damage sustained, and the national treasury looted by the departing dictator, the Somoza dynasty had finally come to an end. And the work of rebuilding the nation was just beginning.

From the start, it was clear that the FSLN had no intention of relinquishing power voluntarily. For nearly eleven years, until its defeat at the hands of the United Nicaraguan Opposition and its presidential candidate, Violeta Chamorro, the FSLN maintained a dominant position in Nicaraguan politics. These years can be described as four separate periods: reorganization and recovery, adjustment and expansion, reinforcement and defense, and negotiation and change.

Reorganization and recovery. The period immediately following the overthrow of Somoza was devoted primarily to reorganization of the government and recovery from the damages sustained during the insurrection. The government, led by the FSLN, declared that Nicaragua would abide by the principles of political pluralism, a mixed economy, and military nonalignment. The executive power was vested in a junta dominated by the FSLN but including opposition representatives. The legislative power was vested in the National Assembly, also dominated by supporters of the FSLN but representing a wide variety of political and civil interests.

The government took control of the financial sector, including banking, insurance, and foreign commerce. It also confiscated the holdings of Somoza and his supporters. Other private commercial enterprises and holdings were permitted, but were subject to confiscation if they were not used productively or if their owner were found guilty of subversion. A tremendous amount of land, much of it previously undeveloped, was turned over to the rural poor through the Ministry for Agrarian Reform. Some of the larger estates were maintained as state farms, but most of the land was farmed in cooperatives or as individual holdings.

The policy of nonalignment was manifested in diversifying economic and political relations. For practical purposes, this meant es-

tablishing diplomatic and commercial relationships with the Social-
ist Bloc countries for the first time in Nicaragua's history.

The preferential option for the poor was demonstrated in several
other programs in addition to agrarian reform. The Ministry of
Health created a unified health system with open access for all citizens. A new Ministry of Housing and Settlements was formed; it
initiated rent control, formalization of land titles, and construction
of low-income housing projects. A Ministry of Social Welfare was
created, which initiated programs for many marginal individuals
and groups. By far the most ambitious effort, internationally recognized, was the Literacy Crusade. The Ministry of Education organized and trained 80,000 volunteers to teach literacy in all parts of
the country. Living and working with their students, these volunteers taught over 400,000 adults the basic skills of reading and writing, thus lowering the national illiteracy rate from 50 percent to 13
percent. In the process the potential and effectiveness of popular
participation for satisfying basic needs was clearly demonstrated.

Adjustment and expansion. The second period (1981–82) was described to me by a vice-minister of education as "years of relative
bonanza." Many of the early organizational problems were resolved
and the new programs began to function more smoothly. Although
there were still some groups who resisted the high level of government control or who preferred different policies, most of the more
vocal critics either withdrew from the political process or left the
country. Even though the U.S government, led by Ronald Reagan,
withdrew its financial aid and began covert promotion of the counterrevolutionary forces, Nicaragua attracted assistance from a wide
range of governments and international groups. Western European
and North American nongovernmental agencies were particularly
helpful in providing technical and financial support, while the So-
cialist Bloc governments emphasized trade credits, personnel, and
education and technical training. The agrarian reform continued
apace: some 60,000 families received title to nearly one million acres
of cooperative farm land. Social programs were greatly expanded.
School enrollment doubled, and new schools, health facilities, and
social service centers were built. Community participation was well
organized. Neighborhood groups, aided by the government, initiated many improvements, such as the installation of water and
sewer systems and electrical lines. In a plan modeled on the Liter-

acy Crusade, citizen volunteers were recruited and trained to carry out national health campaigns. Through these efforts, polio and diphtheria were eliminated, and measles and several other diseases were significantly reduced.

Reinforcement and defense. During the third period (1983–87) Nicaragua was in a virtual state of war. Although the policy of "low intensity warfare" had been initiated by the United States when Ronald Reagan took office, its effects were not serious until the beginning of 1983. The United States stepped up its economic aggression, using its influence to block international development loans, and declared a complete trade embargo against Nicaragua in 1985. Direct acts of sabotage sponsored by the CIA destroyed public facilities and threatened international trade until international protest caused them to be discontinued.

Daniel Ortega was elected president of Nicaragua in 1984. In spite of protestations from the U.S. government to the contrary, the election was judged by many international groups to be exemplary. Encouraged by the Reagan administration, several parties boycotted the election. The FSLN won two-thirds of the seats in the national assembly, the rest being shared by six other parties. A new constitution was written, guaranteeing civil, political, and human rights. As a result of international consultation and extensive national public meetings, the document was extensively revised. It was formally promulgated in January 1987.

Increased support of the counterrevolutionary "freedom fighters" led to more frequent attacks against economic as well as military objectives. Any governmentally supported program or government employee was deemed a "legitimate target" by the counterrevolutionaries. This included education, health, and agrarian reform facilities and personnel. Over 500 schools and 100 health centers were destroyed or closed because of the hostilities. More than 200 teachers and students, and 50 health care persons, were killed by the counterrevolutionaries and many more were wounded or kidnapped.

The economic effect was devastating. The monetary damages exceeded the entire national income. As the defense expenditures rose to over 50 percent of the national budget, the allocations for social programs shrank until the quality and quantity of programs had to be reduced. Inflation became rampant and the economy was on the verge of collapse. If anything, the social and psychological impact was worse. A key element of "low intensity warfare" is to destroy social cohesion and the will to resist. The economic and military aggression produced that effect.

Negotiation and change. The fourth period (1987–90) covers the signing of the Central American peace accords and the Nicaraguan elections of 1990. During these years the deterioration of the economic situation slowed somewhat and the signing of the various peace accords encouraged many people to believe that the worst was over. Although the attacks of the counterrevolutionary forces diminished, the U.S. government continued to support them and to insist on their continued existence, even in violation of the peace agreements. It also continued its economic aggression, continuing the trade embargo and using its influence to discourage economic aid from government and international banks. When elections were announced for February 1990, the United States attempted to influence the outcome through direct and indirect means. Directly, millions of dollars were transfered from the U.S. government to the National Opposition Union (UNO). This diverse coalition of fourteen parties, ranging from the Conservative Party to the Communist Party, selected Violeta Chamorro as its presidential candidate. She was the publisher of the opposition newspaper *La Prensa*, the widow of a martyred Somoza opposition figure, and a former member of the first governmental junta after the overthrow. No U.S. funds went to support any of the several other opposition parties or candidates.

Indirectly the Bush administration attempted to influence the voting by promising to lift the trade embargo, to extend massive government aid, and to promote the disbanding of the counter-revolutionary forces—but only if Chamorro won the election. In February 1990, in one of the most closely supervised elections in the history of Latin America, Violeta Chamorro was elected president, with 54.7% of the popular vote. The FSLN won thirty-nine of the ninety-two seats in the National Assembly. Of the remaining 53 seats, 51 were distributed among the 14 parties of the UNO coalition, while two minor parties won single seats. In the local elections the UNO was even more successful, winning more than three-quarters of the Municipal Councils. Estelí was one of the few major cities won by the FSLN. What the future holds for Nicaragua is anybody's guess.

In the following story of Doña María and her family, the reader will have the privilege of hearing an important part of Nicaragua's history as reflected through the memories of four of its citizens. I have witnessed, read, or been told similar incidents of people all over Nicaragua. But I know of no writing that provides such rich and intimate detail as Dianne Hart has recorded here. The many-faceted account of these lives gives us insights into the day-to-day problems, hopes, and fears of ordinary people living under extreme hardship.

Three points are touched upon in this history which frequently confuse persons unfamiliar with Nicaragua and which I would like to clarify. The first is the meaning of the terms "revolution" and "revolutionary process." For most Nicaraguans "the revolution" does not mean the fighting which led up to the defeat of Somoza, or the moment of victory when he was finally overthrown. Usually, the former is referred to as "the insurrection" and the latter is called "the triumph." "The revolution," or frequently "the revolutionary process," refers not to armed combat but to the ongoing and conscious process of social change. While there is no consensus about its precise goal or direction (defining it is in itself part of the process), there is a general understanding that it is a dynamic and current activity in which all Nicaraguans play a role. "Advancing the revolution" means promoting social change, not invading other countries. Being "involved in the revolutionary process" means being an active participant in community affairs, particularly those which further the common good.

The second is the meaning of "sandinista." It is sometimes used as a shortened version of the name of the political party, the Sandinista Front for National Liberation (FSLN): the party as a whole, its leaders or its members in general, may be referred to as "the Sandinistas." But unlike party affiliation in the United States, membership in the FSLN is not open to everyone. One must be invited to join, and must demonstrate selfless commitment and loyalty before one is accepted as a full member, or "militant."

The term is also used in a more general way to convey a sense of

being like Sandino: nationalistic, heroic, patriotic. Thus the Sandinista Defense Committee (CDS) is not officially a partisan organization, nor is the Sandinista Popular Army (EPS). Although it
may be the case that the leaders of these and similarly named organizations may be militant Sandinistas, the groups are officially nonpartisan. Some would argue, however, that the overlap is so great
between membership in the FSLN and leadership in organizations
that the distinction is academic, and that the FSLN took advantage
of the circumstances to promote its own interests.

The third point has to do with the meaning of reality or truth.
Those familiar with Nicaragua may take exception to some of the
information that is related by the López family. Those not familiar
with Nicaragua may be bothered by the seeming exaggerations and
contradictions within the dialogue. One should not doubt the quality of the translation nor the sincerity of the speakers. When situations are very grave or when they provoke strong emotions, many
Nicaraguans have a tendency to express themselves in absolutes.
When they say "There's no bread!" they may mean just that. Or they
may mean that it is not available at the usual place, that one must
stand in line to buy it, that it costs too much or is only available on
the black market.

One should also bear in mind that people have selective memories. Especially when people are under great stress and when things
are changing rapidly and unpredictably, it is not unusual for recollections to become distorted. In Nicaragua the value of the *córdoba*,
the exchange rate, wages, and prices changed so frequently that it
was difficult to keep current, let alone remember what they were on
any given previous day. Government regulations and office holders
changed almost as frequently.

These issues and many more will become apparent in the reading
of *Thanks to God and the Revolution*. From the mosaic of information
provided by the family of Doña María, the reader will gain a feeling
for the lives of many Nicaraguans which could be improved upon
only by having lived through these years with them.

HARVEY WILLIAMS

Stockton, California
May 1990

THANKS TO GOD
AND THE REVOLUTION

1

Introduction:
The Family and Their City

ESTELÍ, NICARAGUA, was halfway to the Honduran border. I had reassured my family that the leaders of the 1983 Oregon Professional Women's tour would not take us to the border, but when I landed in Nicaragua, I found out that, indeed, they intended to do just that. The border trip was scheduled for a Sunday, destined to be a slow day in Managua, so I decided to go halfway: 154 kilometers north to the town of Estelí. That way I would not break my promise to my family, but I would also be able to get out of Managua. The capital, with the crumbling remains from the 1972 earthquake at the city center, was so different from other Latin American cities that I wanted to see another city in Nicaragua, one that might have a downtown plaza where I could watch people go about their daily routines, observe more of the life I was accustomed to seeing in Latin America, and, I hoped, feel more in touch with Nicaragua. In Estelí, our tour group stopped at the office of the women's association (AMNLAE),[1] where the Oregon women were joined by the armed guards needed for the rest of the trip. We were one of the first groups to come to Nicaragua and were made even more noticeable by the presence of two cameramen from Oregon television stations and two women reporters. On top of that, just before we arrived in Nicaragua the CIA arranged the bombing of the Managua airport.[2] No one wanted to take any chances.

Joan Acker, a sociologist from the University of Oregon, stayed in Estelí with me, and AMNLAE arranged for one of its members, Marta López, to walk around with us and show us the city. It turned out that Sunday was a slow day all over Nicaragua—in Managua, in the war zone, and in Estelí. Marta took us through the cemetery,

3

around the central plaza, and to El Mesón restaurant. With the music from *Flashdance* as a loud background accompaniment, we each had a beer and a grilled cheese sandwich. It was there that we started to talk. She told us what her life had been like before the revolution, how it had changed with the revolution, and how the role of women had changed.

After lunch we went to her home. We met the family members who lived in Estelí: her shy six-year-old son, Miguel; her mother, Doña María;[3] her sister, Leticia; and her brother, Omar. We drank more beer and talked about the war ("a week-day war," according to Omar, who was in the military and in uniform), religion, and creams

HONDURAS

EL SALVADOR

* Ayapal

Escambray
* Jalapa
Santa Clara   * La Laguna de Miraflor
   • Ocotal   * Quibuto
Pan American   Somoto
   Highway   Condega
Pueblo   Pantasma
Nuevo   Ulises Rodriquez
Regadio   La Laguna de Miraflor
                   Sirena River Bridge
Limay   Estelí
San Roque   * Santa Cruz   Jinotega
   La Trinidad

                   Sébaco

Chinandega

Corinto
   Leon   Lago de Managua

Managua   Masaya

Pacific   Granada   Atlantic
Ocean   Lago de Nicaragua   Ocean

         Rivas

N

* - *Best estimate according to Marta.*

Scale
0 10 20 30 40 50

Kilometers

COSTA RICA

Map by Bill Lanham, Oregon State University

to protect them from the sun and aging. Doña María held Omar's machine gun while he danced with us, and the neighbor children watched from the doorway.

It wasn't until I was back in Oregon, once again teaching Spanish at Oregon State University, that the possibility of learning more about the family occurred to me. People in the United States were curious about Nicaragua and the nature of U.S. involvement there. In trying to explain the situation, I often found myself relying on the family's personal story, not on what was told us by politicians from the United States or Nicaragua. The story was more powerful and more understandable when told from the family's point of view. A bond already existed between the family and me—we liked each other—which set up the foundation for the confidence and trust needed for an oral history. I wrote to them and asked if they would agree to work with me on it. They said they would. In truth, none of us had any idea what would be ahead of us. I did not know what direction the oral history would take—the story was, and is, theirs to tell.

It is important that this history be published in English because most North Americans, whose country is the most significant player in the hemisphere, have little understanding of the politics or culture of Latin America or Latin Americans. I strongly object to U.S. policy toward all of Latin America throughout the history of the United States and especially during the eight years of President Reagan's administration, but the only effect that had on this research was that it initially helped establish trust between the family and me. It might sound inconceivable, but the issue of my politics rarely came up.

The family experienced a dictatorship, the fight for revolutionary change, the triumph, and the difficult postrevolutionary years that followed. Had there been no revolution in Nicaragua, the family's story would not have had quite the same interest to me or to the reader; therefore, it was important that the family represent the poor who fought for the revolution and for whom the revolution was fought. The López family members were the poorest of the poor in their youth, and in different ways they all worked for the triumph of the July 1979 revolution. Yet the questions I asked them were always personal ones, and they mention the political only as it is reflected in their lives.

I knew that when we North Americans, in our direct way of questioning people, confront Latin Americans (including Nicaraguans), we receive a more circuitous and perhaps a politer answer than we would prefer. Additionally, in the case of Nicaraguans, history has taught them to be secretive; Marta said that they tell only what they think the listener wants to hear and, until they know people well, only what they believe isn't going to hurt them. Early in the research, it became apparent to me that I would be more accepted, learn more about their lives, and get to know them better if I took a more indirect approach (which is not my nature, as my family and friends would testify) to asking questions. As I worked with them through the years, that approach always *felt* right, and I think it proved to *be* right in the end. Whatever opinions I had of the Sandinista government—positive or negative—I kept to myself, which meant that I did not ask them questions that would lead them to one answer or another, nor did I ask them questions that I thought might send them scurrying back to a safer position. A lot of trust was necessary for this work ever to evolve. So the questions were just about their lives, but the story ends up with a much broader scope than that.

The actual recording of the interviews was rather straightforward. I prepared a set of base questions every year before leaving the United States, and reviewed the previous year's tapes. In Nicaragua, I spent all day sitting at a table in the López house tape-recording the interviews. I had a slick, voice-activated tape recorder that, according to a salesperson at Oregon State University's bookstore, would save tape because it taped only when someone spoke. That sounded like a good idea in the United States, but in Nicaragua the tape never stopped moving; it recorded roosters crowing, children laughing, comments of curious neighbors, and trucks that thundered by a few feet from where we sat. Upon my return to the United States, the tapes, which eventually totaled seventy-eight hours, were transcribed (leaving out the roosters, trucks, etc.). Then I translated them and used them as a basis for talks, papers, an article, and a book chapter.[4]

As any oral historian knows, this sounds easier than it is. Interviewing, preparing questions, and controlling one's impulses to interrupt or interpret are all very difficult. Lives aren't told chronologically or without numerous interruptions, and some events are discussed with reluctance. When one works in Nicaragua, one is subjected to the same difficulties that Nicaraguans live with every day: shortage of water; erratic electricity; little variety in food and often a shortage; transportation problems; difficulty in getting medicine and batteries; the danger of a random or planned attack by the contras; an ever-changing currency rate; and the tension of living or working in a country at war. Even the generosity of the family was exhausting: they arranged their days so that I always had someone to interview. When one of the family got tired, a different person sat down.

Instead of using a question-and-answer format, I have written a narrative that has been heavily edited to remove repetition and confusion and to give some chronological order to the story. I have presented the family as accurately as possible. I ask the reader to trust that I have not eliminated anything of critical importance, nor have I left in more information portraying the family members or their country in one particular way or another in any attempt to interpret for them. When I was in doubt about what they meant, I left out that information or cleared it up with them at a later date. Certainly, the questions I asked them and my responses, spoken or unspoken, have influenced their retelling of their lives. There is simply no way around it. Our friendship grew, and that changed the lives of all of us.

In the retelling, I divided their lives into the following periods: the years before the revolution, the day of the revolution, the post-revolutionary period of 1979–84, 1984–85, Leticia's story from February of 1986, 1985–86, and 1986–87, and the epilogue. Within these periods, I began the oral history with the story of the oldest family member, Doña María, the grandmother; her children's stories follow.

There are some Spanish words that I did not translate because they are used often, and accurate translations aren't possible. A young man could be called a *muchacho*, a *guerrillero*, or a *compañero*. All those words have different meanings that cannot be adequately expressed in English. The words that have been left untranslated and are not later treated as foreign words are the following: *barrio* (neighborhood, but often in a more formal way than we mean it in colloquial English), *campesino* (peasant, rural inhabitant), *compañero/a* (friend, companion, comrade, boyfriend, girlfriend, lover, workmate), *compa* (shortened version of *compañero/a*), *contra* (counter-revolutionary), *córdoba* (Nicaraguan currency), *muchacho* (young man, usually one involved in the struggle for liberation), *guerrillero* (one who actively fought against the Somoza government), *guerrilla* (the organization of *guerrilleros*), *guardia* (Somoza's National Guard), and *pueblo* (town, people, common people, masses). In addition, some of these words would often be treated as plurals in English, but I have left them as singular collective nouns as they are in Spanish, such as *contra* and *guardia*. When Nicaraguans say, "in the mountains," the expression usually refers to mountains in general and has no political significance. However, the use of the singular *mountain*, as in, "He is leaving for the mountain," means that someone is joining the *guerrilla*; it represents a major personal and political commitment.

The Lopéz Family

We began working on the oral history in 1984, and my 1983 impressions of the family deepened; each member of the family proved to be even more interesting than I initially imagined. The grandmother, Doña María, a short, stout woman with soft Indian features, usually tied her long, straight, brown hair back behind her head; she always wore a sleeveless house dress and, eventually, hand-me-down shoes that had belonged to my daughters. In 1985, after I had arrived in Estelí but before I visited the family, I walked through Estelí's central plaza and saw Doña María from a distance as she, with great animation, talked with some young men. She had been sick and had lost a lot of weight. Her ears were pierced, she wore a simple navy-blue dress, and her brown hair hung loosely over her shoulders. A handsome woman with bronze skin, she was past sixty-five, but I could see traces of the beauty—and the flirt—she must have been in earlier years. And as always, talking with men turned her watery eyes into mischievous ones.

Her irreverent sense of humor brought relief to difficult situations; in 1987 I brought some blue sheets to the family as a gift. When Doña María saw them, she immediately said that the family could bury her wrapped in the sheets. Later, in a lighter moment, she told me she wanted to be the first one to go in color. We laughed, and I told her the color was fashionable in the United States right now. She chuckled and said maybe then the people would come to see her because she was being buried in the best color. She loved to be teased, and her comments were often lewd. It always surprised me to realize that I was sitting in a little house in revolutionary Nicaragua listening to an old *mestiza* telling me dirty jokes.

In her house, where most of the interviewing took place, birth announcements, posters, holy cards, and photos of dead children cover the dark brown walls, hanging high and crookedly in random spots, sometimes on top of each other or in the middle of a larger piece. (I have always wished that I could have been there when they decided which photo went where; placing one squarely in the middle of a painting would not have occurred to me.) The house has two dark bedrooms, a combination living and dining room, and one bathroom. The one window area is covered with unmovable wooden slats instead of glass. The living-dining room is furnished with a wooden table, one wooden chair, three plastic chairs, a dresser, a television set, and sometimes (depending on the economy) a refrigerator. They have running water and a door that locks. Every morning, they sprinkle sawdust on the floor and sweep it out. Behind the house, but very much part of it, is the *solar*, an indoor-outdoor kitchen with a dirt floor. Besides two wood-burning stoves, the *solar* has a garden, chicken coop, and clothesline, all walled in by uneven boards placed at some distance from each other. The boards do not keep out the wind and rain; they serve only to mark the area as one's property. One did wonder about the cleanliness of the food, given the fact that flea-ridden animals roamed freely in the *solar*, but Doña María assured me that as long as I ate her food, I would never get sick. I think she boiled everything to death. And had I eaten only there, I probably would always have been well.

The television set makes the house the center of the neighborhood for young children. One Sunday, more than thirty children crowded into the tiny front room to watch an old movie from Spain. The remarkable thing, to me, was that although each child sat on the floor so close to the next child that their arms touched, not once did anyone push or shove, nor was there even the slightest disagreement.

Doña María usually sat right outside the door to her duplex—part of the housing built by the government after 1979—enjoying the breeze that blew through the house. When she saw someone coming down the street with whom she didn't want to speak, she pretended to tie her shoelaces, even though her feet were so swollen that she hadn't been able to tie them for months. At the end of each day, I would ask her how many times she had to tie her shoes, and usually it was only once.

Whenever I could, I sat outside with her. I was sometimes overwhelmed by the sweet smell of rotting fruit combined with exhaust from car engines and smoke from her stoves, but her clever and caustic comments made staying there worthwhile.

The first year I asked Doña María what she thought of the interviewing, she answered, "You'll learn what it's really like here because I'm not going to tell you that I have lived well. That would be a lie." Her children, out of concern for her health and on doctors' orders, asked that I not bring up topics that might make her sad, so I was left with general questions and the hope that, on her own, she would discuss the significant events in her life. In addition, she was intimidated and confused by the tape recorder and small microphones. I always interviewed her last because she needed to watch her children do it before she could. She needed a lot of direction, but ended up liking the process. When she finished her last interview, I remember thinking, "Wow!" It had taken several years, but she was rolling. When I told her this, she responded:

> You say that you think this has been a good interview? I think it has been fun! I thought being interviewed had no value. I don't know why I felt downhearted about this, but I got the courage to do it, and now I feel good. I like being interviewed. I didn't use to, but with time you learn a lot of things. You just develop. I'm no longer afraid to talk to people.

Her daughter Leticia, however, had no trouble. She is the most sophisticated and worldly of the family members and has the lightest skin. She has curly hair, dark sad eyes, full lips—a beautiful combination of white, black, and Indian features—and is short, small-boned, and full-figured. When beauty products were available (she is a hairdresser), her hair would sometimes have a reddish tint, her eyeliner might be violet and so might her lipstick. The colors changed every year. When I took photographs, I gave her a day's warning because I knew she wanted to look her best. Once we went for a walk together, and I was suddenly made aware of all the attractive men she knew in town as they all greeted her on the street or called to her from passing cars. Her dramatic appearance carries through in her presentation of herself and in her storytelling. She is the easiest one to talk with and tells a sad and emotional story—always. She often seems to be on the verge of tears and, in fact, is quick to cry. There is an intense sadness about her. At the same time, she can be determined and strong and is capable of great rage. She will do what she has to do to survive.

During the oral history period, Leticia lived in two different homes in Estelí and one in Managua. They all had a relatively large front room, which is where Nicaraguans put the refrigerator, if they have one, and the rooms were dark, as were the rooms in all the homes I saw. If she could not set up her salon elsewhere, then she would put her equipment in the front room, along with a television set covered by a cloth to protect it from the dust that blew in. In her Managua house, the front room was more like a patio; it had a roof, but three sides were open. One kitchen area was in such a small dark room that I wondered how she could see to cook; another time it was an earthenware stove on the wall of the *solar*. Strutting chickens claimed the small counter as their own, and a pig ran free.

Her younger sister Marta is shorter than Leticia, probably under five feet and around one hundred pounds. She is so small that she wears hand-me-down T-shirts and blouses that my daughters wore when they were ten. Her facial features are tiny, her skin brown and ruddy, and her curly hair cropped close to her head, sometimes with a small tail in the back. She speaks decisively and in a matter-of-fact way, often snapping her fingers to indicate that something happened rapidly or successfully. Her mother's mischievousness and irreverence show in Marta's lively eyes. She is less inclined to drama than is her sister, preferring to state things "the way they are," and seldom cries. Whereas Leticia's way of dressing presents a definite image, Marta puts on what she has, with no attention to style, and feels foolish in makeup. When I went for a walk with her, old women on the street asked her how her mother was, people stopped to ask her about meeting times, and she reproached little children who had the temerity to ask me for a pencil or who were playing near a dangerous electrical cord.

Even though she was the first family member I met, Marta has been the one who has been the most difficult to know; yet, six years later, I might know her best. There is a reserve about her, a need to know someone well before letting her guard down, but after all this time, I am sure that I am one of the few people in the world she completely trusts. Our interviews are complicated, deep, trusting, and funny. She talks faster than anyone I know, and when she starts to talk about sex, we both run to my purse where I have my Marlboros. (I smoke only in Nicaragua and only when I talk with Marta.)

Her younger brother Omar has classic Indian features: dark, straight hair; sad, dark eyes with long lashes; white, even teeth; and dark skin. A strikingly handsome man in his late twenties, he is the thinnest of the family and about 5′ 5″. His most noticeable qualities are a vulnerable sweetness and shyness in gestures and speech that show how easily he could be hurt. His smile is tentative, his tension and nervousness visible.

Omar lives on a hillside overlooking Estelí. In many countries, the location would be a view lot and sell at a high price, but not in this case. The path leading up to his house accommodates only animals and people. The house itself has a dirt floor; the holes in the walls and roof allow some light—there are no windows—and a lot of rain to come in. The tiny living room narrows to a hallway that seems an inappropriate place for the small earthenware stove; this leads to two bedrooms: one for Omar and his wife, the other for the children. In the children's bedroom, there are just two beds for the eight children, and one wire cot (minus the mattress) folded up. Outside they collect rainwater and use that to wash themselves. Wood planks, considered to be inferior material, are used on the exterior, except for the front where the more prestigious bricks are used. A little blue plastic cord serves as the lock to the door. There is no refrigerator or television set; Omar used to have a radio, but it was stolen.

When I walked with him to and from his house, I had the definite impression that the old men he greeted on the road thought I had been a conquest. As they said, "Va, pues,"[5] to each other, they exchanged knowing smiles. How else, people must have asked, could one explain a Nicaraguan man and a North American woman walking away from his house? In reality, at first I was one of the few who was still interested in his old war stories, but as his emotional depression deepened, I almost became a therapist. I listened, and I did so sympathetically. He told me that his family always told him what to do instead of listening to him. He said, in 1985, "When I talk like we're doing now, I feel relieved because someone is listening to me and understanding my situation. Other times, I've gone to my mother's house to talk about my problems, but they just want to tell me what to do. That bothers me a lot." Toward the end of the interview that year, he said, "From yesterday—[when we started this interview]—to today, I've felt a change. I feel better." As the newness of being an oral history subject wore off, as his mental health improved, and as the military demanded more of him, our time together shortened.

Originally I had not intended to interview Omar; the oral history was to be of the three women family members in Estelí (I have never met the family members who live outside of Estelí), but that first year, Omar kept pacing around the table, asking me when I planned to interview him. I had no intention of doing so but finally relented, thinking that afterwards he would leave and let me work without interruption. A few minutes into his interview, I realized that he had to be included. As a guerrillero, he added an important dimension that the women alone did not provide. In addition, he was the one who first involved the others in the fight against Somoza and was, according to Marta, the person her son Miguel modeled himself after, his own father having died in battle. "Omar is the only male he knows," she said. "He's like a father to him."

In the years that followed our initial meeting, I had to struggle not to become an actor in their life story and to remain instead a recorder and observer, to remain on the outside all the while being so close to the inside, to resist the temptation to add a bit of advice of my own. I wasn't always successful. As I look back, I suppose that the first time they saw me cry, they knew that I could not always keep a professional distance. All of them cried at some point in the retelling of their lives, and when they cried, I cried. There are some things that happened to them that even now, years later, I cannot tell without tears coming to my eyes.

My relationship with the family altered my life, as well as the lives of my husband and children. My husband went with me for three of the five trips; two of our children were still at home when Leticia and her daughter visited us; and every summer they saw new slides of a family dressed in the clothes they had sent down the year before. No longer could any of us read an article about Nicaragua and keep the images in the abstract. When the economy worsened, we knew it affected the family. When the contra attacked, we were careful to note exactly where it took place. We repackaged medicines and constantly went through our closets, looking for more items to send to Nicaragua. We chafed when we heard government officials who, legally or illegally, sought more money for the contras. The politics made no sense, especially when you knew the people who might be killed. In every haunting face on television or in the news magazines, we saw the family from Estelí. They became our family, and we theirs.

During the Iran-Contra Hearings in 1987, shortly before my last trip to Nicaragua, I watched stonily as Oliver North rationalized his expensive security fence by saying he had received threats from terrorists and worried about the life of his young daughter. I wondered how Marta's son Miguel differed from North's daughter. Why was her life more important? Why did our multiethnic country sympathize with such an ethnocentric point of view? To Miguel, Oliver North was certainly as much of a terrorist as Abu Nidal was to North's daughter. To North, and to many in our country, the political became personal. It did to me, too, but I was thinking of a small, wide-eyed boy who played in the streets of Estelí, Nicaragua.

Doña María told me in 1987 that I had worked miracles and that my visit was her favorite part of the year. Later Marta described "the miracle" as one that brought her brother and sister to her mother's house more often:

> You wonder why my mother said you worked miracles? You work miracles because my sister has come often and brought some things to eat, and my brother came the other day, and just now he sent money with Irene. Even though they know the troubles we have, [when you're not here] they never ask if we've had something to eat that day. Never. So I tell you that you work miracles with your presence.

Later, she added, "While you've been here, there has been unity."

Once, a U.S. photographer in Nicaragua took me off guard by asking the kind of question I asked the family, which was, "What surprised you most?" Without stopping to give it much thought, I answered, "How much they fight," and a North American who has spent years in Nicaragua immediately agreed. The closeness of the Latin American family is real, but not without contradictions to the

North American viewer. Even they realized that it confused me; in 1986 Marta said, when she criticized Leticia for seldom visiting the family, "I'm worried about what must be happening in your head. I'm telling you one thing, and my sister is telling you another. Am I telling you the truth, or is she? Who is? I would wonder, too."

Needing to be with one's family, even though they fought when they did get together, was first priority in any decision. The economic and emotional ties are stronger than they are in most North American families, and so are the conflicts. They judge each other severely on how much time they spend with the family and carefully measure how much help—financial and otherwise—each one provides the other.

Marta eventually integrated her complaints about how much time the others spent with her mother with how available they were for interviews. In 1986, she said:

It seems to me that Leticia changed while she was in the United States. Look, what she was really worried about in the United States wasn't my mother. Instead she worried about the problems with her husband. If she had been worried about my mother, she would, at this very hour, be here. And she knows that you're here. She should say, "Good, Diana's going to be there; I'll go to see her." But as you can see, she's not here. She should be here to show appreciation because we all love each other and understand that the work you do is to help people understand the situation.

The contradictions also exist in attitudes toward feminism, love, and women—and men—in the revolution. The successes for women are numerous in revolutionary Nicaragua, but more in a broad sense than a particular one. Leticia praised the strides made for women, but even her young daughters forgave the philandering of their father with the comment, "You know how men are." Leticia objected and said, "I might be a woman, but I still have my dignity," as if it weren't normally possible to be a woman and also have dignity. Marta, a tough feminist who taught women to drive tractors and to defend their cooperatives, is wanted by the contra for having taught women to do these things, but even she says that it's better that her lover have another woman than for her to have another man.

Again I said nothing, afraid I would take away the rightful pride they felt in their accomplishments by pointing out what I perceived as their failures. Feminism from my perspective as a college teacher in the United States married to an obstetrician-gynecologist was altogether different from the perspective of Leticia and Marta. My resolve was unleashed, albeit to someone outside the family, on my way home one year when I unexpectedly spent a few hours in Honduras (traveling in Central America always provides surprises) and met a Sandinista who was studying law in West Germany. He proudly told me that he had children in Nicaragua, Florida, London, and Bonn, and he had never considered marrying any of the mothers nor supporting any of the children. I became so disgusted that I ended up saying something like, "Until you Sandinistas get your act together about women, you'll never get your revolution off the ground." Oddly, he agreed with me; so might have the family, but I said nothing like that to them. I did not want to be judgmental, and preferred that whatever conclusion they came to about feminism in Nicaragua should be arrived at without hearing comparisons from me. I often tried to suggest a more critical viewpoint, but neither one of the sisters took my lead, possibly because these discussions were emotional ones that didn't allow for more objectivity. The contradictions remain.

I became exasperated with their decision-making process. It seemed to me that when they had to make a major decision, they did so on an emotional basis rather than a pragmatic one. They discussed their options endlessly, but no one asked questions of any knowledgeable source before taking action; they made assumptions based on either no information or hearsay, and then wondered why things hadn't turned out as they wished or expected. Again, I found it difficult to be silent, but only once did I interfere and push for a decision; that happened in February 1986 when Leticia was in Oregon and couldn't decide if she should go to Miami. It was ten minutes to five o'clock on a Friday afternoon, and the travel agency would soon close. We had talked about it all week, made phone calls, and frankly, the discussion had worn me down. I had earlier encouraged her to go to Miami, and at that point I said, "Yes or no. Tell me now." She said yes.

At times, they pointed out differences in our cultures, as did Marta in the following story:

There's something I'd be interested in knowing, especially about the women [from the United States] who come to Nicaragua. There are some who like a certain Nicaraguan man, or maybe the man and woman like each other. I'm not sure, but it seems that in the school here where Spanish is taught to foreigners, they prohibit the North American women from having relations with a man. If I go to another place, and if I like a man, and we want to have an experience, as they say, we have it. That's all there is to it. But it seems to me that the North American women aren't like that, and I don't know why. The school must think that if a Nicaraguan man goes with a North American woman, it's because he's interested in getting dollars from her.

On the other hand, I heard about this place in the United States—I don't know if it's true, and I don't remember what state—where you can go with your lover. You and your lover can have relations with other people, and you return together to your house as if nothing happened. This would never happen in Nicaragua.

I also became the person in charge of small facts. If the family members were asked in my presence how old they were, they would turn to me for the answer, and I was never sure because no one had been able to give me a definite birth date. Sometimes they gave dates that varied by ten years. How long could a person exist in the United States without knowing his or her birth date and social security number? Not long. Leticia, as she got closer to forty, started to give her age as thirty-five, which probably says more about similarities than differences in both our cultures toward aging.

Often the numbers given to me were out of what I considered to be a logical order; for example, the family would say, "people had ten, nineteen, or eight children," whereas I probably would say that "people had ten or twenty children." On top of what seemed to me to be an unusual way to think of numbers, they also gave me a total after they listed the numbers. It was never the correct sum of the numbers they had listed.

They also described quantities of people—how many they could rely on or how many helped—in different terms from what I would use. In 1987, Leticia, while talking about her stay in the United States, spoke as follows:

No one in my family helped my children while I was away. The only one who did was my father. And Marta was concerned about them. And

Raúl always went to Managua and brought them beans, oil, rice—things they couldn't get there. He was the only person who visited them. So I had a lot of disappointments. That's when I realized that the only person my children have is me. And their father.

By the time she finished the description, it seemed that her children had many people looking out for them, but she, as did all the family members, started out and ended by saying "no one."

When I talked with them, I could never betray a secret, nor disclose that I knew something about one of them that had been told me by another in confidence, nor let on in the slightest way that I had made a judgment. This was not easy. I have always tried to be completely honest with my children and to explain everything to them, but I watched quietly as Marta prepared to leave for the war zone while she kept it a secret from her son Miguel. The family insisted that it was better that way; otherwise, Miguel would cry. As I witnessed his screaming and howling when the jeep pulled up to the house and Marta got in, it was all I could do to keep silent.

When I first interviewed them, they framed every situation as having taken place before or after the triumph. As the years went on, they told their stories beginning from my last visit. They described people as being as white as I am, or as having hair like mine, or as being as tall as I am. My arrival became a major event; Marta in 1986 said that "for entertainment, I have a beer, and you come here every year and we talk. That's it."

After that first summer, people in the United States asked me why I would want to go back. Hadn't the family told me everything? But in a country that has gone through what Nicaragua has, there are always many changes. One's personal life is closely tied to and affected by the many decisions made in Managua and Washington.

So it was in 1985. My husband and I left the United States just as the news magazines were full of stories about the contra attack on La Trinidad a few miles south of Estelí, and the airport newspapers told of the kidnapping of a Witness for Peace delegation. Tension stalked the streets of Estelí. The first two years I was astonished at how few secrets they had from each other and at how well they got along, but by 1985 they began to lower their voices and talk about each other, knowing that my sensitive tape recorder picked up even their whispers. Sometimes they would take advantage of the fact that my tape recorder was off to tell me something they didn't want committed to a recording. Certainly some of this was caused by the anxiety the family and the entire city felt after the threat of war, but it was also caused by the strengthening bonds between us. They did have secrets, and those secrets became mine.

One secret is their names. "Oral history . . . gives sudden importance to those who were rejected before, to those relegated to anonymity."[6] Certainly, in the past the López family had been relegated to anonymity, and in a sense they still are since they have chosen to use pseudonyms. Leticia, in 1984, said, "When you finish the story, you'll decide whether to use our complete names or not; it will depend on the situation we're in." As I write, they still do not want their names used. To keep their names secret, I have had to alter some facts but nothing that takes away from the truth of their story. That is not to say that I do not worry about writing something that will hurt someone; I do.

As my work continued with them every summer, it became apparent to me that the family did not want many people to know what I was doing. At first, I told people in Nicaragua that I was working on an oral history. As time went on, however, I talked less and less with other Nicaraguans and fellow North Americans. Depending on the situation and the person asking the question, when I was asked what I was doing in Nicaragua (and that is the first question anyone ever asks), I usually said I was visiting friends, especially when I was asked by either a tourist in Estelí or by someone who lived there. And the family taught me to simply remain silent or to shrug my shoulders and say, "Nothing." The reasons for secrecy are many and complex, ranging from their concern about my safety to their worry that people would think they were making money from this endeavor. In 1985 Leticia expressed more worries about me than about the family:

We have run risks from the moment we were born in Nicaragua, but I worry more about you. That's why I'm not sure that you should talk about it; we have said practically nothing, not even to my [father's] family. When people ask, you can just say, "I'm here in Nicaragua because I want to learn about it." If that doesn't work, you can say that you are here to study the Christian base communities: "I have a friend here who belongs to one."[7] I really have talked with no one. They've asked me; they're not so foolish as to think that we aren't talking. I did explain to our [North American] friend Carlos[8] that it's better to have a verbal testimony of what we are living through in Estelí told by people at the moment they are experiencing it. It's a *testimonio vivo*, a living testimony. Nonetheless, it's always good to be reserved. One never knows. Time passes, and you don't know [what will happen].

In 1987, she added more political concerns:

> Since we aren't working with an organization, someone could come and think that maybe we're working against the government.[9] I've thought about the questions you ask and know that, more than anything, you're interested in the true story of a family. If it were simply political, you wouldn't ask me these personal questions about my life.

They eventually hid me from AMNLAE; in 1986 Marta told me that "if AMNLAE came here and found us working, it wouldn't justify my not being at work. They'd think that I stayed home to do this work instead of staying home to take care of my mother." That day, we did the interview with the front door closed, which meant we talked in an almost entirely dark room. Miguel sat right outside the door, playing with his friends, but with the instructions to tell anyone who came that his grandmother was sick. In 1987 Marta, referring to both AMNLAE and the problem of dollars, said:

> We don't want everyone to know what you do here because people will think we are making dollars by doing this. They will think that we just *say* we have difficulties when we really have a pile of dollars. There are people in Nicaragua who do these things in exchange for a lot of money. Some of the people in AMNLAE, like Maricruz and another friend, know what you do, but most don't know and for the same reason. In general, there's an obsession in Nicaragua with dollars. Dollars are a headache.[10] People wouldn't believe that you give me whatever you want and that you give it to help me, not to buy me. But they do know that you come every year to visit us.

Marta went on to explain the rigorous secrecy that she had to maintain in her everyday life:

Some people from the city give the contra information about the work people are doing, for example, with AMNLAE. The contra announces on their radio that they look for the leaders of the community, those in AMNLAE and in all the organizations. For that reason, it's best that you not use our real names. Sometimes when I go around to the different places, they invite us to some activity; someone I don't know says, "Let's dance."

"Okay, let's dance."

"What's your name?" he says. And I invent names.

"Where do you live?" And I say another place, not Estelí.

"The address of your house, what is it?"

And some say, "I know you. I've seen you in another . . ."

So I say no, even though I know I've been there. It could be that the person is interested in me even if I'm not interested in him, but it could also be to learn what work I do. That's why we don't use our real names. We got used to using pseudonyms from the time of the insurrection. If your work was done secretly, for example, in the guerrilla, your family wouldn't be bothered if no one knew your name. But if they knew your name, your family was tortured, your home was burned. You should never say more than is necessary. It's better to answer with only what we believe isn't going to hurt us, especially if you don't know the person well.

They also kept my identity a secret from neighbors and relatives, sometimes for personal reasons; according to Doña María in 1987:

Some of the neighbor women come by, now that you are here, wondering who you are, who has come. They say to me, "Who's she?" I say, "A friend who visits us every year." I don't have to explain anything to them. Not even my sister knows, and she lives nearby. My mother and sisters never loved me, so my sister isn't like a friend or a sister. Why should I tell her anything about you?

I took hundreds of photographs of the family; although I often showed slides of them when I gave a presentation, none of the photographs has been or ever will be published.

Another secret that had to be kept was Leticia's illegal entrance into the United States in 1985. She and her daughter ended up in Nevada, and I arranged for them to fly to Oregon. We picked her up at the airport and spent the evening around the kitchen table, catching up on all the news from Nicaragua. It wasn't until she had gone

to bed that it occurred to me to ask her exactly how she had gotten
here. Was she legal? When I asked her the next morning, she said,
"No," which immediately changed the plans I had made for her.
She continued to use her pseudonym as she spoke to university and
high school classes, and I carefully monitored the interview she had
with a reporter from Oregon State University's student newspaper,
the *Daily Barometer*, and any other contact she had. She had told a
North American friend, Carlos, the truth. She said, "I trust him, so
I told him how I got here. My family knows, and you do, but you are
the only ones who do."

They have given me permission to use some of their personal
secrets in the book; I'm not quite sure why. Maybe they think that
the family members won't read it since it will be in English, or that
my world is so far away that little secrets in a book published here
will have no impact on their lives, or that by the time the book is
published, it won't matter anymore. I don't know.

Every year, I left less than U.S. $100, which I divided among the
three adult children. It seemed an appropriate amount, not too
much and not too little. I wanted to help: they took off work to be
interviewed and made a delicious lunch—soup, homemade tortillas,
and limes—for me. However, I did not want them to become depen-
dent on me; I wanted the money to be a gift rather than direct
payment for the story of their lives, and that is how they always
viewed it.

Once in 1985, when the tape recorder was off, Leticia and Marta
asked me that if I left any money that year, would I please give it all
to Leticia? They told me that Omar gave the money to his wife, and
she squandered it; Leticia would invest the money for the common
good of the family. For example, in 1986, Leticia, while talking about
a piece of property she intended to leave Omar, said, "I managed to
buy that land with some savings, including the money that you left
last year." I agreed to leave the $100 with Leticia, but I was always a
bit uncomfortable about it, especially as the extent of Omar's poverty became more apparent to me and even though he told me, as
had everyone else, that Leticia took care of them. A further com-
plication for me was that although Leticia had planned to give Omar
the property, her husband refused, in Leticia's absence, to give him
the deed. I didn't question Leticia's intentions, but the end results
seemed to be different from what she had originally planned. Con-

sequently, I did not always honor their request and secretly slipped small amounts of money to Omar; eventually I went back to giving them separate amounts. No one asked why, and I didn't explain.

They often gave me an accounting of the money. Marta told me in 1986, "With the money you left us last year, I was able to buy a fan for my mother to use at night. She couldn't breathe and needed more air." In 1987, she said, "I pay for the house monthly, but I used the money you left last time to pay for this year and part of the next year until February."

Keeping track of the fluctuation of the córdoba in relation to the U.S. dollar was always difficult. It may help to remember that it was one digit to the dollar during the Somoza years; in the first years of the revolution, two digits, and by 1986, four digits. For example, in the Somoza years, the córdoba rate to the U.S. dollar was 2, 5, and 7 córdobas.[11] By September 1983, when I first went to Nicaragua, there were 28 córdobas to the dollar and the same a year later. However by August 1986, there were 1200 córdobas to the dollar (rising to 1400 in a week), and by August 1987, 5000 córdobas to the dollar (rising to 5500 in a week). The move to five digits came later: by January 1988, there were 20,000 córdobas to the dollar, and 50,000 by February. The rates I've quoted are the ones tourists would legally get at their hotels or at a *casa de cambio*. One can only imagine how much the black market rate must have been.

Late in 1985 Leticia made her trip to the United States. She returned to Nicaragua, arriving a month before I did in August 1986. By then, her mother's health, which had always been a concern, had deteriorated. The family had been saddened by Leticia's departure and then subsequently hurt by how little attention she paid them after she returned. The economy had worsened in her absence, and everything was harder. President Reagan's 1985 economic blockade had earlier cut off Nicaraguans' access to parts, equipment, and dollars, and the impact was felt in Nicaragua. U.S. aid to the contras increased. And Marta, the difficult times weighing heavily on her, said:

> In case I die and you come next year, remember that the family is not just one person. I hope that this would not affect your visits to the house; instead I would ask that you help us more because the visits help a lot. Talking—forgetting some things and remembering others—it's good.

In 1987 when I landed at the airport, I was immediately aware of the worsening economy. In exchange for the U.S. $60 that foreigners are required to change, I received an unwieldy stack of córdobas; I left the airport wondering where I was going to put all the money. Within a few hours, I saw small but symbolic changes. The old córdoba coin that was used for public phones no longer circulated because it had no value; therefore, no pay telephones could be used. Most of the taxi drivers I knew from previous years could not work because their cars had broken down, and they couldn't get parts. Water was turned off two days instead of one day a week in Managua. Beans, the staple of the Nicaraguan diet, weren't always available, but when they were, it was only on the black market that you could get them and for a high price. In Estelí, Doña María and Marta were embarrassed that they had no food to make lunch for me the first day I was there. Marta said:

> My mother feels bad because the first day you were here, she couldn't offer you food or anything due to our situation [with her sickness and the economy]. Leticia brought a chicken yesterday to make soup with, so she feels better because she wants to be able to offer you something when you come.

Marta, as she reviewed the years and our relationship, and maybe sensing that the oral history was coming to an end, said:

> There are times when I remember everything I want to tell you, other times, I forget. There have been things that happened, and I want you to know, so I say, "I'm going to write and send them to Diana." Then I say, "No, better to wait until she comes." I didn't think to take notes and have them ready when you come. So many things happen to me, good things and bad things. Then I forget.
>
> What made me happiest this year is your visit with the family. I haven't had any other happiness, only problems during this time. The only happiness is that you're here and that you're interested in knowing what the situation really is. You're doing a lot for us, and we very much appreciate your visit.

I looked back over the years, too, and thought how fortunate I was to have chosen people I like—indeed, love—so much. Even so, I couldn't protect them. Nicaragua and its people were showing the stress of the years of struggle. So was the family in Estelí. All I could do was tell their story.

Oral historian Elena Poniatowska says, "In the strictest sense, oral history is almost always related to the vanquished, the defeated, the earth's forsaken ones, that is, the people. Oral history walks side by side with defeat, not victory."[12] It is up to the reader to decide whether the family members have been victorious or vanquished. Maybe neither. Or both.

Their City: Estelí, Nicaragua

There are somewhere between 30,000 and 80,000 people in the city of Estelí, Department of Estelí, Las Segovias, Region One of Nicaragua,[13] according to the estimate I've been given. North Americans, basing their sense of how many people fit into a certain amount of space on their experience in the United States, usually underestimate how many Latin Americans there are in a city. Whatever the number, Nicaraguans would describe it as a mid-sized city. Certainly, in the eyes of Estelianos, size has nothing to do with the importance of Estelí in Nicaragua's history.

All through Nicaragua's recent history, Estelí has played an important role. Insurrections against Somoza's guardia occurred in Estelí in September 1978 and again in April and July 1979. By 1978, Estelí and other Nicaraguan cities "lay in ashes."[14] The people of Estelí continued to fight against Somoza, and he, in turn, ordered his air force to bomb Estelí for thirteen days. It was the last city he retook.[15] Today the city is often called Estelí Heroico (Heroic Estelí), and once Marta told me that they no longer put the accent mark on the *i* in Estelí because the city didn't want to be under anything.[16]

In 1985 the contras attacked the small town of La Trinidad just to the south of Estelí. Nicaraguans knew that the real target was Estelí. Up to that time, I had referred only to a city in Nicaragua, but that summer I asked the family members if I could use the name Estelí. My argument was that Estelí was becoming almost like another character in the account of their lives. It would have been impossible

to tell their history and not refer to the incidents of that summer
without naming Estelí. They agreed.

Located in a valley in the hilly tobacco area of Nicaragua, Estelí is
far from the oppressive heat and ugliness of Managua. From the
surrounding hills, it looks like a picturesque Central American town
tucked in a valley, dominated by a cathedral, bordered by the Río
Estelí, and divided by the Pan American highway. When you enter
from the south, the National Institute of Nicaragua is on the left. A
boulevard divides the two principal streets, each going one way.
You pass El Rosario School, the Pepsi agency, and a small park
called Ildefonso Velásquez with merry-go-rounds and slides, followed by the Casa de la Novia, the only place that sells wedding
outfits, and a florist next to it. Then comes the hospital, the business
district, and Central Park.

The park, called the Sixteenth of July, is the heart of Estelí. Around
it, they sell fruit, roast meat, and *vigorón*—a typical dish—made of
yucca, crackling,[17] and salad. The Cine Estelí is on the north side,
and on the south is the Teatro Estelí. According to Leticia, "on the
north, there are large houses that belong to people who've lived
there since I can remember; nothing happened to the houses in the
war. Around the park there is the Court and the Government House.
In the center is a fountain and monument of a mother with her
child. There are big rocks with writing on them that have been there
since I was little and played in the park." Marta described the park
as having "a lot of acacia trees. At the head of the park is a cathedral
where almost all the people go to Mass on Sundays. Around the
park people sell roast meat, *nancites*,[18] papaya, fried potato chips,
cotton candy, roasted or cooked corn, a corn liquor called *chicha*,
cool drinks made of *pitaya* or the seeds of *jícaro*, and earthenware
jars and flower pots."

Cars, trucks, jeeps, and motorcycles thunder through the busy
cobblestone streets. The farther one goes from the park, the worse
the streets are; there, a few cars go by, as do riders on horses and
donkey-drawn carts. During the day, the business district is lively;
people stand in line to buy fabric and other hard-to-obtain goods,
and vendors display their vegetables. Women stand around the central plaza and sell cotton candy, corn on the cob, chips, and sticky
sweet things. Everyone spits—anywhere, everywhere, and at any
time. Helicopters routinely hover over the city; people talk about

the sonic booms created by U.S. spy planes, but what makes them scream and run is the regular late afternoon rainshower. When it is not raining, the town is dry and dusty.

On a particular Sunday night in Estelí, life went on in the central park as it had for decades, varying only in small details, with the revolution nowhere in sight. An old Mexican movie starring Antonio Aguilar was playing in a battered theater; when it let out, people spilled into the park. An old-fashioned *paseo* took place: groups of adolescent boys and girls walked around and around, looking each other over. The young men's unbuttoned shirts waved in a gentle breeze, and the acacia, palm, and madroña trees rustled, giving a tropical feeling to the evening. A sloth hung upside down from one of the trees. A six-year-old boy sold *elotes*,[19] while the older boys wrestled with each other. Children played on well-worn swings, slides, and teeter-totters and ran through an old-fashioned bandshell; some approached the few foreigners and asked, "*¿Cuál es su país? ¿De qué anda? ¿España?* Where are you from, Spain?"

The chanting and music from the Assembly of God and the Pentecostal Churches reverberated down two of the dimly lit streets that spread out from the park. In other streets, people could be seen in the sparsely furnished front rooms of their homes, rocking in their chairs under bare bulbs and watching television. They all watched the same old Spanish movie, creating a stereo effect as the program echoed down the street, leaving an impression of Estelí as a city of television, rocking chairs, and Jesus Christ.

Marta described the homes in Estelí as "coffee-colored, like the color of the earth or of wood. The streets are wide enough for two vehicles. There are new buildings that we didn't have in the time of Somoza. For example, the fire station has been built on the spot where the jail I was imprisoned in used to be. There are new homes of people who lost theirs in the struggle; the government helped them rebuild, and the people built them better than they were before. There are new factories and a lot of traffic: cars, carts, donkeys, horses."

Omar spoke of a fairytale city, "a fantastic city. It's like a city in a story that someone reads—a city so valiant that it could not exist— and suddenly that person found Estelí and saw that there was such a city. It's hard to explain because Estelí, for me, is the most beautiful city in Nicaragua. And maybe that's how it would look to that person who reads about it, even in comparison to cities in foreign countries where there are better houses and better buildings."

Although Omar views Estelí as beautiful, he is not blind to the poverty—his own and the city's. "None of the streets is the same. There are hills, inclines, rises, and other streets are flat. Some streets have paving stones, others don't. Some are dirty, some clean. Some have trees on the side, others don't. At times, some have dirty water running down the street. We have only a few big buildings: the Bank of America and the Government Office. Estelí is a commercial city, but still there aren't many businesses. The majority of the owners are of campesino origin and don't have the money for big buildings. For example, in poor homes where Irene and I live, there are no walls, only empty sacks hung up, or pieces of wood. In the homes of the rich the walls are of concrete and so is the floor, but our floor is dirt. Roofs are made of zinc or tile. Some homes have electricity, others don't and light their homes with a candle or with gas. The majority have electricity and water. Where Irene and I live, you have to carry the water from a well or haul it from a stream."

Omar went on to describe a fountain with no water, a library with no books, a dirty city with no sanitation. "The city isn't clean because it lacks sanitation. The park isn't pretty; it doesn't have much decoration. We don't have any recreational centers, or not many. There are two parks, one small and one large. The large one is a whole block, 400 square meters. There's no water fountain—it's empty and dirty. There are few trees and few places where you can sit. There's a library, but it's not open much, has few books, and part of it has deteriorated. It really doesn't exist. There are three secondary schools, eight primary schools, a football and a small baseball stadium. The university from Managua gives classes on Saturday and Sunday."

In the surrounding area, according to Leticia, they grow "corn, beans, potatoes, rice, and *el pipián*,[20] which is used in soups and stews. Mother uses *quiquisque*, which is like yucca; they use the yucca more in Masaya and the *quiquisque* here in Estelí. And there's tobacco here; cotton is grown in hotter places, like Chinandega and León, and coffee is grown in more mountainous places, like Jalapa and San Juan. The tobacco crop produces more income for the country, but the most important crops are beans and corn." Marta added that they produce tomatoes, onions, and *chiltomá*.[21]

The family members described the people in Estelí with great affection, distinguishing them from people in other cities. Leticia said that the people "are nicer. They're more hospitable, more understanding, and less prejudiced. In Matagalpa, they're more know-it-all types and always criticize. I don't see that much in Estelí. In Managua, people are far apart; people don't know anyone, not even their own neighbors. If you asked where someone lived, no one knew. But if you come here and go to a house and say, 'Do you know where so-and-so lives?' they'll tell you if they know, and if they don't, they'll try to find the person for you. It's easier to have friends here."

Clothing styles in Estelí are simple, and people's features are distinct. According to Leticia, "people dress simply, but most like to look nice. Even if the fabric is cheap, they want to look good. The features of the people are pretty. Nearby in Santa Cruz, the women are prettier than those in Estelí. They're white women with green eyes. Very beautiful. Or blue eyes. In Estelí, most people are good-looking—there's a big difference between here and Masaya or Managua—the people of Estelí have finer features, more distinguished. In Managua people have more luxuries, but they're fatter and browner. Maybe they're sunburned due to the climate. In Masaya the people are brown and have straight hair. We call them *aindiadas*, Indianlike."

Marta talked about the campesinos in Estelí; "the people of the city dress differently from the people of the countryside. The campesinos wear work clothes—some with patches—and boots. The city people wear more elegant clothes because they work in an office or have more contact with other people. When the campesinos come to the city, they wear clothes like those of the city, with shoes of the city."

Omar spoke of the ethnic mix and class differences. "There are Chinese who are Nicaraguans, and blacks who don't come from the Atlantic coast but are Estelianos.[22] The ones who have the hardest character are those who come from the bourgeoisie; they're ugly and hard. The rest of the people—the poor—have a friendly and happy character."

The family has always lived near the river; Marta mentioned its potential for destruction and its benefits. "When it rains a lot, the river rises, widens, and washes away the houses on the river banks.

The town has to be ready so that we can get the people out before the river takes them away and they die. We use the river sometimes to irrigate the tobacco and vegetable crops. A lot of people go to the river to wash clothes and to bathe."

The family declared that Estelí's spirit and courage make it stand out in Nicaragua. Leticia says that "Estelí made a difference because many guerrilleros were from Estelí, and they made people conscious of what it took to make a revolution. Estelí is heroic because it was the first city attacked by Somoza. The Somozas always believed that Estelí was their enemy, that it was the most dangerous part of Nicaragua. They knew that Estelí was the city that would create and make the Frente Sandinista. And so it was that the second city Somoza attacked was Estelí. And the third. And now, in 1985, with this recent attack, it's the fourth."23

Marta agreed: "Estelí was the most combative of the cities. We listened and carried out the decision of our people to fight the guardia. I'd describe Estelí as a city that is a lover of peace."

Omar was the fiercest in his pride; his first reasons were historical and personal. "Estelí is combative and brave because generations have all followed that path. The majority of students fought against Somoza, and their mothers bequeathed to the other children their example. Many of their ancestors went with Sandino and fought against the Yankee intervention in 1900. From generation to generation, they transmitted this hatred toward the invaders. We followed the examples of Leonel Rugama, Rufo Marín, Filemón Rivera, Enrique Lorente, René Barrante—all old combatants [of the Frente Sandinista] who died.24 We, as Estelianos and Segovianos, confronted the guardia when they were powerful and we had nothing. We came out of this [encounter] with a spirit that made us feel brave and ready to follow the heroes who fought to the end. Estelí is a warrior town. The young people have been examples and have passed it down to another generation of young people, to those who join the cachorros.25 The majority of the cachorros are Estelianos or are from Jinotega and the North Zone. The young get it in their heads that they want to be like their fathers or their uncles, so they go with the cachorros. My photo, taken at the northern war front, is in the museum in Managua. I was the only Sandinista [in the family]. They saw that I was fighting the guardia and followed my example, and now they are all Sandinistas. And Marta's son Miguel wants to be what I am. So it goes."

Then Omar talked about Estelí's national and international reputation. "We're a people rising in rebellion. That's why Estelí is famous. But as they say, he who suffers most in war keeps getting screwed.[26] Somoza bombed the city many times. The contra wanted to get hold of Estelí because we've been an example on a worldwide level. Taking this city would be a political and military triumph for them. It would recover the morale they've lost by not having been able to take even an unimportant town; taking Estelí, an important city throughout the world, would bring them fame. They'd be able to say, 'We took the most important city,' and get a lot of publicity. Estelí has always been the vanguard, and it continues to be an example for the towns in Segovia and the rest of Nicaragua."

Contrary to what the family members believe, Estelí may not be known throughout the world, but those who live there think it is. Estelianos are proud to belong to a community that is one of the toughest and most determined in Nicaragua. While I would not call Estelí beautiful, it does have a certain charm about it that may not be apparent on one's first visit. However, in comparison to Managua, it seems like Heaven. I could hardly wait to leave the heat of the capital and arrive in the cool tobacco highlands around Estelí, and I always loved sitting in the central park that I set out to search for in 1983. After spending years talking with this family of proud Estelianos, even I began to think of the city as Estelí Heroico.

2

The Years before
the Revolution

The family and I began the series of interviews in 1984. They reached back in their lives to tell me about their early years and the time that led up to the insurrections that toppled Somoza.

Doña María

My name is María López. My mother never told me the date I was born, the year, or how old I was. That's because when I was three, she gave me to my godmother, who brought me up. Neither one of them ever told me. I imagine that I am 65.[1] I barely remember my father. While I was still living in Condega with my real mother, she sent me to spend time with my godparents so that I'd get used to them. I remember well that they put me in a hammock so that I could play and get accustomed to being there. My mother gave me to them as a present. She kept her other children, and never did I have the affection and love of a mother. My life is a sad story.

My mother still lives in Condega. She doesn't like to hear that I was treated badly in the house where she sent me to live. I was brought up to be afraid of everything. My godmother made all these marks on my arms and legs. My mother says she sent me there because she wanted me to grow up in a different atmosphere—she was poor and couldn't give me anything—but it was worse.

I remember kneeling by my godmother and learning the first letters. She was sewing, and when I couldn't make the letters, she'd hit me. I had a good enough memory, though, and I learned. Around the age of six, I could read any sheet of paper. My godmother rarely took me to school—maybe one or two months—and my godparents didn't teach me a trade. Today I can read very little, but I can write my name and the names of my children.

The man who brought me up, my godfather, was a lawyer. He supported the family, because my godmother didn't work. He was nice, but she wasn't. He was educated, wouldn't tolerate hearing a bad word, and was good with everyone. Papa died when he was eighty. He didn't hold a grudge against anyone, not even if they threatened him. She died two months after he did. They loved each other a lot. They lived very united. They had no children, so it was just the two of them.

I didn't meet Sandino, but I heard people talk. I first heard of him when the Liberals fought the Conservatives. Papa was a Conservative, and we fled to the mountains. I was so small that I was still playing with dirt, making little animals. Later, I heard that Sandino was in the mountains. The Liberals looked for him so that they could kill him. Luckily they didn't find him.[2]

Around eighteen or twenty, I got married to a man named Ricardo. I lived in Condega, and he worked there. He came to the house and asked permission to visit. Everyone was afraid of him because he was evil. Once, when they told me he was arriving—coming from somewhere—my body shook, and I fled to Estelí, where I worked on a little farm where I made five córdobas a month. I wasn't used to the work nor to chopped cabbage, which is the food they ate. Again, he came to look for me. He was a bad man who intimidated me. He hit me and gave me a bad life. Even the priest was intimidated. Ricardo told him that if he didn't marry us, he would kill him.

A couple of years later we came to Estelí. I was with him for four years, and we had two children. Diego is now about forty-three, and Adela is forty-two. I had to work in order to have clothes. He didn't even give me a dress. He treated me badly in front of people. And he drank.

Ricardo was a guardia for the first Somoza. He liked Somoza. I saw that Somoza; he was robust, brown, and very repugnant. It was said that if people didn't suit him, he had them killed and thrown in the ocean. They'd disappear and never be found. Ricardo was one of the first guardia at the time when they made twelve dollars—not córdobas—a month. Later they made sixteen, then twenty, then thirty—all dollars. I didn't get a divorce from Ricardo because there's no divorce when you get married by a priest. Ricardo married another woman in a civil ceremony. He beat her, too. He died when he was quite old. He was ten years older than I.

After that I lived with a blacksmith who's the father of Leticia and Leonardo. He loved only Leticia, not Leonardo.

I worked for people in Estelí who had money. Later I made tortillas, and Leonardo delivered them. Leticia sold desserts for a Turk by going to the buses.[3] I started washing clothes in the river—I didn't know how to do it, but I did it—and was paid twenty-five cents a dozen. The rain would fall, and the river would rise. It got all the clothes dirty. I'd wash again, dry the clothes on the bushes near the river, and deliver them so that we could get money to eat.

The father of my daughter Norma was an assistant in the guardia.[4] He was the same as the others; they were all alike. I made braids out of palms and sold them for fifteen cents so that we could eat a tortilla and have some sugar. He lives in Managua. He was already old and retired before the revolution.

The birth of the children was sad. The neighbors helped me and gave me something to eat. The children were born at home in bed, and I'd get up from there to look for food. Six of my children died as babies. The neighbors helped because when I gave birth, my children didn't have a father. The fathers left me.

Marta's father wanted to take me to Costa Rica, but I refused because I had the children and I wouldn't leave them. Better to stay here and suffer than leave them and follow him. He was good and made sure that I had clothes, shoes, and money. He didn't like it that I beat the children, and he didn't hit me. I was with him three years. I gave birth to two of his children who died. He was married to another woman but didn't love her because she was ill-mannered. He left her and went to Costa Rica. Just as well.

The father of Omar and Pedro lives in Jalapa, and he didn't help me, either. It didn't matter to him if I ate or not. He filled up at his mother's while I was hungry at home and had to drag firewood from the hills so that we could eat. We lived in the same barrio; when I first saw him, I said, "Very good man." That wasn't true. He was reserved, never talked, and didn't help. But he didn't fight and didn't like it that I hit the children.

The children and I lived in houses made of boards for six córdobas a month. The price rose to twelve, then to twenty, and I lived

here and there, all the time renting. The day that Omar's grand-
father died, Omar's aunt kicked me out of a house—Omar so little
and Pedro a baby. They kicked me out because they didn't love me,
old as I was. I found another house for twenty-five córdobas; a doctor there was good to us and gave us a month's free rent for Christmas. From there I went to another house. Always ironing. I made
twenty-five córdobas a month and had to buy the firewood to be
able to iron. I couldn't even buy a liter of milk. I had eggs and
exchanged them for the milk. Leonardo had to cook because I was
ironing. Pedro was sick and spent three years vomiting and having
diarrhea. I don't know what was wrong. It was probably because I
had nothing to give him.

That's how I learned the jobs I did. I suffered and learned to do
everything, to be a woman. I knew nothing. The people who brought
me up taught me nothing. They had money, cows, a house, ma-
chines, and the ability to teach me, but no interest in teaching me. I
remember that I had a good memory. I would have learned well.

My Leonardo was a good son. He worked hard to help me. He
made two córdobas a day on the tobacco plantations and later three
a day as a helper for the bricklayers. He'd tell me that someday I
wouldn't have to wash other people's clothes, that he was going to
get new teeth for me and find a way for me to have glasses. "Some
day," he said, "life will change." But it wasn't like that.

He was working for the bricklayer one day when his boss said to
him, "There's a trip to Ocotal." Leonardo thought, "They're going
to send me!" So he took off his work shoes, put on his sandals, and
came home. I was in the bedroom and he said, "Mama, I'm going to
Ocotal. Don't wait for me because I'm going to deliver some bricks."

"Aren't you going to eat?" I asked.

"No," he said. So I prepared some food for him and put it in a
bag, and he left; he went down the street, saying good-bye to all his
friends, and Omar ran after him with a soft drink.

In the afternoon a man came and said, "Your son is in the hospital."

"Which son?"

"Leonardo."

"No," I said, "he's working."

"He's there in the hospital."

They brought him back dead. But they didn't tell me. Leticia was working in one house, Marta in another, so I turned off the radio and left. We all went to the hospital where we found out that he was dead.

I left to look for the box to put him in. He had given me a gold chain, and I was going to pawn it for the box. But it turned out that I didn't have to spend any money; the owners of the company paid for everything.

Leonardo respected me and loved me a lot. He didn't drink—not that I knew, anyhow—and he didn't smoke—unless he hid it. He worked in tobacco, bricklaying, carpentry, shining shoes, whatever he could to help. He wasn't lazy. He was nineteen when he died [in 1970].

We were deceived in that we thought that the person who had hit Leonardo on the highway was in jail. Leonardo had stopped on the road to put water in the van, and a speeding bus hit him. But the driver paid a bribe to Colonel Meneces, a Somoza man, and was let go. Meneces was a bad man and eventually had to flee Nicaragua. He died of a heart attack in Miami.

All the Somozas were alike to me, always coming and making propaganda. I understood nothing because I knew nothing. I did know, though, that there was one person who was good with the poor—René Schick, a president we had for a few days.[5]

Somoza was the owner of everything. We always lived under him because, for example, they gave you money to register to vote. I could go to a table and get two córdobas; I would go to another for another two córdobas. I went around getting money. Pedro walked from table to table doing that, too, and then went out to drink.

Leticia

I'm Leticia. I was born May 30, 1947. From the age of seven, I worked full time selling food that I carried on a tray on my head. I sold *tamales*, *elotes*, and corn already cooked in its leaves.[6] The corn, for example, sold for one córdoba, and I earned twenty cents from each córdoba. I knocked on doors and asked, "Would you buy some *elotes*?" I did this every day of the week and, if I had to, on Sundays, too. I worked twelve hours a day. On Mondays we made a soup called *mondongo* to sell to people who drank too much rum on Sunday; it makes them feel better. There were five sisters who did the cooking, and when the soup was ready, I picked up the bowls at the homes of the people who had ordered it. Then I took the bowls to the sisters; they dished up the soup, and I delivered it. Later, around the age of ten, I sold pies to people in buses for a woman who was very kind to me. Whenever I finished selling, I'd go to the river to help my mother. She washed clothes in the river. The clothes were in heavy bags, and she couldn't bring them on her own.

Some days, there was nothing to eat or no wood to start the fire when we got up in the morning. We had some friends who looked after a farm for a rich man, and they gave us green bananas that we half-baked in the remaining cinders when we didn't have wood for a fire. Sometimes we ate a piece of bread in the morning with a cup of coffee, and that was all we ate until the night, when—if my mother had gone to wash clothes, and if the clothes had dried, and if she had been able to deliver them—we'd eat again. In those days they paid her around two córdobas for a dozen pieces of clothing.

It's difficult to study and work without having food. A child can't do it. When I picked up a book to study a lesson, I couldn't remember anything. My head would start to ache; it would feel heavy, and I'd have to stop studying. I felt I couldn't go on, and my brain wouldn't help because it hurt.

I always had to pay for the rent and buy food because I was almost the eldest. I say "almost" because my mother has two other children older than I am, but they were brought up by their father.[7] So I was the oldest. My brother Leonardo was two years younger than I.

My father still lives in Estelí. Ever since I can remember he hasn't lived in the house with my mother; he lived with another woman. I love my father a lot. He'd always visit me, and I'd visit his family. I even lived with them for a while; they cared a lot for me.

I finished eight years of school, but I was late—almost eighteen— when I finished. I had a lot of problems. For a few years I went to school in the evening. I started school whenever I could but then would have to drop out halfway through the year, which would make me lose the whole year. I always had to work, and that came first. My mother would sometimes get sick, so I'd have to look after her because the other children were small. I had to make the meals, so sometimes it would get too late for me to go to school, which is why it took me so long and why it gave me so much trouble.

In spite of the problems, I always wanted to be different. When I was about thirteen, I went to a store to ask for work because the stores always need people who can more or less read and write. The owner sold clothes, fabrics, shoelaces, and hardware. He was a harsh man and treated me badly. When I made a mistake with the prices, he'd shout, "That's not right!" I needed the job, so I'd try to forget those experiences, but many times I cried because he shouted at me in front of the clients. The store owners were the powerful people of Estelí; they still have their stores but had to divide the inheritance among several children who now have the stores. I made less than I made selling food, but the work was different.

While I was at that job, a friend of mine had a brother in Managua who worked at a hat factory and wanted to start a shoe shop in Estelí. Before coming to Estelí, he asked his brother to find him a salesgirl. His brother asked me to change jobs and work there. He offered to pay me the same amount, but I realized I'd be treated better, so I accepted. I worked there for about three years, from age thirteen to sixteen. After a while, the sales weren't too good, and he told me he couldn't keep on paying me and I'd have to leave. I knew I needed to work but didn't want to leave because I was fond of them, as they were of me. So I told them it didn't matter, they need not pay me—just give me food—and I'd keep on working until sales picked up. The man accepted, and I stayed. Then my grandmother died, my father's mother, whom I loved a lot. Her death bothered me, and I had to miss work for about eight days while we went through the mourning period. Since I didn't report to work, they hired someone else, even though I thought they liked me since I liked them so much, and I had told them about my grandmother's death. So I didn't have a job.

A man came to my house and asked if I wanted to work at his store. Before the war it was a big store where they sold all kinds of electrical items, cameras, radios, records. They thought I was a good worker. I sold a lot—probably because I was good at convincing people to buy—so the owners were happy with me, but I was always looking for a way to improve myself. The woman who took over while the owner was away used to ask me to curl her hair—to put rollers on her—and dye and style it. She used to say that I must like it because it came easy to me. I told her that it was impossible for me to think of becoming a hairdresser because it was very expensive. She gave me the first push. They used to receive *La Prensa* newspaper, which was the equivalent to what is now the *Barricada*.[8] *La Prensa* opposed the Somoza regime, and the fact that they received it made me realize that they weren't supporters of the government. One day she said, "Come," and showed me the newspaper. "Look," she said, "here they are offering a scholarship from Argentina, but it's only a correspondence course." Then she said, "Would you like to apply?" I think you had to send U.S. $35 to apply, so I said, "Yes, I would, but I can't because I haven't any money." She said that she would give me the U.S. $35 so that I could go to the bank to buy the draft and apply for the scholarship. Then I mailed it, and about a month later I received my first lessons. I worked at the store during the day and studied in the evening. Sometimes, in order to study my beauty lessons, I'd get to sleep at midnight or one in the morning. I sent the exams to Argentina to be corrected, and they would send me the grades. My grades were good. I did this by mail for a year until I graduated, also by mail. I was about seventeen or eighteen. By that time I was earning about five hundred córdobas at the store, which I used to help my mother.

When I began the correspondence course, I started to save a little money by doing without some things because I wanted to leave Estelí and go somewhere that had an institute where I could get a degree as a beautician. A correspondence course doesn't provide the actual practice one needs. Then, just by chance, a beauty school— a branch of a Managua school—opened here in Estelí. It cost 3000 córdobas, way too expensive for me, even though I had my savings, [but I went]. I'd work all day, then go to the elementary school, and at eight o'clock at night I'd go to the beauty school and get home about midnight. The days went by, but it was terrible for me because I knew my money was running out. I wasn't learning anything because the woman didn't teach us well enough. She charged us the monthly fee, but we weren't learning. So one day when Gloria, the owner, came, I asked her if she would let me study at her Institute in Managua and give me a job. She said yes, that it would be fine, and that my lessons would cost five hundred córdobas a month.

So I took the risk and left. Life is harder in Managua because everything is so distant. I told Gloria that I didn't have much money left because I had been paying for my studies and hadn't learned much. I felt I had to start over again, even though I had already spent 1500 córdobas on the Estelí branch. She said if I hadn't learned anything, that was my problem. She cared only about money. I arranged with her to start school and help her in the house as much as I could in order to earn my meals. She told me I had to wash my own clothes and pay for the lessons.

I started studying at the Escuela de Belleza Gloria. I always had this gift of being able to work with hair, but I became more aware of this when I saw other friends who had been at the Institute a whole year and still didn't know much.

People came to the Institute with a little paper that said, "Coupon for free hair styling," or "Coupon for free nail care." We wouldn't charge them because we practiced on them.

Gloria was a selfish woman who cared only for herself. We, the poor, were disregarded. It was terrible to feel like such an outcast. I shared a room in Gloria's house with another student, and we always ate in our room from plates we held in our hands. The only food she gave us was *gallo pinto*, beans with rice all mixed up and fried. We never got a piece of meat or a piece of cheese. We worked from eight o'clock in the morning to eight at night seven days a week—we always worked on Sundays because that's when people get dressed up—but we didn't get home until ten because we had to wait for a bus. She didn't charge us for the food, but she made a lot of money from our work. I was there only six months, thank God. The Lord was by my side; he knew I couldn't stand that life for too long. I couldn't even buy food off the street because I didn't have any money. When my mother managed to send a pound of *cuajada*,[9] I'd share it with my roommate; her mother would bring her cream or *cuajada* when she could—they were poor, too—and we'd share.

I realized that in spite of everything, the Lord helped me. He was always by my side, because of the forty-five girls who graduated, I was the one to whom Gloria offered a job in Matagalpa. I was eighteen years old. I graduated on April 30, and on the first of May—the next day—I started work. I couldn't even stop in Estelí.

I had a place to live in Matagalpa because Gloria had already arranged everything. The woman in the house where I was going to live owned a beauty salon. She didn't know how to run it, so Gloria told her that I'd manage her salon if the woman would rent the room to Gloria. I would also teach students. Thank goodness, the woman in Matagalpa was kind. She had been a poor, hard-working woman but had managed to improve her life. So I landed in a good home.

This is when I began another stage of my life. I started to work at the salon and on the publicity for the school, and people enrolled and took beauty courses. I worked for the woman and for Gloria. When a student practiced on a model, I worked with the paying clients but also supervised the students' jobs. Our teachers had used the same method with us. More or less twenty girls were graduated from my first beauty course in Matagalpa.

I liked this part of my life because—especially when you teach—there is always something different. That selfishness I had often felt no longer existed because I taught everything I knew. Some of my students have their own salons in Costa Rica, others in the towns of Chinandega, Jinotega, Matagalpa, Sébaco, and Limay.

I earned a total of six hundred córdobas a month. I always sent my mother money to pay for her house, and I bought things I needed. But there were times when Gloria picked up the money the students paid her and said, "I'll pay you later," and went to Managua without paying me. One day she stopped paying the woman who owned the salon. Gloria was a scoundrel of a woman who wanted all the rewards for herself. The owner of the salon and I decided that I'd no longer work for Doña Gloria and that the woman wouldn't let Gloria rent her salon. So Gloria left, without paying either one of us.

Gloria had never given me my degree; she wanted to have a way to hold me back so that I would always work for her. One day, when I no longer worked for her, I asked her for the degree, but she said that it hadn't yet been authorized by the Ministry. This wasn't true; she had it but never gave it to me, which is why I can say she's a bad person. Those who follow a bad path never end right, poor thing; she lost everything with the earthquake. Absolutely nothing remained of the salon. In spite of all she had done to me, I went to look for her, but I couldn't find her. She disappeared; I never saw her again. One day I was in a bus, and I thought I saw her at a corner waiting for a bus. I'm almost sure it was she. I felt like asking the bus driver to stop so that I could get off and talk with her, but I didn't. She must have left Nicaragua after the triumph because her husband had a government job and was close to Somoza. Their house was a mansion.

I kept on working for the woman in Matagalpa, and one day my first teacher from Estelí—the [only] one I did learn from—came to the salon and asked me if I wanted to teach beauty courses with her. It's funny the way destiny works out. The teacher was a certified professor and authorized to award diplomas. We got along fine at the salon and in the school. I helped her teach the beauty classes, so she gave me a beautician degree. She knew that I had already obtained my title and that Gloria had practically stolen it from me.

One day I told them that I had decided to move on. I didn't have much money to buy the equipment I needed, but I had managed to save a little. I had asked a man to make a small table of wood. I bought a mirror to put on it and rented an apartment with a friend. In those days, there were stores that gave credit, so I asked for a drier and paid a small monthly installment. I put up my sign and started to work. I called my salon the Centro de Belleza Leticia. I was about twenty years old then, and I felt good about the salon. Liberated. Whenever I had a slow day, I'd come to Estelí to see my mother. I'd give her a little money; then I'd leave. I liked Estelí, and I wanted to stay there because it was where I was born, but at that time in my life, Estelí brought back bad memories for me. I felt sad when I went there, probably due to all the difficulties we went through with my mother when I was a child. We were hungry because my mother was on her own. She has always been on her own. I always admired her, maybe because I was the eldest and could understand the situation a bit better. She always had to wash and iron to support us, which made me feel sorry for her. Going back to Estelí made me remember all those things.

And then I met Sergio. His sister came to my beauty salon one day to have her hair cut and to invite me on an outing to a farm. She and her friends didn't know me and weren't even my friends; nonetheless, I thought they invited me because they liked me. That wasn't so; there was more to it. Sergio's sister was jealous. She thought her boyfriend was in love with me, but that wasn't true. He was a friend of mine because he worked with my roommate at a creamery. He'd come to visit, but he wasn't in love with me. She thought he was, so she and her friends invited me on the trip. They wanted me to see that she was his girlfriend. I went, but took it very naturally because there wasn't any truth in what she thought.

When I was going to the farm, I got into the truck that we used for the trip, and Sergio was in it. He was sitting somewhere in the truck and moved so that I could sit down beside him, and then we drove off. We started to talk about everything but nothing related to falling in love and all those things. We went to the farm on February 14, 1970, and spent the day there; we walked and had a party and a *piñata*. The farm was nice; it had a big river where we went swimming. Then I realized that he had fallen in love with me and I with him. We returned home that same day, at night. He went home to bathe and came back that night to see me. The girls who had invited me to the party were happy—they no longer worried about the boyfriend—and became good friends of mine.

During the first week of March, they planned another trip to the farm for Holy Week. This time we spent a whole week on the farm. It was during that week that we became engaged. He was just starting his first year at the university; he was twenty-one and I was twenty-two. His family welcomed me to their house—they invited me to lunch—but they didn't think it was serious; they thought it would pass. I visited them a lot, and they also visited me. When Sergio told his mother that he wanted to marry me, she said, no, that if he married me—this was the month of March—she wouldn't help him with his studies, and he would have to leave her house. We were married on April 4, 1970. We married quietly, without his family knowing. I wrote to my mother and told her that I had found a man I was going to marry, but I was having only a civil wedding—not a church one—to see if it would work out.[10] I hadn't known him long, but I was sure I was in love because I had another boyfriend before for two years and had never felt so in love with someone as to get married. My mother said that there wasn't any problem and that I knew what I was doing. She met him after we were married.

He continued to live in his house and I in mine because his mother helped him pay for his studies in Managua. His family had money, so he had never worked before. He would go to Managua on Monday, return to Matagalpa on Saturday, spend Saturday and Sunday during the day at home with me, and go to his mother's house at night. We lived this way until one day, about three months after we had gotten married, I told him it was time to fix our situation. When he told his mother that we were married, she told him to leave. He told her to forget about any inheritance, to forget everything, [which left him] practically in the streets with no help. I told him that as long as I had work and until he found a job, he had to keep on studying, and I was going to help him. So that was how it was. He left to study, and I helped him pay for his courses. From that time on, I didn't go to his house anymore. Time went by like this, but one day he got sick, and his mother came to see him. I welcomed her. "Please come in and sit down." She said hello and all that. Afterwards, we were on speaking terms, but she would always say things to me like, "If my husband were alive, you wouldn't have married my son because he wanted to take Sergio out of the country, to Spain or somewhere else." His father wanted Sergio to marry a professional—a doctor or lawyer. I'd say to her, "These things are set by destiny." She hurt me a lot with the things she said, but I tried not to show it. Sergio was good to me, but his family didn't like me because I was poor. They had money, so they never regarded me as the perfect wife for my husband.

I got pregnant with Marisa six months after we got married. I was happy because I was going to have a child but sad because I knew that our situation in those days wasn't the best in which to have a child—I was the only one working. But then Sergio found work at the Sears store in Managua, where he earned five hundred córdobas a month. He continued studying at night at the university.[11] This way he was able to pay for his classes and his food. I paid for his clothes, transportation, and some other small items. I always helped however I could. I continued working; I never stopped. I don't remember ever not working.

When Sergio's father was alive, he gave Sergio a small piece of property in Matagalpa, maybe ten by fifteen yards, and Sergio sold it to help us. With that money, he then rented some land in Matagalpa and built a *galerón*, which we used as a carport to protect cars. I looked after it while Sergio was in Managua. This helped us financially.

I'd been on my feet working all the time, and by the time our daughter was born, I was weak and tired. A friend of my mother's lived in Matagalpa and often came to my house. She told me that labor sometimes began when the water broke and sometimes with blood. There was a doctor who had always seemed to be a friend. My husband paid him. It was a sacrifice, but I didn't want to go to the hospital free. It wasn't pride; it was fear. I was afraid, not because I wasn't brave enough to have a child—I was brave enough—but it was because I had seen many terrible things happen in hospitals to women. Nurses treated them terribly and said rude things, and I was afraid of that. Sometimes women had their children in their own bed because the nurses said, "You're a fool if you think you know when you're going to have the baby. You aren't going to have it now." Then the woman had her baby alone in bed. That's why it horrified me to go to the hospital without having paid. Both the doctors and the nurses treated people that way. At times they didn't even change the sheets; they wrapped people up in sheets soaked in blood. To prevent all that, my husband talked with a doctor who lived near the house and paid him to take care of me.

When I began to feel bad, I told the doctor and went to the hospital. He had already arrived and told the nurse to give me a serum that they put in the vein to hurry up the delivery. He said he was going home to eat. I didn't feel good because the pains began at one o'clock in the morning, and by the time I told the doctor, it was already six in the morning. Sergio was studying in Managua. This was May 22, 1971. They put a nightgown on me. The nurse went to look for the serum, but she didn't return. No one came back, not the nurse and not the doctor.[12]

A friend of mine who lived in Matagalpa came and said, "They said that the doctor left and will come back tomorrow." It was almost two in the afternoon. The water had broken, but no one knew it. My friend said, "You're not going to stay here. I'm going to take you to La Trinidad.[13] You can't stay here because you'll die."

My friend had a little car. She got me up, dressed me, and put me in the car. The people in the Matagalpa hospital didn't even realize I was gone. I was nervous during the trip because I thought I'd give birth in the car during the one-and-a-half-hour drive to La Trinidad, [but I didn't]. Marisa was born about 12:30 in the morning, about twenty-four hours after the water broke. I had trouble because I didn't tell the nurses [at La Trinidad] that the water had broken, and they waited for that to happen. Marisa almost asphyxiated inside the womb. She was born a little bluish, and they had to put her in an incubator. The hospital had nurses from the Atlantic coast—brown-skinned, affectionate, good—and they treated me very well. There were good doctors there, too—foreigners. The hospital has a good reputation. They are Adventists, a religious sect.[14] I think it cost 1500 córdobas on top of what Sergio had already paid in Matagalpa, but you could make payments.

When my first daughter was four months old, I was already pregnant with the second one, and we moved to Managua. Sergio was working for the Central Bank in the Department of National Census. He did the census in communities; he got the names of the people, what land they had, and so forth. Then he became supervisor of the national census and always had to travel. He had to go to places that were far away and sometimes didn't return for a month. Since he had to travel so much, I took responsibility for the family and the house, and at the same time, I had to work. Sergio and I saw little of each other. I was very sad because, for all practical purposes, I was alone. In Managua, we moved into the top floor of a two-story abandoned house, but two months later there was an employee cutback, and Sergio lost his job. So we came back to Matagalpa because he had no work and I had clients there. We spent two months in Matagalpa and lived two weeks in his mother's house. She didn't like me; she was possessive, and I didn't feel good there. In those two weeks, I began my little salon again and worked with the people who knew that I had returned. Through my friends, I looked for a place to live. Then a client, one who liked me a lot and knew the problems I had at home with my husband's mother, said, "Look, Leticia, I'm going to ask my father to rent you a garage." Sergio said we didn't have the money to rent it, but I had made up my mind. I told him I'd work, and with that money we would be able to pay for the house. "Let's do it," I said, "and if you don't, I'm leaving."

"Stay," he said, "I'll do it." He went with me. Immediately I made a division in the garage, put my salon in the front, and began to work again.

The earthquake took place two months after we left Managua. The house we had lived in was completely destroyed. We had lived on the second floor, and that part sank. If we had been in it, we would have died. But God is great, because two months later, they called Sergio back to work. Again he went to Managua and returned to Matagalpa for week-ends. We still didn't see each other much because I had to work all week, including the week-end. We communicated very little. Time passed, and they sent him to supervise the census in the mountains. He had to quit his studies because he couldn't return to Managua every day. He lost three years of studies for the sake of his work in the countryside. He asked for a transfer to Managua in order to start his studies again. He said he'd quit if they didn't give him that opportunity. The bank agreed because he was a good employee. This was in 1975, more or less. Our third daughter had already been born.

Sergio lived in student housing in Managua. When I decided to go to Managua, he said he wanted me there, but he thought life in Managua was so expensive that we wouldn't be able to support ourselves. In Matagalpa I had my work, but I told him that I was sure we'd be able to live in Managua. I felt bored and completely alone in Matagalpa. I made the decision against his will, and told him that if he didn't take me to Managua, we'd have to separate. Let him choose, because I practically lived alone. We almost never saw each other. He drank a lot because he had a lot of freedom, and he took a lot of liberties. He was irresponsible. He didn't see what problems we had in the house; he didn't know if the girls were sick or if I had a personal problem. He knew nothing because we didn't even have time to talk. He'd get to Matagalpa on Saturday afternoon around four o'clock because he had to work in Managua until noon. Once he got here, he'd go out—walking and loafing. After that he'd come back, then leave again and go to parties. He came home at dawn only to sleep. It was the same on Sunday. He'd leave early Monday morning for Managua. So we hardly talked.

When he saw that I had decided—I really had decided to do it—he said he'd look for a house in Managua, which he did; but he had to work, so I looked for a house, too. I talked with a woman who was building a house and explained my problem to her. It didn't have electricity or anything yet, but she—to help me—told me she would rent it. So I went back to Matagalpa, arranged my things, and caught a bus with my three children.

At first it was hard because I didn't have a lot of work, and Sergio earned very little. Life in Managua is always expensive. He asked me what we were going to do. With a small amount of money that I had, I bought some things cheaply in the Managua market—fabric and shoes—and sold them. I'd go with my friends to Matagalpa, sell the things, and return in the afternoon. I did this to be able to buy food. I also sewed. I didn't know how to do it—all I had done before was repair children's clothes—but I began to make dress patterns and clothes. I had a sewing machine that I had bought on credit while I was in Matagalpa. As I saw that it was going well, I began to sell ready-made items: dresses, blouses, sheets, and pillowcases.

Time passed, and I asked Sergio why we didn't buy some land to build our own house. So he sold the little carport in Matagalpa and everything else we had for 12,000 córdobas, and with that and our savings, we bought the land for 30,000 córdobas. What we did next was save his salary to buy material for the house; my earnings supported the family and paid household expenses. Sergio worked with another man who knew carpentry. He made us a little house plan because it was a little house. It still is a little house. My brother Pedro was still alive, and he helped us build the house because he was a good bricklayer. Both Omar and Pedro worked with us and built the house in a week. It was Holy Week, their vacation. Some walls of a previous house were still standing after the earthquake, so we used these walls, plus some wood and small pieces of concrete. The house was built without bricks, without floors, without doors, without windows. When it had a roof, we moved in and little by little added the windows and door. About eight yards in front of the house, we built a *portón*, a big door [with a wall], so that we could not be seen from the street. It was also for security since we still didn't have a door on the house. We put in running water, but we couldn't do everything at once because we had no money. A neighbor gave us electricity; we bought the wire, and she passed the electricity from her house to ours. We paid her for what we used.

Meanwhile Sergio continued studying and finally received his degree in business administration. He still worked for the bank, but sometime afterwards we decided to return to Matagalpa for reasons of health. He felt very tired, and I did, too. Managua had been a hectic place to live. But more than anything, we left because the Managua climate bothered me; I was skinny, and the heat seemed to give me tachycardia, a rapid heartbeat. But Sergio also felt that he wanted to be in a more peaceful place. So we went to Matagalpa where we lived one or two years, and then one year here in Estelí, and then back to Managua, which is where we were during the struggle for liberation.

During those years, I worked indirectly for the Frente. But much earlier, when I was thirteen, I had begun to think about politics. My first boyfriend was Oscar Benavides Lanusa. Now he is a hero, a commander, and a revolutionary martyr, but then he studied accounting and worked for his father. I met him at a party in the house of my grandparents on my father's side. Oscar and I became boyfriend and girlfriend, as young people do, but he was a very serious man with very formed ideas. I was mature. I don't know if it was because of my work or what, but I was always mature. I always took things seriously. So we went to parties and movies together. He was twenty-two when we met—this must have been around 1960—and he was already working clandestinely. At that time, I didn't know that he worked for the Frente. We didn't talk about it at the beginning because he didn't know me well. He didn't know that I had never liked seeing the injustices we saw in our childhood.

I never liked to see rudeness, even as a child. I remember once I saw a guardia hit a drunk with his gun. Because the drunk couldn't walk, the guardia hit him again and again. I remember being very small and yelling at the guardia. I felt such a repulsion for the guardia. I remember well the street, the corner, and my being halfway down the block when I screamed, "Why are you doing that? He's drunk!" After that I couldn't contain myself, and I ran away crying because I felt so powerless. I knew I could do nothing. Although I never liked the guardia, I can honestly say that among them, there were some good people, humble men. Some were campesinos and easy to get along with. But there were some that were rude to the people. I didn't like those things, and I could never be quiet about it. When I don't like something, I always say it. That has been my defect.

Anyhow, I began to watch Oscar, and at times we had disagreements because he would disappear for three or four days. I told him that I thought he had another girlfriend, but he told me that wasn't true. He said he spent time with his family in Santa Cruz. I half believed him, but not really. One time after we had been going out for a year—I was about fifteen and still going with him—he gave me the only party I've had. His present to me was fabric, white with gold stripes, for a dress. But I have a bad memory about the party. A good memory on one hand, but not on the other. It was midnight when the guardia came in a jeep and asked for the permit that we needed to have for parties. We didn't have it because Oscar had said that he wasn't going to ask permission to have a party. He already had his own convictions. The guardia closed the party down and said if we started it again, they'd put us in jail.

Oscar had a lot of confidence in me and began to tell me certain things. He said, "If you want to work with me, you'll help me work with the other compañeros." He told about meetings with Doctor Dávila Bolaños, Filemón Rivera, Ricardo Rodríguez, Julio Benavides, and other compañeros who later died.[15] He never told me their names; I discovered only with time who they were and that they had confidence in me. The only thing I knew was that we had to give parties and charge for them. Each person paid two córdobas to enter, and then I picked up that money and gave it to him so that he could give it to the Frente.

One day Oscar told me that he wanted us to get married, a civil wedding, nothing more. I don't know why, but I became frightened, and I told him no because I was too young. I got so nervous that my teeth chattered. I told him that it wasn't because I didn't love him, because I did. He was my first boyfriend, and I loved him a lot. But he didn't believe me. Then he went to the mountain without telling me. Our relationship was just left like that. We didn't finish it or anything. That was the last time I saw him. He never again came to my house.

When we say that people have gone to the mountain, it means that they have renounced everything. They give up everything good about life in the city. They are ready to suffer everything that happens on the mountain—food or no food—for the people and for the struggle. The people who make that decision risk their own lives and give them up by saying, in a sense, "Here is my life, and I hand it over for the sake of change." The slogan is "Free Homeland or Death." The people who went to the mountain proved that with more than just words.

Oscar lived on the mountain for eighteen years. When he was a prisoner in the Tipitapa jail in Managua, his mother, poor thing, walked from town to town to get there to be near him.

He died on May 17, 1979, exactly two months before the triumph of the revolution. He never got married. He had a Cuban girlfriend, though, because he trained in Cuba for a while. He became a great hero of the Frente Sandinista, like Tomás Borge, on that level. He was a compañero of Borge's, of Daniel Ortega's. And for me he was, well, he left me good memories. I don't have a bad memory of him.

My political involvement in the later years was also clandestine; not only did I cover for my brothers but also for compañeros who would have to leave Estelí because they had been detected. My mother didn't know that my brothers were working for the Frente. I was the first in the family to realize that Omar was working as a courier. One time Omar disappeared, and my mother became sad because she didn't know what was going on. Later Omar and I talked. I told him to tell me the truth, and he did. I asked him, "Aren't you afraid?"

"No," he said, "I've made the decision."

I was living in Managua, but I often came to Estelí because I always remember to visit my family. Sometimes Omar wouldn't be there. Then suddenly he would appear, the same day, in dark clothing—green shirt and green pants—not clothing of the Frente but in dark clothing so that he couldn't be seen on the mountain. There hadn't even been any insurrections or anything at that time.

Marta

I'm Marta López. I was born on February 16, 1960, in Estelí, Nicaragua. My father, a car mechanic, lives in Costa Rica and abandoned my mother when we were young. According to my mother, he was the best of all the men who fathered her children, but I didn't grow up with him and don't see him as something important. Our mother brought us up without him.

We were so poor that even though our mother worked, so did we, starting at age seven. My day began at six in the morning and ended at eight at night. I worked in the house of rich people for fifty córdobas a month. It was difficult; there were days when we didn't eat because we had no food. I earned very little, not enough to pay for the house or for the water, the electricity, not even the food.

I couldn't go to school because the people I worked for didn't give me permission to study. I started to go to school at night when I was eight and eventually finished the sixth grade. Sometimes a neighbor who went to school during the day helped me read and write. I continued from the second grade to the third and skipped grades because I was always trying to understand the readings better.

When I was nine, I found work for my brothers Omar and Pedro and me in the *tabacalera*, where the tobacco is produced. The process includes the sowing, then taking it to the *sarta*, which is what we call the threading of the leaves. Then the leaves are put out to dry and finally passed through another process. My work was to pull off the tobacco in the field, leaf by leaf, from four in the morning to six in the evening for five córdobas a day. There were times when we got up at that early hour and knew that we'd have to go all day without eating. There was nothing in the house to eat, and there was no place to borrow food because everyone else was in the same situation. Pedro got sick a lot, so they wouldn't let him work any longer. That left just Omar and me. Seeing that we didn't earn much, the bosses offered my brother additional work making cord and string. That way he made five córdobas a night and taught me how to do it. So we worked during the day at the *tabacalera* and made ten córdobas more at night by working at home.

The tobacco companies were associated with the Somoza government and also with the Cuban *gusanos*[16] who came here to make money at the cost of people who needed to work. We had to accept what little they paid us because there was no other work. I had a problem with the bosses; they wanted to take advantage of my economic situation, of my misfortune. They tried to pressure me to live [and sleep] with one of them. I was ten years old, and it frightened me. Omar and I quickly quit the job. Then he got work at the factory during the day, and I took care of children. At night he made rope, and I helped him. I worked for a family from six in the morning to seven at night. That family was more considerate than others had been. I didn't eat there because I knew my own family didn't have good food, but they let me take food home to share with my family in the evenings.

For years I took care of children, but I also mopped, cleaned, scrubbed, and cooked. The majority of people with money bring up their children poorly and let them do whatever they want to people they hire. If, for example, you took some of your relatives to the house where you worked, the children would pinch or hit them, stick out their tongues, and throw food. Since they were children of rich people, we could do nothing. We had to put up with it. We had to work.

When I was fourteen I got a job making airmail envelopes for letters in a printing shop where they make letters and things for when people die—cards for mourning. I learned to make them well; it was the only place in Estelí that made envelopes, and I made a little more money than I had before. I tried to earn more by going from house to house after work offering the cards for sale. I liked both making envelopes and selling them. I worked there until I was fifteen. When the owner died, they closed the shop, leaving all of us jobless.

I went to Matagalpa to work, again taking care of children. The family was nice and used to give me their old clothes for my family. Their children were small and not poorly behaved. I liked them a lot. I stayed only eight months, though, because my mother got sick. The owners of the house she lived in were trying to evict her. In order to support herself and the family, she washed and ironed clothes for the owners, but they weren't satisfied with that as payment for the rent. When I returned to Estelí I looked for a little room, and I took her there. The room was in bad shape. The water kept coming in, and there wasn't enough room for two beds, only for one bed for four of us. We had to use a *tijera*, a sort of canvas bed on poles that could be folded up.

Pedro and Omar learned to be bricklayers, to build houses. They were poorly paid, and their hands were all beat up by the hard work. But they earned more than I did, so it helped. At that time we all began to go to school more often.

I got another job cleaning house. I had gone to school but didn't know much, so the people at that house told me that they'd give me some time off to study, and their daughters helped me understand the lesson. That's when I finished the sixth grade.

We were still living in bad conditions: the neighbors treated us badly, my mother cried all the time, and we believed that people humiliated us because we were so poor. But we had hope that some day we would live, not better than others, but better than we had before.

Here in Estelí, principally in the barrio El Calvario, was where the Sandinista Defense Committees began as a mechanism to hide the organization of the compañeros working in the clandestine struggle.[17] Most people were unaware that we were organizing. We did it to help the guerrilla; for example, when the guardia captured a muchacho, the Defense Committees tried to free him. The nucleus of the Committee was only 120 people: only that many knew what was going to happen and what the muchachos were doing on the mountain. The committees worked in total secrecy. I didn't belong at the beginning, but I started to help in 1977 by hiding people in our house after I realized how involved my brothers were. That's when I first heard about Sandino and how he had fought for the campesinos and for the working class. At first I was confused and didn't understand. The guardia said one thing, and Omar said another. Somoza said that Sandino was a communist and wanted the people to die of hunger. He said that there were communists in Cuba, and they didn't feed all the people.

All my life Somoza was the only leader we had. He came to Estelí once when there was a parade in which the boxer Alexis Argüello rode a horse. Somoza was always behind a protective glass; in fact, most people in Nicaragua saw him only behind that screen. He was fat, tall, robust, with big cheeks and big glasses, and wore a black tie and black jacket. He told us that we were poor because we did not work so hard as those who had money. We tried to work harder, but nothing changed. The rich exploited us in such a way that it wasn't possible for poor people to improve themselves, not even to learn to read. We lived in ignorance.

I was confused until Omar explained it to me. He was probably only sixteen when he talked with me about all this. Omar was our teacher and guide, and Pedro and I were his pupils; he'd teach us how to organize ourselves, what to do up on the mountain, all that. When he explained it to me, he did it simply but fearfully at the same time because he was afraid I wouldn't understand and would divulge what I knew. When I learned about the clandestine groups, I also learned about the Frente Sandinista. I worked with [one group] the Northern Frente, without knowing who had the most authority, without knowing the commanders. I knew only their delegates because those in authority were clandestine, working in an orderly but secret way for their own security.

Later Omar asked me to hide things—my mother didn't know anything about what we were doing—like bags of corn, beans, and rice with guns hidden in them. After the guns were given to us, often delivered by a trusted friend who had a taxi, my brother would come and show me, "These are .45s, these are .22s, and those are .38s." I didn't know anything about guns. Then he'd say, "Put these in this bag, that in the other; we'll take them to separate places in Nicaragua." After that, he'd tell me, "Tomorrow, at such-and-such a time, two compañeros will come." He'd give me details: what they looked like, how long their hair was, and how their eyes were. Then they'd arrive and ask me if any housing was available around here; that was the code. I'd tell them that there was nothing available and then invite them in. As soon as they were inside, I'd hand them the bags. They'd leave and take the bus. I did this maybe eight or ten times.

Or a couple would arrive looking like boyfriend and girlfriend, but that was only so that other people thought that they were. The next day they'd come back, as if they were lovers going on a trip who needed to change clothes in my house and get provisions. A bag of this, a bag of that. But inside there were guns. I helped by knowing when the provisions would come and then listening for the knock on the door. There was always a lot of tension and fear. Our mother didn't know and laughs at us now. She knew something was going on, though.

The clandestine work was difficult because you had connections with people who knew what you were doing and who you were. That was the danger. At any time the compañeros could become prisoners and divulge the names of other compañeros. At the moment of their capture, you'd have to go to the mountain, even if those who became prisoners said nothing, even if they died in jail without telling. Out of fear, you had to go to the mountain.

I went to Managua where I got a job as a waitress in a restaurant; the salary was small, but I was helped by the tips. I returned to Estelí once or twice a month.

What happened is that during those days Omar had a compañero, another bricklayer named Antonio. They all worked together in secrecy for the revolution. Antonio and I saw each other in Managua. He couldn't go to Estelí because there he'd be recognized by the guardia. We'd be with each other in my sister Norma's house in

Managua for a week or three days, depending on the work he had to do. Clandestine work and clandestine love.

I stayed in Managua a year. By the time I returned to Estelí, I was pregnant, but I didn't even realize it. I didn't understand anything about that. I talked with Omar, and he told me I must be pregnant. I was around seventeen.

When Miguel was born, a nurse named Doña Cecilia took care of me. She still lives here. She loves my boy and still calls me the "scared one" because I was afraid. Antonio wasn't here because he had to secretly travel between Managua and Masaya and couldn't come to Estelí. I gave birth in a *tijera*; it's comfortable enough if there isn't a bed. There were no medicines for the pain. Doña Cecilia worked at the hospital and was aware of the situation because one of her sons was working for the guerrilla. She found an injection and gave it to me so that I could give birth quickly. The pains started at three in the afternoon, and he wasn't born until ten. By then all the neighbors were around. They brought a weighing machine—one of those scales to weigh food—and hung it from a string, put my boy in it, and weighed him.

I took my son to Managua once to show him to his father. We were there three days, and then he told me to go back to Estelí because he couldn't stay in one place for long. We saw each other only three times after the birth of the child. Miguel was five months old when Antonio last saw him. We didn't see each other again.

It's difficult to know if Antonio and I would still be together if he had lived because as women we're learning to value our work as women and as wives. For me, perhaps I can say yes. But there would have been changes. I've seen, among the compañeros who fought in those times and who lived together, that many of them have had to separate. It was a difficult situation where they didn't see each other often. A man would look for a different woman, and the woman would look for another compañero. I haven't had another lover. But who knows, in each second there can be a change. Each hour has a change.

I was given an opportunity to do some work for the Frente. I spent probably five days in Honduras, maybe seven in Guatemala, and six in El Salvador. I delivered papers to certain people and was told to find out what I could. The people didn't know me, but I had their descriptions and their addresses. I'd arrive and ask for a person by a pseudonym. Sometimes we'd go to a park, a restaurant, or a little cafe so that we could talk without risk.

I traveled in a truck with the owner, as if I were his wife. His business was delivering things, like clothes, that people had sent for. He worked all over Central America and knew the problems everywhere. His work wasn't clandestine, but mine was. I learned that there were many people ready to come and support the liberation of Nicaragua. And there were places our people could go, if they had to. I reported to the Frente when I returned. By mouth, not on paper. Papers talk.

Omar

Much of this testimony was told to me in 1984, the first summer of the oral history work. When I returned a year later, the Sandinistas had just celebrated their sixth anniversary and had run a series of articles in their newspaper, the Barricada, *celebrating the battles that led up to the triumph. Almost casually, Omar got out one of the articles based on an interview with Walter Ferreti, a military commander. In the article, Ferreti mentioned Omar as one of the people the commander still remembered. There was also a photograph of Ferreti's notebook, showing a list of the guns checked out to the squad Omar belonged to. Near the bottom of the list, a signature read, "El Esteliano," which was Omar's Managua pseudonym, along with the number and type of the gun he checked out. This prompted him to tell more about his story and, by his own admission, provided relief to his mental problems.*

I'm Omar López. I was born July 1, 1961. I started to work as a shoeshine boy when I was six. I remember a lot from my childhood. For me, it has been a source of pride that I worked and didn't become a delinquent. I remember the river coming into our house, and we had to run to another house carrying everything—tables, chairs—on our backs. I also remember that, as a child, I wore short pants and even though I shined shoes, I was barefoot. It was a difficult job because it didn't pay much, not enough to eat. We had to give what we earned to my mother for her to buy food. Those who shine shoes today make more than before; now they earn 25 córdobas per shoe. I used to make only twenty-five pennies.[18] That's 200 córdobas they make daily and I, in my present job in the military, make only 10 córdobas. They make more than I do![19]

From childhood to adulthood, we've had to work all the time, stay on the honorable path shown to us by our parents, and follow their advice. But really, we were brought up by only our mother. We haven't had a father to support us and give us advice. It has been only our mother. Perhaps that's why we have always gotten ahead. Our childhood was very sad.

I finished the fourth grade. At the age of twelve or thirteen, I began work in construction as a bricklayer. I was always looking for a way to achieve something, so I started as a helper and continued until I learned to build houses. That was my work before I became involved in politics. I also worked in agricultural business; for example, I made ropes that are used to tie boxes, horses, cows, and that are used to make girths and bridles for horses.

My life has been different from that of my sisters because I grew up alone with my mother. Pedro and I were always the smallest and lived at our mother's side. My sisters have had better opportunities than I've had. Maybe because of that, I didn't study much. It was difficult because I had to work and also learn a skill for the future in order to have some value. I've achieved that: I learned to be a brick-layer, or you could say, a builder, and I have a profession, too, in the military.

I saw Somoza in 1974 when he was campaigning in the city of Es-telí. Somoza always made promise after promise to get himself re-elected, but the people's lives never changed. Later, when I was working for the fire brigade here and in León—in 1977 or '78—I saw him close up when he came to congratulate us. He was always be-hind a glass case like a watch display. He never shook hands with the people. He was always protected. His appearance had two stages: at first he was fat and didn't have a moustache, but with all the trouble the Frente Sandinista gave him, he started to lose weight and get thin. He even grew a moustache and spoke in another lan-guage, almost always in English. He had an odd accent in Spanish; he didn't speak in simple language but like a well-educated person.

He didn't speak like we Nicaraguans speak; we're a little backward in speaking Spanish. He spoke it perfectly. He expressed himself well, but it wasn't in a way that would convince the people.

I joined the Frente Sandinista in 1976. At one point our family rented a house near the cemetery, and it was there I met one of the leaders of the Frente, José Benito Escobar. One day I went into his house and, by chance, I heard him talking about the Frente, but I didn't understand what the Frente meant. Escobar saw me listening and called to me, "What did you hear?"

I answered that I heard what they were saying.

"Would you want to join the Frente?" he asked.

I said, "I don't understand what it is."

He said, "The Frente is an organization that's going to overthrow Somoza's government, which oppresses us."

I told him I was too young for that.

"That doesn't matter. The important thing is that you cooperate with us."[20]

I was the first in my family to believe in the Frente and to get involved in the political movement; then I involved everyone else. The first job assigned to me was that of a courier, delivering papers from one part of Estelí to places in Matagalpa or Managua. The insurrection was October 1977, and a friend of mine had to leave for the mountain.[21] After he left, I was inactive for a while because I didn't keep in touch. Later I met up with my friend Tacoleón; he involved me with the Frente once more and assigned me the task of recruiting five people for the mountain force, which I did.

We lived near the highway, and I kept having problems with the guardia. One time in 1977 the guardia caught me and imprisoned me for three months. A lot of people knew I was working for the Frente, and they turned me in. The guardia came while I was sleeping at my mother's house. I heard a car and then saw four guardia getting out. I didn't even have time to get up. They pointed their guns at me and told me to get into the vehicle. I didn't resist because I didn't have a gun. They put a hood—a closed bag—over my head and took me to the barracks. At three in the morning, they began to question me. They told me I had to tell them where we kept the arms and where we had the camp. I wouldn't talk, so they hit me with a piece of iron; you can still see the scar [on my forehead]. I hit my mouth when they threw me to the floor. The next day they threw cold water on me after they had put thick salt over my body to make the wounds sting. Then they applied electric shocks between my ribs. Two shocks straight from the electrical outlet—whish, whish. I was unconscious for about an hour. After this they didn't question me any more since I didn't talk. After some time, another commander took over the barracks. The new commander, Melgara was his surname, was a kinder man, and he got me out of there. He told me that I should leave and not get involved in politics anymore, that the guerrilleros were thieves, that they dealt with marijuana, that they were rapists, and that I was too young to get involved in all this. I promised not to get involved again, but I was already determined to continue the fight.

Then I saw Tacoleón again. He told me to go with him to the mountain. I left without telling my mother I was leaving; I just got my clothes and left. I really have been my mother's favorite; she loves me a lot, and I didn't want to see her suffer because I knew I'd probably die, and then she'd die. Sometimes I'd disappear for a length of time with the excuse that I was going to see some friends in the community of San Roque, but I was really working for the Frente. My mother didn't even know I had been imprisoned because she hadn't been at home when the guardia captured me. After all that, my only alternative was to go to the mountain.

So I left. This was at the end of 1977 in December. I had never been in the mountains before.

We say, "*El se va para la montaña.*" [He's leaving for the mountain.][22] The saying is impressive, and it impressed me. I had heard the guerrilleros talk about it as if it were a mysterious subject. I thought that when I arrived at the camp, I'd meet big bearded men, but it wasn't like that. Instead I met young people, smaller and younger than I was. I was probably seventeen or eighteen. There were fifteen-year-olds there.

Before I went, though, I received guerrilla military training, maybe every week or two for three months in a safe house right by the river in Estelí. But it wasn't [the sort of] training where you learned a lot because it took place in a house so little that you couldn't even go to the patio to do maneuvers; you could only talk.[23] On the mountain the training was every day and hard: perspiring, running, hitting each other, and getting in shape. It started at four in the morning and lasted until five in the afternoon, sometimes without food because there was none.

When I left Estelí for the mountain, I walked with a sister of Irene's[24] to a hill you can see from my mother's house. When we reached the cypresses, her sister's husband was there to meet us. Irene's sister had been in the Frente for a long time, and her husband Filemón had known I was going to arrive. He took me to a straw hut where I spent the rest of the day. A woman was there with six children. She had an oven where you bake bread in her house. There were lots of lime and fruit trees and some cattle. I spent all day waiting for the compañeros; they arrived around five o'clock, just as I went to get firewood for the kitchen. One was called Mario and the other Martín. They asked me if I was ready to go with them and if I really felt competent to put up with isolation, hunger, and cold. They had a list of seven people who had been trained at the school in Estelí. The others on the list had already gone to the mountain; I was the only one missing. I arrived last because of problems at home; it was just Irene and me, with her two children. Then her brother died at nineteen from epilepsy. That made my leaving difficult. He hadn't been able to feed himself—we had to do it—and he hadn't been able to walk.

I had to decide which group to join. Within the Frente, there were three groups that fought differently. There were the Terceristas, and most of the students belonged to that. I went with the other organization called the Prolonged Popular War, and the Proletarians—the poor—went with what we called the Prole, which had fewer resources.[25] The Terceristas had more support because they either belonged to families with money or were advanced students. The Prolonged Popular War had mostly campesino people, and the Proletarians had some groups of campesinos. It turned out that Mario and Martín were Terceristas and wanted me to go with them because there weren't many in their group. But Filemón, the husband of Irene's sister, told me to wait for Isauro, who was with the Prolonged Popular War.

The people in the hut gave us beans and a tortilla. Later I asked where I was going to sleep, and they told me to sleep on the floor. I put out a blanket and a cape to protect myself from the rain. We were spread out on the floor, and while a compañero was cleaning his gun, it fired. The bullet passed near my head. It surprised me. The compañeros touched me to see if I was all right, but I told them it was nothing. They took away the other compañero's gun and penalized him by not giving him food in the morning.

Isauro, the commander, arrived about nine or ten the same night. Isauro is his pseudonym; his name was really Cristián Pichardo. He said to me, "You, muchacho, are going to come with me." And to the Terceristas, he said, "He goes with me."

But Martín said, "No, I'm going to take him." They were arguing about who I was going to go with.

Finally Isauro said, "Who do you want to go with? Are you going with Martín, or are you going with me?"

I said to Isauro, "I'm going with you."

"Right!" he said. "We'll leave at three in the morning. What pseudonym do you want?"

"I am going to call myself René."

"No," Isauro said, "not that pseudonym. We'll give you one now, and in the camp, we'll call you something else."

It was the three of us: Isauro, Filemón, and me. We left at three o'clock. It was dark, and we couldn't see because of the trees. I was in the middle, Filemón went first, and Isauro was behind. There was also a campesino to guide us, but he was farther ahead.

I fell many times because I couldn't see much and wasn't used to walking in the dark. When we passed near a house, a muchacho was taking out the cattle—in this place they milk them at four or five in the morning—and he saw us. Isauro talked with him and told him not to tell anyone that we had passed by. About seven o'clock, we rested in a place where there were few trees. We ate only a few pieces of candy because we didn't carry water or food with us. At nine we started walking again and approached a house where there was a big door and dogs that barked at us. We went in, and the campesino gave us a tortilla with *cuajada*. We left there about eleven and walked until four, when we got to Santa Marta where there aren't many people or roads. The campesino left at this point because from then on, he no longer knew the route. We climbed a hill that was almost a thousand meters high, and we had to come down it very carefully. It took us almost two hours because there were many rocks and trees.

I was confused because I had not expected to walk so much. I had thought we'd go to the camp in a vehicle. I was walking, but I didn't want to; instead, I wanted to tell them that I wanted to go back. In my mind, I was thinking, "I've already walked enough, but I can't return. They won't let me." It would put their lives in danger if the guardia got me and made me talk. So I kept on walking.

We arrived at another house around six in the afternoon and asked the people if Antonio, a muchacho, could take us to the other side, but he'd gone to the town of Pueblo Nuevo. "When will he come back?" we asked.

"He'll come about nine tonight."

"We'll wait for him." So we waited and talked with the people. We were in the house, and Isauro asked me what I was thinking about. I told him that I wasn't thinking about anything. Then I said that I had joined the Frente Sandinista because I had really suffered, as had all of Nicaragua, from the dictatorship we had.

"We're on a good path," he said, "and I like what you're thinking."

Around eight-thirty, the muchacho came from Pueblo Nuevo, talked with Isauro, and agreed to take us.

I had a bag on my back that was very heavy. I had some wire in it, a blanket, two pairs of pants, two shirts, and thirty pounds of dynamite. They didn't really need the dynamite; carrying it was a test to see if I had the strength or capacity. The others carried things, too, but nothing like soap or toothpaste. We walked from nine until three in the morning and got to Regadío. The muchacho went to a house near the road where there was another man who collaborated with the Frente. The muchacho asked if there was any chance that we could stay there a while, but the man said no: either the guardia would come, or the neighbors would turn him in and say that we were guerrilleros of the Frente.

After the muchacho told us that, Isauro said to him, "Look for some house where we can go. We're exhausted." I was wearing low shoes, not boots, and my feet hurt. The shoes always came untied, and I'd stop to tie them and then have to run to catch up with the others. Fortunately, the muchacho found a house where the owner let us spend the night if we were gone by the morning.

When we got to the house, Isauro asked me, "Do you have any candy?"

"I have only eight pieces."

"You take two and eat them, give me two, and give two to Filemón." Then we each drank a glass of water.

The campesino said, "Spread out here on the floor because there's no other place to sleep." We used our clothes as pillows. In Regadío it's very cold, so the campesino got out some empty corn sacks and said, "Cover yourselves with these." He also gave us six small, round loaves of bread, which we saved, and some canned sardines. I put one can in each pocket.

At five in the morning Isauro said, "Let's get going and catch the truck that's going to come by here." And in fact at five a truck brought milk to Regadío and went on to the Sirena River bridge. Isauro asked the driver, "Why don't you drop us off in Condega?"

The driver said, "I can't because I don't have any gasoline, but I can drop you off at Piedra Azul."

"Good," Isauro said, "let's go to Piedra Azul."

We left with the driver, but about fifteen miles from Condega, he pulled over to the side of the road to repair his truck, and we saw other vehicles coming from Condega. Isauro said to the driver, "Listen, friend, do you know if the guardia is in Condega?"

"Yes, they are. They're searching everyone who comes and goes."

"Then we'll stay here and not go through Condega."

I asked, "Then how are we going to get to the camp?"

Isauro said, "We're going to cross these hills." I couldn't go another step, not one more step, but I didn't say anything; I just said in my mind, "I can't walk anymore." Then I began to think, "No, I've walked this far; I'll keep going."[26] So we began to walk.

I asked Isauro, "Is the camp far from here?"

"We're near; we're near."

I knew it had to be a lie.

It was about six in the morning. We had been let off on the Pan American highway near a house with cattle in a corral. We crossed a river and walked on a little path, one where only carts or small vehicles can go. An hour later we were near some houses, but Isauro said, "We can't go near those houses. We have to take a detour to the other side." We went down another way so that the people wouldn't see us. Isauro did the guiding with the use of a compass and some notes he had written in a little book. We walked from eight in the morning until one without resting. There were many hills, and I always fell behind. It was hot during the day and rained a lot. We rested under some trees.

Isauro said, "Do you have any candy?"

"Only two," I said.

Isauro said, "Climb the *jocote*[27] tree and get down as much fruit as you can." I climbed it and got down a pile. The fruit—small, yellow, and sweet—is high in the tree. I must have gotten three pounds of fruit—some ripe and some that weren't. We ate a lot, and I put two pounds in my bag. We rested while we waited for the rain to stop and then started walking. My shoes were of no use. They were open, the soles had holes, and my shoe strings had broken. So we walked, and again I fell behind. They had more experience than I had; Isauro had lived in the mountains for more than five years, and Filemón, three. They walked quickly, and I slowly. They had to wait for me every four hundred meters. About four o'clock, we stopped at the mouth of a river. The water was clean, so we drank a lot.

Then Isauro said, "Get out the two pieces of candy."

I got them out—they were each about an inch big—and I said, "But there are three of us."

He got a stone and a piece of plastic. He broke the candy but ended up with a pile of tiny pieces, so he gave a little handful to each one of us.

Then, about four-thirty, we arrived at a little house of a friend of Isauro's. There was a woman in pain—in her belly, in her stomach—because she was going to have a baby. Her husband wasn't home. She was there alone with three little boys and a little girl. The two little ones were crying because they hadn't eaten. There was food, but the mother couldn't get out of bed to give it to them because she couldn't stand the pain. There were some beans in a pot but the fire had been too low. We found some wheat tortillas—they are black ones that people make when they have no corn—and fed the children and ourselves. The woman was in a *tapesco*, which is like a rough bed made of wood, but it's not really a bed; instead of lying on a mattress, she lay on empty corn sacks. In front of the bed, there was a folding screen made of corn stalks tied together with the bark of a tree.

The woman was complaining about the labor pains, so Isauro said to me, "This woman is going to give birth. Heat up some water." I began to heat the water, and he took care of the woman. He struggled for a couple of hours because he didn't have much experience. I gave him the water and went outside. I don't know what happened inside because I didn't look. I talked with the children about where their father was. They told me he had gone to a friend's looking for a pound of salt. Filemón is the one who actually delivered the baby. Isauro cleaned up with the water and a cloth. Filemón had seen a delivery before when a compañera on the mountain had a baby, but even though he hadn't helped then, that experience served him well this time.

The child was born, and the woman was fine and went to sleep. The father returned with the salt but also with the smell of liquor on his breath. Isauro scolded him. He asked him how it was possible for him to leave when his wife was in that condition. The man said he was doing an errand and the woman hadn't told him when she was going to give birth. An argument started.

Then Isauro said to him, "I need you to get us out of here, off this mountain, and take us to the highway that goes to Elí."

"I can't," he said.

"Stay here then," said Isauro. "Do you have money?"

The campesino said, "No, I don't."

"I'm going to leave you money, but I'm not going to give it to you," Isauro said; "instead I'm going to give it to your wife. You'd drink it up." He gave 3000 córdobas to the woman.

We left about six in the afternoon and walked until ten-thirty toward the highway that goes to Elí. We slept under some trees until three in the morning, when we began walking again, arriving at a roadside around seven o'clock. We asked for rides on the highway, but the only one we got was for two kilometers.

Isauro said to me, "You're falling behind; walk faster. We need to arrive today. Or tomorrow."

"Tomorrow? Why did you tell me that it was right over here? You said we'd arrive today."

"We'll be at the camp soon," he said. "I was joking!"

We walked from nine in the morning until three, when we reached La Laguna de Miraflor, a valley with maybe fifty little houses and an artificial lake. There were houses on both sides and a little place where they sell popsicles and soft drinks. We had a drink with bread—the first we had in so long. And we rested.

The way we dressed, as civilians, protected us because it's winter all the time in that zone, and the campesinos work all day. Isauro wore a hat, so did Filemón, and I had a cap with a bill. We were all beat-up, Isauro with campesino boots, Filemón with rubber ones that campesinos wore, and I with pieces of shoes. People looked at us because they didn't know us, but they didn't give it much importance, even though we didn't look just like them.

Isauro said to me, "Do you think I look like a campesino?"

"No," I said, "you don't."

"Why?"

"Because of your glasses." He wore big glasses.

"What shit! I go around thinking I look like a campesino, but I don't!" I laughed. Besides the glasses, Isauro had a big moustache, and he's white.

"I don't look like one?" he asked again.

"No, you don't."

We continued and arrived at a hacienda called Venecia, where they raised cattle. We didn't try to go in; we just went by slowly on the side. About two miles away there was a little hill called Cerro del Fraile. Instead of going over the top, the people went through the middle of the hill—it's a natural cave of five hundred meters—and came out on the other side, which we did about five-thirty in the afternoon.

I asked Isauro, "Are we near the camp?"

"Now we are," he said.

We went through the middle of coffee plantations, and he said, "Get out the sardines." I was happy. He cut open the can with a knife and got out the bread. He gave us one-and-a-half loaves, and he had me cut up some plastic and divided the sardines in little bags for each of us. He asked me, "Did you bring a spoon?"

"No," I said.

"Then I'll show you how to make one." He got a piece of wood and began to carve. "This is how we make spoons on the mountain." I ate with the one he made.

Later he said, "If you want, you can get some water to drink just down there." When he said that, I realized that he knew where there was water. It had to be that we were near the camp. At six o'clock, he said, "Let's go." We continued walking.

"How many hours away are we?"

"We're getting there."

We went on a small road and then climbed through some coffee plantations. There were a lot of *guineo* plants.[28] Isauro told me to get some fruit down. "How am I going to do that?" I asked.

"Get a knife, and cut the plant through the center. Then pull with a leaf, and the *guineo* falls off." After I did that, he said, "Put them in your backpack."

"I can't carry any more than I have!"

"Put them in!" So I did. But first we ate half of them.

"Now I'm going to explain something to you," Isauro said to me. "In the past, we made a lot of mistakes with compañeros we brought here who later deserted. They left the camp, and many of them turned us in. You'll forgive us, but we have to blindfold your eyes from here on."

"No! If you do, I won't walk!"

"Look, it's for your own good and for the good of all the friends you're going to have in the camp." They told me to tie on my pack and bag; then they put a handkerchief, a black and red one, over my eyes and turned me around five times.[29] "Hang on to my belt," Isauro said.

I hung on. Filemón went first, Isauro in the middle, and I came behind. I walked, but I also fell. We went slowly. I could feel that we were going lower. We went through water up to my knees, and when we went through a stream, up to my neck. There was lots of mud, and branches hit me in the face. I calculated the hours. In the mountain the crickets begin singing about six o'clock; the frogs and toads sing about an hour after the crickets. After the frogs, there is a silence, and the crickets begin again. I say we walked two hours. At that point, Isauro said, "Be quiet; we're almost there." He whistled. There was no answer, so he whistled again. Then they answered. The other guerrillero was up higher, but Isauro made a mistake—it was very dark, and we didn't carry a lamp—and he missed the entrance. "Wait for me here," he said. "Don't move." So there I sat, with my eyes blindfolded. I lifted the scarf up, but I couldn't see anything. It was all dark. I pulled the scarf back down when I knew they were coming. He said, "It's through here; hang on again." We went near the banks of a river, and he said, "Hang on tightly. Here the earth is smooth and soft, and you can easily slip." As we walked, my bag got tangled up with a branch, and I ended up pulling Isauro from behind; I broke his belt, he fell on the ground, and I fell after him. He asked me if I was all right, and I was. He went on ahead and came back to get me. They had whistled again, and four guerrilleros came and took my bag. I felt so relieved. Isauro said, "Take off your blindfold," and I did. There was a hill a little higher than a house to climb before we got to the camp where it was flat. I looked up toward the camp but saw nothing. They said, "Grab this root."[30] The root hung from the trees and was used to climb up to the camp, but it was very smooth, and I fell twice. I kept at it until I got where I could feel rough sand or rocks where they had made ditches. It was about one o'clock at night when I arrived, and I couldn't see any one, only the four compañeros who came with me. They said, "How do you feel, brother?"

"Pretty well beaten up on the legs. It was hard."

"You'll get used to it," they said.

"What do you have to eat here?" Isauro asked.

"Only *atol*," they said.[31] "It has to be heated up a bit." They heated it, but I didn't want to eat. "Eat it," they said, "it will make you feel better." So I ate it.

"Now where do I go?"

"We have to make a hammock for the compañero." That very night they wove a hammock for me to sleep in, and then told me to hang it up. I looked for two trees and hung it between them. But when I tied it, I didn't do it very well, and it fell to the ground. Everyone laughed.

Isauro scolded all of them, "That's not the way to receive a compañero. You have to help him." They all agreed.

It rained from time to time that night. I was lying down and getting wet. Another compañero said, "Compa, if you want, you can use my piece of plastic and sleep below my hammock where I'm sleeping."[32] So I lay down under his hammock and kept dry that way. I didn't sleep, though. I was sad and missed my mother.

I was happy to see the compañeros' faces in the morning. There were forty of them. Some young, others old, some bearded, and some not. Some had guns, others had pistols. There were machine guns, some carbines.

At five in the morning, there was a formation, everyone in line. They asked me, "How are your legs?"

"They hurt."

"Then don't do any exercises today; go help cook."

I asked the cook how I could help; he said, "Go look for some firewood."

It had been raining all the time, making it difficult to find wood that would burn, so I returned and said, "I can't find wood; there's only wet wood."

"Bring it."

I wondered how he was going to burn wet wood, but I brought it. The compa began to scrape off the wood until all that was left was the part inside, the driest, and he made little chips, kindling wood, out of it and put it on the fire. The wood was from the *ocote* tree.[33] He lit it with a match, and we began to make the coffee. There were three jars of milk, so I said, "Why don't we make coffee with milk?"

"Good," he said, "mix up the milk." He put the coffee on the fire that was in three big rocks under a plastic sheet; it had started to rain again. After we made the coffee, he said to me, "Let's make *gallo pinto*. Fry the beans." I fried the beans, and he made the rice on another little fire. That was all. No tortillas, nothing.

When they finished the training and exercise, they all clapped and yelled, "Food!" They sat in a circle, and we gave them old cooking oil cans—some had their own old, beat-up cans—and spoons. There were forty spoons to hand out, and apart from mine, five were left. After they ate their *gallo pinto*, we poured the coffee with milk in the can. That way we washed the container just once; we had to conserve the water because the water came from far away and it was dangerous to bring it.

Then Isauro said to the compañeros, "We have to give you the final touch." That was the five servings of *gallo pinto* that were left over. Each person got an equal amount, a little spoonful.

At nine o'clock we studied. Sometimes we read the diary of "Che" and studied guerrilla warfare, such as ambushes and attacks.[34] We did that until noon, when they told me to go cook again and make the same *gallo pinto*.

In the afternoon, we rested. At about three Isauro said, "Let's give you a pseudonym." He called everyone together and introduced me. "This compa has come to join us, to live here. He's your brother. I want you to understand him, and I want those of you who are experienced to help him. Learn to value this compañero, help him however you can, show him what you've learned on the mountain. We're going to give him a pseudonym now, and you tell me which one."

Some said that they wanted to give me the name Roberto, others said Carlos, others said Miguel. There were a bunch of pseudonyms they wanted to give me, but Isauro said, "None of those."

So I said, "Why not call me René?"

"No," he said, "not that one. We had a compa called René, and he stole a pistol from us and 1000 córdobas. It'd be a shame to carry the name of that traitor."

"Okay, then."

"What other name would you like us to give you?"

"Pedro."

"Not Pedro. There's another in the camp named that. I'm going to give you the name César. César Augusto Salinas. You have to learn to value this pseudonym and learn why you have it.[35] You're the only one here who'll be called César."

Isauro was the commander. He assigned people to different jobs. There was always someone in charge, an officer; they took turns being like the owner of the camp. For example, the camp had to be kept clean. The officer made sure that everyone, instead of throwing out a cigarette butt, buried it so that we left no trace.

After two weeks, they sent me to wash dishes in the stream. Before going, I'd seen a jacket—it was very cold—that had been thrown on the ground and was dirty, so I said to the officer, "Why don't they use that?"

"It's no good," he said. "It's dirty, and no one wants it."

"I'm going to take it," I said. So I did. I went to the stream and washed the jacket. The stream was so cold that no one bathed in it— not many, anyhow. No sun came through the trees, and it was always foggy. When I was going down to the stream, I saw a little place where the sun managed to shine through the trees. After I washed the jacket, I spread it out on that spot to dry. Then I saw that the zipper was broken, so I ripped it out and threw it away. While the jacket dried, I washed the dishes.

The following day, other people went to wash dishes and found the zipper I had thrown out. They brought it up and gave it to the officer. He called me over and said, "You're penalized because this is a crime. If the guardia were to discover this, they'd climb up and capture us."

I asked, "What's the penalty?"

"You're going to bring firewood all day. You'll make five trips for firewood." I got a machete, and it took me all day to haul up the firewood. They had made me see my error.

After I had been in the camp for a month, it was my turn to be the officer and give orders to others. Isauro was the commander, but if I ordered him to wash dishes, or if I ordered the second-in-charge to bring firewood, neither of them would get angry because we were all friends.

The commander is the one in charge, and after that, there were ten chiefs of the squadron—political chiefs, training chiefs—who never were the officer of the day. They were chiefs and didn't like to order a lot—well, they did the same thing as the officer did because they were the heads of groups and had a lot of responsibility. But the officer of the day stands in the middle of the camp and gives out the day's orders, such as who will stand watch. Others were told to clean or bring firewood. All day we trained by walking up to ten hours to make our legs strong. We had a course through the middle of the trees where we ran. We had an orchard where we grew a few things. In the winter, there are no crops, so the campesinos' food helped us.[36] We had four or five hundred *quintales* of corn and beans and rice.[37] We ate those three things, but we really didn't eat much. We had no trouble with coffee because it was the coffee plantation area.

We made hooks where we hung containers to dry after we washed them. We made some little tables of bamboo and a big one of little pieces of wood; we covered the big one with a plastic tablecloth. Some compañeros ate there and some at their hammocks. When I was at that camp, we moved four times.[38] We either burned the tables or threw the pieces of them in many different places.

There were a lot of campesinos in the camp, about seven from that zone. There were about eight students. The rest were workers who didn't have a profession. There were professors and a doctor. Not all the camps had doctors, though.

The campesinos and students are different from each other. The campesinos are more humble than the students. The campesinos are quiet. It's easier for the students to talk, and they do. The campesino is short and brown, and in that zone, they were even shorter. The students are more agile, but the campesinos are stronger; they can run and walk better and endure more hunger. The problem of the students is that they lived a life of more comfort than the campesinos. They lived in better houses. In the camp, they had to face the fact that there was no electricity, no television, no movie theatre, while the campesino, on the other hand, never had any of those things. That's a big difference.

There was never any prejudice against anyone. It was explained to us that since the campesinos supplied the food, the guerrilla couldn't exist without their participation. At the same time, the guerrilla couldn't exist without the intelligence and support of the students. The same for the workers and the support they gave. All these different people helped give us more experience; the students taught the campesinos to read and write, and the campesinos taught others to grow corn, so there just were no problems. We were more than friends; we were brothers and sisters. That was made clear once when a campesino brought two chickens, forty-five tortillas, and ten pounds of *cuajada* to the camp. At the same time, a student's mother had sent with a courier some jelly—fruits mixed up with honey—and a box full of bread. The campesino and the student put the food on the table of the officer, who said, "This is for everyone." The officer divided the food for lunch but saved one chicken for one day and one for another. Everyone had the same to eat; no one ate more than anyone else. It was the same when the amount was small.

After I had been in the camp for three months, Isauro said, "Let's have a military operation. Let's train and prepare ourselves to confront the guardia." I felt happy and, at the same time, afraid; I had just a tiny pistol.[39] He said, "We're going to take La Laguna"—the place we had gone through and stopped for a soft drink. He continued by choosing compañeros: "You're going, and you're going." He selected everyone but me. He didn't want to take me. "How do you feel, César? Do you feel competent to go?"

"Yes, I feel good; I'll go."

"Are you sure? You won't be sorry?"

"No," I said to him.

"Good, then let's go."

I had already made a pack—I had learned how to do it—out of a sack. We left around four in the afternoon in order to be in the town about seven because it was three or four hours of walking to get there. It was the first time I had left the camp, so I watched exactly where we were going to learn where I had been for three months.

We got there but couldn't enter because there was a lot of traffic from Condega. Finally Isauro said, "We'll wait until the next day." At nine in the morning, we entered La Laguna. It turned out that our intention was not to confront the guardia—they weren't in La Laguna—but to begin with a political act and let the valley know that the Frente Sandinista was there.

The people were happy to see the guerrilleros and gave us food—chickens, bread, jam—that we put in our backpacks. Then, with no trouble, we withdrew. We got back to camp and ate well. The following day, the guardia came to La Laguna after they realized that the Frente Sandinista had been there. The people didn't tell them how many of us there were. They said we were a thousand guerrilleros, but there really had been only thirty of us. The guardia was afraid!

Isauro, or someone else, made contact with another guerrillero camp, and they delivered some better arms. I turned in my little pistol, and they gave me a big gun. I felt more confident with it. It was a .30.05; that's the only name I knew it by.

The hardest part was the illness I got after six months. I had problems with my lungs; I couldn't walk much and couldn't breathe. It was as if I were being asphyxiated, especially as I was falling asleep. I'd have to jump out of the hammock because I'd get tangled up. I couldn't breathe and would fall on the ground, suffocating, until someone gave me water. Isauro said I had to leave to be cured. It's a lung infection; the same problem my daughter has. I also got what they call mountain leprosy.[40] It's like having pimples or holes on the skin—big ones—that bleed. You get it from being bitten by a mosquito. It was all over my body, like a sore everywhere. My clothes would stick to my skin when I slept, and when I got up the clothes would peel pieces of the skin away. I couldn't sleep on either side or on my back because it was everywhere. The doctor gave me some injections, but they didn't help. He said, "We can't cure you here; let's see if we can get you out."

They took me—I had to walk—to Condega where my mother was. I didn't tell her anything about what I was involved in, but she knew; I had a little beard and long hair. I told her I was going to Estelí, but I didn't tell her that I was sick. I was with another compañera, and the guardia was watching from their posts because there had been confrontations here in the southern front with the guerrilleros. The guardia was checking young people to see if they had scratches. I had a pistol and a lot of ammunition—so did the compañera—and we put them in the sacks of beans. I told her to go first and I'd follow, but I'd avoid the guardia watch post by going over the mountain. She went, and farther out, past the watch posts, I caught the bus. When I got to Estelí, the guardia already knew I was coming. Someone in Condega told them. Two guardia dressed in civilian clothes followed us from the Estelí bus stop. I went to a house where my mother used to live, and I changed clothes because the clothes I was wearing had stuck to my skin and I was bleeding. I hid the clothes under a pile of firewood. I put on some clothes that belonged to Pedro; they were in the room I used to live in. I looked out at the two men who were parked on the corner. We left and took a taxi to the bus stop. The two guardia followed. When we got in the bus, the two guardia did, too, but they didn't say anything to us. At Santa Cruz, about nine kilometers from Estelí, I said, "Let's go to another camp." We took a little path—now uniformed guardia followed us—and ran to a *solar*, where we hid. We heard a guardia come by slowly, and the owner told him that he hadn't seen us. The guardia said we were in there and came in. He shot my compañera, and she shot him. The others from Security came and shot at us, and we responded but ran away at the same time. Three guardia died, and my compañera was wounded in the arm. The guardia didn't try to follow us.

We went to the camp about eight kilometers from Santa Cruz, where I made plans to go to a doctor in Managua. I stayed in a corn field for about eight days. Finally a muchacha came to tell me that the connection for Managua was ready and that I could leave. They took me to the Barrera family, who were later killed by the guardia in Honduras. When the Barrera woman saw my shirt full of blood, she told me to take it off and lent me a very large shirt of her husband's. They took me to Managua, where they had a brother who was a radiologist. When they said, "We'll go to the hospital tomorrow and get you through hospital security," I was afraid and got out my pistol to take along, but they told me that to take it would be dangerous. We went to the hospital by car, and the man drove by a big group of guardia. I immediately thought he was going to turn me in. I grabbed him by the neck, and said, "Drive over to the other side, or the two of you will die."

"Don't be afraid," he said, "I'm not going to turn you in." And then he drove over to the other side. "There's no problem," he said,

"I'm the same as the Frente; I cooperate with the Frente." He got me through the hospital security, and I got some injections. I was cured after staying with the Barreras in Managua for a month. That was August 1978.

Then the Frente took me back to Santa Cruz. While I was in the camp, the guardia realized that we—only nine guerrilleros, no more than that—were there. Three hundred guardia came. We fought them for only fifteen minutes; we didn't have much ammunition. A helicopter came, and we ran away because there were just too many of them. When they realized that they weren't able to capture us, they killed the peasants living next to the camp, who had given us food. They threw them—a family of twelve—down a well.

One of our compañeros was wounded, and we had to carry him. Since I had the most experience, I carried him for a kilometer. Then another muchacho, who was later killed on a corner in Estelí, carried him. After a while, we put the wounded compañero on a horse. He couldn't stand it, though, because of the bullet in his leg. He got nauseated and then unconscious. The guardia were all around us; we stopped a vehicle and told the people that they had to take us (we forced them) to a nearby clinic. But the compañero died from the bullet wound.

It was up to us to take him—but how?—to his home, about five or six kilometers from Estelí. We got him to the house where my mother used to live and put him in a *tijera*. We wrapped him in a sheet to take him to his family. A friend of mine, who had a taxi but worked with the Frente, said he would take the dead compañero to where he was going to be buried. "We'll leave about three in the morning," he said. But he was late; he came about five. We put the compañero in the trunk. At the guardia watch post, they were checking all who came and left. The taxi driver knew the guardia so he gave him one hundred córdobas, and then the guardia let us pass. We hadn't noticed that part of the sheet with blood on it hung outside the trunk. As we pulled away, the guardia saw it and tried to stop us by shooting. We had to fire back, but no one died. We got away and took the body to the muchacho's family. We explained how it happened, and his mother said she understood. The funeral took place right there in the community, and we went back to the camp.

After a month, Isauro took me back to the other camp. I was there until the insurrection of September 1978. Then the Frente told me that we should prepare ourselves for the insurrection, and I should return to Estelí, [which I did].

I was sleeping when I awoke to the sound of shots. That meant the Frente had entered Estelí. When I left, Pedro said he wanted to go with me, but I told him not to, that he'd better stay because he was too young and too nervous. He insisted, but I told him to look after our mother. He stayed in the neighborhood for quite a while, but I left. I fought near the Calvario Church, near the Rosario School, and all around the Estelí area.

When I returned, I could find no one in the house where I had lived. Some people told me that my mother and everyone else had gone to the Valley of San Antonio. I went there and found them. From there we went to La India. They stayed, and I came back, always in contact with the Frente.

That first camp was important. From there, I went to another camp and met other friends, but I was never in the other camps that long; after that it was one month, two months [at a time].

In some camps there were as many as eighty or ninety of us, but we were mobilized; instead of staying in one spot, we walked day and night. It seemed that we never slept. We'd spend five days walking, then return, but not to the same place.

The routine was usually the same. We began to make food for the compañeros at three in the morning. At five we did exercises to stay in shape and to keep our spirits up. Afterwards we had a breakfast of beans, rice, and coffee. There were no tortillas or potatoes. We often didn't eat after that because there was nothing to eat; what there was, we had to save for the next day. We all were skinny, very thin. There's no sun in the mountains, so we were white, with beards.

About eight or nine of us spent the day standing watch. When the rest weren't training or had finished their work, they sat on their plastic sheets. The sheets were small, about the size of a bag. We covered ourselves with them when it rained, and it rained all the time. We huddled up to get warm. There were no blankets.

When there was nothing to eat, we walked through the mountains looking for something. At times we caught deer and killed them; I was the cook and cut up the carcasses. Eventually we got some old oatmeal containers and ugly beat-up milk jars to drink from. The spoons were made of soft wood, as were the plates.

Once, with Commander Germán Pomares, we ate a snake.[41] They're delicious and thick. We took out the intestines but kept the skin to make a belt. We cooked the snake in water and salt, nothing else. But it was good because we were hungry. Not everyone ate it, though.

Sometimes there wasn't even snake. Then we ate fruit from trees and roots we dug up. We ate monkeys. Delicious. They looked like children. You could only suck the bones. But that's how we survived. We drank water mixed with mud—black, black water—because there was no clean water. We didn't boil it which is why we suffered from stomach sicknesses. Sometimes we could light a fire but at other times, we couldn't because the guardia would come if they saw the smoke. We ate raw meat without cooking it. When you're hungry, everything is delicious.

Living in the camp was nice. You know everyone is your compañero. If I had a blanket, I wouldn't just cover myself; I lent it to the other compañeros. If I had some food, I wouldn't eat it alone; instead, I'd give a little piece to everyone. We'd been taught to do that, and it was good.

3

Insurrections and the Time of the Triumph

In 1984 the family members told me of their different roles in the increasingly intensive struggle to overthrow Somoza, and how the time of the triumph was seen by each of them.

Doña María

We suffered a lot during the insurrections because we were poor.[1] Omar worked as a bricklayer, and Pedro worked and drank a lot. Poor thing. One night during the first insurrection, we were sleeping when we heard shots on the corner. Omar said, "Lie down on the floor." He knew that the Sandinistas were entering the town, but I didn't know that. They didn't tell me because I'm very nervous and get frightened. We threw ourselves on the floor, and bullets flew. Pedro refused to get up; he also knew what was happening. Then a piece of shrapnel hit a suitcase near us.

We left quickly because we knew that by morning the guardia would be coming along the highway with tanks, firing shots over houses. Little Miguel, Marta's son, was around three years old. We went to a valley called San Antonio. We walked all day, [feeling as if we were] dying of hunger. We took Pedro along because he had thrown bottle bombs, and the guardia had shot at him. We had to beg him to go with us. Finally I just took him. From our family it was only Marta, Miguel, Pedro, and me, but a lot of other people went with us. They helped me carry the child.

We stayed in schools and homes as refugees. I had brought some córdobas with me, so Pedro—in terrible shoes—and Marta went to

79

buy food and milk for Miguel. People were good and helped us; they brought us beans, corn, everything to make a meal. Twice we had to go there as refugees. The second time Omar showed up. He had looked for me in Estelí, but I wasn't there. The guardia was everywhere, but he got through and found me.

I was often afraid because I didn't know what my sons were involved in. I was afraid that the guardia would look at them to see if they had beards or scratches on their elbows and knees.[2] I was afraid because in La Trinidad, where Pedro had gone to look for food, they didn't like Estelianos. They still don't, not in San Isidro, either. They didn't like us because we were Sandinistas. Now they're Sandinistas, too, but they still don't like us.

We moved everything to Condega, where some friends helped me. My family in Condega didn't help; my brother has money, a house, cows, and a little place to sell things, but he despises me. Friends found a house for me. If the rain got me wet in the house, they took me to another and another until we found a good one that had a door with a lock, everything. And cheap. They gave me food, corn, and helped me.

Pedro had been shot and came to Condega where I washed his wounds and was curing him. We were walking together to my mother's house when a plane of Somoza's flew over. Pedro said, "Walk in the middle of the street." The plane looked for people who ran like clowns from here to there. To run is bad. Then he left me at the door and said, "I'll be back. I'm going to look for some pills for you and milk for Miguel." It was a lie. He went to join the Sandinistas, wounded like that, without being cured. The plane was still flying overhead, so we lay down in the house. The plane followed, through the mountains, the van that Pedro was in. Fortunately, trees covered the road and made it hard for the van to be seen. Soon planes dropped bombs on a town outside Condega. I went to my sister's house, but she didn't help me, just gave me the shade of her house.

It was when we were living in Condega that I realized that my sons were secretly working for the Frente. I found out little by little. I knew everything was hidden, and I was afraid. [I started to realize what was happening when] Omar came with a muchacha. His clothes were dirty, and he took them off to wash them; you couldn't let the guardia see you in clothes that were dirty and muddy from the mountains, so I gave him clean and ironed clothes. He took off his guns, hid them in the bags of beans, and covered them with towels.

Pedro didn't show up. Neither did Omar. After the revolution, we were told that there'd be no more rum, drugs, killings—nothing. That made me happy because I knew that Pedro drank a lot. I said, "My son's going to be healthy." He loved me a lot and was good, but not when he drank rum. When he didn't drink, he was good. He loved little Miguel and didn't like it when I hit the child or when I scolded him. He was like a nursemaid to Miguel.

When we came back to Estelí after the triumph, I saw the muchachos returning, coming down the streets, and I looked out to see if my sons were coming. Only Omar came, around August. But the other one didn't. I didn't see him again. I even looked in the newspapers and went to towns with a photo of him. When he didn't show up, I had to know he was dead. The other children told me, but I suppose I already knew. Pedro died near Santa Cruz, two months before the triumph, in May. The compañero who took care of his wounds there later told me that Pedro had been born to die.

At times it seems like a lie. I wait for him. I talk with him. I have his clothes here—his pants, his shirt.

Leticia

Pedro didn't know that Omar worked for the Frente, nor did Omar know that Pedro did. The first we knew about Pedro was when he was shot in the leg. He was walking at night, secretly, in Estelí's barrio Rosario, and they shot him. He managed to drag himself to the house where my father lived, and he hid there.[3] I don't know where the bullet came from, but it was the same kind the guardia used. The same bullets were also used by the *orejas*, which is what we called the people who worked with the Frente and turned people in to the guardia.[4] Someone, maybe a person connected with the guardia, saw him go by and shot him.

My father came and told my mother. I was in Managua. Marta went to the hospital. The government's security forces began to investigate and ask questions. But there was a nurse in the hospital who worked for the Frente. She told the people from [Somoza's] Security that Pedro was so sick that he couldn't talk; this way the guardia wouldn't get annoyed, and Pedro wouldn't be tricked. When she saw that things were getting more dangerous, she got him out of the hospital through a window without the guardia knowing it. I had to take him to Managua. We went by bus, and it took a lot for him to hide that he was injured. If the muchachos were seen with wounds or scratches on their knees, they were put in prison. It was a crime because the guardia thought that a scratch indicated that you had been practicing to make war against Somoza. If I fell and scratched my elbows, for example, I could have been put in jail. Wearing boots was also prohibited.

I took him to my house and then to a hospital called Centro Dermatológico, where they take people who have skin problems and mountain leprosy. It was a hospital of the State, of Somoza, and we told the doctor that he had been wounded by shooting himself. We went there every day by bus. It was always a risk because the guardia always looked to see who was wounded.

When my brothers had difficulties in Estelí or on the mountain, they almost always came to my house in Managua. In that way I felt I was helping. After the September insurrection, they could no longer return to Estelí because they'd be recognized by the *orejas*. To go to Estelí would be like putting yourself in the wolf's mouth. They needed clothes for the mountain and would come to Managua for them, or they would come to rest or to get treatment after they had been wounded. Not even my husband knew my brothers were involved in the Frente nor connected to the mountain. Toward the end, he realized what they were doing, but he didn't say anything to me. And he never stopped me from helping them.

When they arrived with muddy and torn pants or boots, we had to bury the clothing at the back of the patio so that no one would notice. We had to do it at night when everyone was sleeping. My clothes were all that was left for them. I was very thin then, and my clothes fit them. So they would change clothes and return to the mountain.

One time, around midnight, when my brothers were sleeping in my house along with my husband and children, we heard shots and the jeeps of the guardia going around and around looking for someone to catch. In those days, if they found anyone in the street after eight at night, they took them away. I had been sleeping, but I woke up immediately. I always expected something, especially when my brothers were in the house. I thought the guardia was coming to take us or kill us. My husband didn't know. He was innocent and so were my children. I asked God, "Help me, help us, My Father, don't let those people stop here." I heard them stop at our door and get out. They left their engine running, took their guns out, and got them ready to fire. I listened and got up without turning on the light. I ran quickly to my brothers without my husband's knowing. They were sleeping with their clothes on; they always slept prepared. "Listen," I said, "a jeep is here. You'll have to run. Get ready." They were already ready. "But not yet," I said to them, "because they might not come here." But after I said that, I went to the living room in the dark. Neither my husband nor the guardia could see me. Then I opened the *portón* so that the guardia would think that there was no house behind it and that the *portón* belonged to the other house. I knelt on the floor and asked God to help us and not let those men come to the house. I prayed that they would leave, that they would leave, that they would leave. Then, instead of choosing our *portón*, they went toward an empty patio that was on the other side. They walked over, looking for who-knows-what. They looked and looked and then got in the jeep.

I heard one of them say, "I think there are people behind that *portón*." They were talking about my house. "We have to look behind that *portón*. Maybe they jumped through it."

The other guardia said, "Yes, maybe they're there." Who knows who they are looking for. My brothers had earlier been chased by the guardia, and maybe the guardia had information about them.

The other guardia said, "No, there's nothing there." Then they got in the vehicle and left. I felt my heart come back to my body. That's how I spent the Somoza years.

I remember the first time I voted.[5] It was between Somoza and Dr. Agüero, the candidate for the opposition Conservative Party. I was young, probably about fifteen, and was working at the Almacén Sony. Apparently we believed that we actually had another candidate besides Somoza. Afterwards we realized that it was the same thing: there had been an arrangement between Somoza and Agüero. It seems that [Agüero and his friends] were manipulated by Somoza, or that they had put themselves in the situation. But we were deceived. I personally believed that Agüero was about to be president, and I sincerely liked him. I thought we were going to have another government, and I didn't vote for Somoza. I was already working with my boyfriend, and I knew what our situation in Nicaragua was. I knew how we were living and what was ahead of us.

When I went to vote, I was not as misled as the poor campesinos who were told, "Look, here's where you will make your mark." It was some people's job to give those directions. But I was more or less prepared because my boss was an opponent of Somoza, and he had told me how it was. I voted in a two-story house, and above the table where I voted—in the ceiling—there were holes. They said the voting was secret, but above the Somocistas were watching to see who voted for Somoza. I looked at the eyes above, arranged the papers just so, bent my head over them, voted, immediately doubled the ballot, and quickly put it in the ballot box. The rest of the people weren't prepared. In each house, they gave you two córdobas. You registered, voted, and got your money the same day. Most people voted for Somoza because they were used to it or they were afraid. Most were afraid. But sometimes you left fear a little behind and went forward.

The day of the triumph was a day we'll never forget. In Managua, we had the barricades of the muchachos on one side, and two blocks away we had the guardia. Thank God I didn't become too frightened to give food to the muchachos who came to my house to eat. If I hadn't been so sure, I might have been afraid, but I was confident the muchachos were fighting for a just cause. If, for reasons of destiny, they hadn't triumphed, it wouldn't have frightened me to die. For me that was a great experience; I began to have more courage, and I knew we were going to triumph, even when the muchachos retreated to Masaya.

Omar had been fighting near our house and told us they were going to withdraw; we knew it'd be an opportunity for us to leave. And Omar wouldn't need us. There was a calm, a moment of peace in what had been almost a month of war. One morning we left Managua looking for a place near the Carretera de los Viejos. We were looking for refuge from the war—outside of the city there was little combat—and went to a little farm that belonged to a compañera of my husband's from work. She had earlier said, "Whatever happens, you have my house at your disposal." Another family went with us. We took some things that we could carry, but more than anything, we took food. The material things we left behind. We didn't know what would happen.

While we were at that farm, a helicopter landed at the next farm, right next to where we were, full of guardia. The owner of that farm was a guardia commander. We got scared because we believed they were going to kill us. There were lots of refugee families in the house with us, and all the men hid under the beds because they had no guns. It turned out that the commander arrived to pick up the few things that he could carry because he was going on a trip. He put what he could in the helicopter and left. When we saw that, we knew.

Much earlier I had made a red and black flag and kept it under a pile of things. In my heart I was sure that the triumph was going to happen, and I had the flag ready for that moment. By the time the triumph was announced on the radio, the guardia commander had already left in his helicopter. I ran to get out the flag and showed it to everyone. I put it on the antenna of the old car we had—we don't use the car anymore because it doesn't have a battery—and everyone cried and laughed. We screamed with happiness.

We drove the eighteen kilometers back to Managua to look for our families. Along the highway came cars full of muchachos, of compañeros. I don't have the words to explain how we felt: those faces, crying from happiness, crying no longer from the pain of seeing our brothers die but instead for the triumph that we were experiencing. A new life was beginning, and that day was just the first one.

Marta

My brother Pedro began his role in the revolution as a courier. We all knew that within the struggle we could lose our lives or get wounded, and Pedro was the first. In 1978 he was wounded during a revolutionary operation that took place in the barrio El Rosario and taken to a house. The people at the hospital said they wouldn't treat him until we deposited a certain amount of money that we, as poor people, didn't have and couldn't pay. He had to stay in the house where he had been taken while I tried to find some money. We finally arrived with the ambulance and took him to the hospital; they gave him a bed, but not inside the hospital, and left him there to bleed.

In those days I cleaned the house of a family we trusted, a Christian family; they were good to my son and gave me clothes that belonged to their boy. They paid me only a small amount because they, too, were poor. I asked them for help. They told me not to worry: they'd borrow the money, and afterwards I could repay the amount with my work.

I went to the hospital and told them that since we were trying to get the money, they should start treating my brother, but they said no. One of the nurses, who was the wife of one of the guardia, took me by the hand to a phone and told me to call the guardia and tell them to come. I said no. She said, "Then your brother will not be taken care of." So I called. A car full of guardia came. They asked me what had happened to Pedro. I said that I didn't know. They called him a Sandino-Communist. I said I didn't know anything and told them the hospital should take care of my brother. The people at the hospital asked who was going to give me the money. I told them that the people I worked for would. The guardia took me there in a jeep, and my boss gave it to me. That's how we got the 1000 córdobas we needed. In those times that was an enormous amount for poor people. I made only 5 córdobas a day.

It was late at night when we got the money to the hospital. After we deposited the money, they told me to find a person who would donate blood. I said that I didn't know anyone who would do that. Then they said to just go and look for someone, but the guardia wouldn't let me go. Instead, twenty-two of them in three cars took me to the place where Pedro had been wounded. They had me there from midnight to one in the morning. The guardia asked me whom Pedro had been with, but I said nothing.

Dr. Selva, who was well recognized here in Region One as a doctor who helped the guerrilleros, had just been at a meeting at the home of one of the muchachos.[6] The guardia had broken up the meeting with tear gas. When Dr. Selva realized that Pedro was one of the muchachos, he came to help him. Because Pedro hadn't had medical attention and had lost so much blood, the other doctors said they'd have to amputate his foot. But Dr. Selva consented to do a graft from another part of Pedro's body and put it on the part just below the knee where he was wounded.

The guardia sent men to guard Pedro so that he wouldn't escape and so that they could see all those who came to visit. It made us afraid to visit often. Dr. Selva told us not to worry because he was going to get Pedro out of there. He and Dr. Dávila Bolaños hid Pedro among other friends, and he did escape.

Not knowing what day the doctors were going to get him out, I went to see him at the hospital, but he was gone. The guardia caught me and asked me where he was. I said I didn't know, maybe they had sent him to another hospital. The doctors said that he had been transferred. At that moment, when the guardia couldn't find Pedro, we became prisoners. I had to report to the barracks every day to tell them everything I heard.

One night sometime later, at eleven-thirty, we heard a lot of vehicles stop, and the guardia surrounded the house. They damaged the door to get us. Omar was taken to one jail and I to another. But first they took me to a place in the outskirts of Estelí where one of the guardia put a pistol to my head and said that if I didn't talk, he was going to blow my brains out, crack my head with the pistol. I told him I didn't know anything and what happened to Pedro was an accident, but they said I was covering up. I did know everything but wasn't going to talk because then we would all die. A lot of people would die. They pushed me back into the vehicle and brought me to the barracks. I stayed there a month.

I was in a small cell, full of water and dark. I couldn't even lie down; I could only stand up. It was about four by five feet. No bed, no toilet, with water halfway up to my knees. There was a ledge to prevent the water from running out when the door opened. There were no windows or bars, only darkness. I was there for a month. You can go without sleep for a month by having faith and knowing you're going to get out of there. I was afraid because the guardia could come at any time, do things to me, and I couldn't do anything about it. But I never lost my faith.

In the mornings they'd let me out to clean the guardia's toilets and to mop, and then they'd put me back in again. The food consisted of half a tortilla with beans. I hardly ate because I wasn't hungry. They wouldn't even let my mother bring me some blankets or food. They wouldn't let anything reach me. They threatened my mother by telling her it would take 6000 córdobas to free me. We had nothing, not even a cent. All she could do was cry. She thought they were going to kill all of us.

There was a government representative who was a friend of Somoza's. He had a lot of farms and property here in Estelí and was the one who gave the orders around here. Since only the people with money could talk to the Somocista, my mother sent him a letter through the firemen because Omar used to be a fireman. The firemen all spoke for us and helped us get out of there. They told the Somocista that we never got involved in anything and that we were humble people who helped put out fires. We also paid 1600 córdobas borrowed from one of our relatives. Finally, after about a month, they freed me.

Before I was freed, one of the guards, a fat one, came to say that if I'd live with him, they'd let me go. But I said no. I said that I had nothing to do with anything and that they could just keep me there because I wasn't going to talk about things I didn't know. He said, "Well, you can stay here and rot. You can stay here and rot in jail together with your family." I didn't say anything, but I cried.

When I got out, it all seemed different: the light, the streets. I saw it all differently, and I felt sad. My mother hugged me and cried. Then I went to look for my brothers; we greeted each other happily. My boy was happy. But I saw everything in sadness. I'd been locked up for a long time, and that produced changes in the way I saw things.

After they let us go free, Omar said that he couldn't live in Estelí any more and asked me to go with him to the mountain. I told him that I wasn't going with him because of my mother. So he left and didn't come back. Pedro left, too. The muchachos like my brothers had only small pistols and bombs made with bottles and gasoline. It frightened the guardia. They thought the muchachos had big guns, but they had only simple little ones.

In 1978, close to the September insurrection, we started to prepare the support activities for the fighters who would come down from the mountain to Estelí and Condega. One morning at dawn, we heard the shots and all the excitement of the muchachos coming to town. Pedro came to warn me to get all the families out and take them to another community. I told people that if they wanted to leave, we'd show them the way. We left by road with five families from our neighborhood. My mother got sick because none of us had eaten anything. My child had only water. When we were crossing a creek, we could hear the bombing [of Estelí]. The situation was hot. One of our relatives was carrying a radio, so we could hear from Honduras what was being said about what we were going through. We arrived at the community about midnight.

We slept in a little wooden school with other people from Estelí. Later, a family we had met walking along the road came to the school and invited us to stay at a small house of theirs. We fixed it up but didn't have anything to sleep on, so we made a bed by hammering sticks onto some pieces of wood, and there we slept, the three of us. One of the muchachos from the Frente left us money to buy milk for Miguel. He said, "We're going to have to organize the people. We need to find a cow that we'll kill and cut up; then we'll distribute the meat to the people." He also told me to get some rope. I went with the muchachos, and we killed a cow with stones because we couldn't make any noise firing shots. We cut up the animal with knives and penknives. We were never short of food because the muchachos would always come to kill an animal and distribute the meat. We stayed there while the September insurrection lasted, about a month. Miguel was about two years old. He was small but was just beginning to walk and talk. He'd play on his own.

Once my mother told me to go back to the house we rented in Estelí and return with a candle, a glass with a wick. So I went through woods and more woods until I got to the neighborhood of San Benito Escobar in Estelí. When I arrived the muchachos questioned me, "What are you doing here?" I told them, and they warned me that the guardia had set up posts and gave me information on how to get to my house. On my way back to the refugee camp, I saw the planes bombing the city.

When it was all over, we returned to the same house. Pedro and Omar didn't, though, because the guardia would have recognized them. The guardia, for three months, came to the house at midnight, standing guard to see if I went anywhere. I had to go every morning at eight o'clock to the jail, present myself, and say if I had seen my brothers or not.

I tried to fool the guardia once in order to warn Omar that they were watching me. I received a message to meet with him, so I went to a restaurant and ordered some food. Omar and some other compañeros arrived and sat at my table. Just after they sat down, the guardia arrived and started to hit one of my brother's friends. Then someone turned out the lights so that we could escape. The guardia had planned to kill us.

After this, life became very difficult. We didn't have anywhere to stay, and we didn't know what to do. My mother went to live in another community outside of Condega. From then on people, including us, started to prepare themselves for the April insurrection. It'd be a strong one because the muchachos had stolen some powerful arms from the guardia. My family all went to Condega, but I stayed in the small room in Estelí, ready to send bags of rice and beans with guns inside to the mountain.

Later I got a job as a maid in Condega, and we moved to a small house where there was room for only one bed. Pedro joined the guerrilla in the mountains and fought the guardia. We were closer to him in Condega, which was necessary because the doctors in the mountains didn't have medicine to take care of him. He, in his condition, continued the fight and told us not to worry about him. He said we'd triumph and he was going to continue working, in one form or another, with the revolution.

In April, when we were in full insurrection, Pedro was transferred to one of the communities near Estelí to do some work. There he was denounced by a spy and ambushed on a road along with four other muchachos. Everyone was wounded, but only Pedro died. He could still talk when they took him to a camp; he said that it didn't matter if he died, but that we should continue the struggle. A friend of his came to tell us. My mother didn't know about it until after the triumph.

The battle that pushed out the guardia was city by city, and it happened in Estelí on July 16, 1979. At that time I was in the community of San Antonio. I knew we'd triumph because we had confidence in our vanguard and in the direction we were going. The insurrections had shown that the combatants would overthrow the dictatorship in spite of the heavy barrage against us.

On July 19, I was in Estelí in the barrio of José Benito Escobar. The situation wasn't calm yet, but there was a lot of work to be done, mainly downtown. That day I'd gone to tell my family that they could leave San Antonio and return to Estelí. I came right back, though, because we had to clean up the barrios. There were dead bodies in the street, and they had to be handled by a special brigade. Some bodies were covered and carried away. Others were burned. The bodies were mainly guardia. There were a lot of them. There were barricades, destroyed houses, and the water was contaminated. The special board in charge of cleaning up the city's barrios created a brigade to clean the areas overgrown with bushes. We were instructed not to use machetes because there could still be unexploded bombs or mines in the bushes and in *solares*; a blow with a machete could set one off, killing anyone nearby. People were beginning to come into town. We started to put things in order by finding food and a way to cook it. We did the same as we had done before; we found one of the compañeros who went with us to find cattle to kill.

At the moment we heard of the triumph, we were at the home of a relative trying to organize the distribution of the meat. We had cut up cattle to hand out rations for the whole city. There was a lot of happiness; people fired shots in the air and banged pots and pans. We were happy because of the victory, but there were many families that had lost their sons and other families that didn't know where a family member was. So we were happy but also sorry for those who didn't have their sons.

Later we went to Managua to see who was left alive. It was there I found out that Antonio had died. It happened in combat, in the withdrawal to Masaya. The guardia threw all its strength into it and attacked them by plane and with a strong barrage of bullets. I know that was when he died because my brother Omar was with him. A paving stone [used to make the barricades] hit him in the chest.[7] It was the final battle, the one of the liberation.

Omar

On the mountain, we had one single idea. We knew why we were there and why we walked with a gun in our hand. We took an oath when we arrived: "I swear before the homeland and before the memory of Carlos Fonseca and Augusto César Sandino to go ahead without weakening.[8] I will not take a step backwards. If I fail to fulfill this oath, the blood of heroes and martyrs will spill on me, and the justice of the guerrilleros will be my death."[9] This oath made us think. We knew the objective was to overthrow Somoza, to have a change, to have a revolution. Other groups fought in different ways, but we fought with guerrilla warfare. Some groups fought in the city, and others fought outside the city, but everyone's objective was to overthrow Somoza and his guardia.

The first time I had to stand watch, I was frightened because there were animals, some snakes—big ones—and monkeys. But I got used to it. One time about midnight, I was cooking a deer we had caught and disemboweled. I was cooking, but I was also sleeping; I was all by myself and thinking about my family. It was at night, and I was alone. Crickets were the only thing I could hear. Everyone was sleeping. A little tiny animal arrived—*tiqui, tiqui, tiqui*[10]—and climbed on me and began to kiss me on the face. It was a tiny fox with no hair on his tail. He left and went to the table to look for food because he wanted to eat—*tiqui, tiqui, tiqui*—but he didn't find anything because there was nothing to eat. I went to the cooking pot, got out some rice, and gave it to him. He ate and left. Then he came every night to look for food. Always when I was alone.

We also had a little rooster. We carried it with us from the time it was a little chicken. But it grew and got big. It sang every morning and before going to bed. But one day we had nothing to eat, and we had to kill the rooster. He had been walking with us for five months, up and down the mountain. He had a name; it was Benito. The day we killed him, everyone was crying. They ate him, and they cried. Everyone cried for the poor rooster because we were used to walking with him. He was cooked in water. And a little salt. He made just a little bit of soup.

Sometimes when a compañero and a compañera got married on the mountain, we had a party in the camp. The campesinos would come with guitars and an accordion and cheer up the mood. The commander would take the place of the priest and marry them. It wasn't a valid marriage; it was just for the time we were on the mountain. We respected the women. Unless we married someone, we didn't sleep together. The women slept separately and the men separately. There was no disagreement, no weakening. We were all like brothers and sisters.

I got married on the mountain to a compañera called Dora. She was white with blonde short hair. We were in the north zone, but she was from Managua. Her father had a lot of money and came once to look for her; we hid her because she didn't want to return with him. She wanted to stay with us. The commander married us, and we had the party. We were married only five days, only five days together. She was carrying a gun in her hand when we went to get food. She was climbing over a wire fence when her gun dropped to the ground and shot her under her chin. She was shot about five in the afternoon and died about one in the morning. We didn't have medicine or doctors. For me it was a blow. It affected my mind. I wanted to shoot myself. I stayed sad for almost two months.

Others died, leading that life in the camp. A compañero died of a fever because we had no pills to save him. In Estelí, during the war of April, a compañero called El Toro died. We had come from the camp to fight with the guardia. He was in the Barrio Rosario, and I was on the corner fighting with the guardia when the guardia's plane flew over and dropped mortars. It blew him to pieces. That was another blow for me. We loved him a lot.

All in all, I stayed in the camp for five months, returned to the city for three months, then went back to the mountain for two months, and returned again. In other words, I didn't stay a long time on the mountain. Instead I'd come back to the city to look for food for the compañeros. From 1977 to 1979, I was on the mountain for ten months and in Estelí, hidden, for four months. In the city, I'd sleep one day in one house and the next in another. I slept in Estelí, or Matagalpa, or Managua, or San Roque. I brought people to the mountain, along with food and medicine. A priest helped me with the food, and so did the nuns from El Rosario school.

During the time when I was going back and forth, the guardia would show up when I visited my mother. We were always persecuted by the guardia. During one of those times, we had a problem in which all of us who were in the house were taken to jail. They held me for about three days until we paid a fine, a big one. From then on, the hatred towards the guardia grew stronger in our home.

I kept working for the Frente and always felt that same hatred for the guardia. They kept coming to look for me. They'd come dressed as civilians or in uniform, but they never found me. I finally had to leave home again. I went to Managua, and so did Pedro. He showed up wearing boots; if the guardia had seen him in those, they would have shot him right then and there. So I took them from him and gave him some boots of mine, civilian boots. Later I came back to Estelí and found him wounded, using crutches. I was training some people, and he asked me to train him, too; he said he wanted to go to the mountain with me. I said he couldn't go because he was still limping, but he insisted so much that I finally had to take him. I told him to report to Commander René, but René realized that he couldn't stay on the mountain because his leg was too injured. They decided to bring him back to Estelí. Later he participated in the April insurrection.

Like all Nicaraguans, Pedro was a happy guy. We were very different; we didn't think alike. He wasn't a responsible person and never took things seriously. He was nervous and smoked too much. He also drank too much. He wasn't the kind of guy to go steady with one woman; he liked to have several women. We were different in many respects, but when it came to the revolution, we thought alike. He just lived it in different ways.

Because the guardia kept looking for me, I couldn't go to the mountain any more. I had to go to the southern front and work with the guerrilleros who had been in Costa Rica. I was there for two months, and that's where I met Commander Gaspar García Laviana. We worked together for a month. He died fighting in the inferno in Rivas when I was in Managua.[11] I talked a lot with him, and I asked him why he had abandoned the church. He told me it was because in the church he'd done nothing against Somoza; now he was going to do something but with a gun in his hand. He said it was better that way because it was of no use to preach the word of God in Nicaragua when the guardia was killing the campesinos; it was better to confront the guardia with a gun and, in that way, truly liberate Nicaragua. I always knew him by the pseudonym of Martín. On December 18, 1978, I heard on the radio that Father Gaspar García Laviana had fallen in combat. I cried a lot that day. I left for the mountain, for the northern front, to tell the other compañeros—they didn't have a radio—that the guardia had killed Martín. We admired his ideas, and his leaving hurt us.

In April, I was in Estelí leading other compañeros in our fight against more than 3000 guardia, but there were only 300 of us. The guardia was closing in, so the commander ordered us to a zone near Santa Cruz but ordered me to return to organize people. On my way back, the guardia at the south post stopped me and asked me where I was coming from. They detained me for two days. When they released me, I went back to Condega and started to look for my mother. I couldn't find her; she'd moved somewhere near Santa Rosa, so I had to stay with an aunt of mine who didn't really want to have me in her house because she was scared that the guardia would come. She asked me to leave. My being there endangered her children. I didn't have anywhere to stay and had to return to Managua.

Later I returned to the mountain. We went through great difficulties. Sometimes we'd eat, and sometimes we wouldn't. For a period of six days, we ate only fruit we found in the woods or ate a salty-tasting leaf, but we really lived on just water.

With Commander Germán Pomares, we fought for three hours in the Valley of the Jícaro. A total of nine guardia were killed, and one of our compañeras died there, too. The guardia managed to push us back to Honduras, and we returned to Nicaragua by the Coco River, walking nine days without food until we reached the La Rica camp. By then the blisters on my arms and body were so unbearable that they decided to send me back to the city again. I returned to Estelí but didn't know where my mother was. I had tried to stay in contact with her but couldn't go home; if I did, it was at night.

A guardia stopped me in May 1979 about some pencils he had lost. He hadn't really lost them; he was just looking for trouble. He said he was going to get the patrol car from the barracks, so I said, "You'll be dead before you reach the corner." Again I had to leave Estelí in order to avoid being imprisoned once more.

I went to Managua as a courier for the Frente, but [just at that time] the national strike organized by the Frente began, with the objective of getting people together to overthrow Somoza.[12] When the strike started, there was no way to get back; there was no vehicle traffic, so I had to stay there. Pedro had already been sent to Santa Cruz. This was May or June 1979. I lived at Leticia's house in Managua. I found myself empty-handed. I had no support. No one knew me. The insurrection was starting, and I wanted to be united with guerrilleros. I went to a trench and talked with some of the muchachos. I told them to take me to their chief, whose name was Chombo, the pseudonym for Walter Ferreti. They took me to someone in charge, and I explained that I was a guerrillero with the Frente in the north. He asked me some dates and then said, "Okay, go with that column. You have more experience than they do, so help them."

The final insurrection began. I ended up in the Oscar Pérez Cassar[13] Squad formed from the most experienced combatants in Managua and named after a martyr who died in an insurrection. The column became the best in Managua. We were outstanding guerrilleros. We fought the guardia everywhere in Managua's Colonia Centroamérica, in Paraíso and Santa Rosa.

But at the beginning, I didn't have a lot of confidence in them. I signed up for a gun at a meeting where they asked us where we were from—our name, address—in case we died.

They said, "Where're you from?"

"I'm from Estelí."

"What's your pseudonym?"

"Give me El Segoviano [The Segovian]."

"No, the woman already has that one.[14] She fought with me and has the name. I'll give you the name of El Esteliano [The one from Estelí, The Estelian]."

So I became El Esteliano and stayed that. I told them that I was "César," but they said no. The more I said "César," the more they called me El Esteliano. "Hi, Esteliano!" So it stuck.

I told them my real name was Omar Antonio Martínez, not Omar López, but they wrote down Omar Antonio Martín instead of Martínez. I didn't give my real name for security reasons. The one who was doing the writing had been with the guardia, so I didn't trust him.

Leticia was nervous because I was involved in the war, and she'd cry. One day I was behind a barricade near her house when the guardia bombarded a church opposite her house with a tank and planes. Approximately twenty people died, and some children were wounded.

The day after that, I was ordered to retreat to El Edén bridge, where we fought the guardia for eight hours. One of Somoza's planes was dropping five-hundred-pound bombs on the people of Managua, and one of the bombs fell at the end of the bridge; it buried most of us and a whole family. Almost a whole block of houses disappeared because of that bomb.

That was June. We continued to fight, but with the constant bombing by Somoza's air force, the use of mortars, the scarcity of food, and the fact that the Frente was running out of ammunition, we decided to change tactics and make a massive move towards

Masaya. The order came from the military staff: Carlos Núñez, William Ramírez, and Walter Ferreti. All of us fighting in Managua went in the direction of Masaya, which was already liberated by the Frente, but only those of us in the Pérez Cassar Squad knew where we were going; the other columns didn't know.[15] They sent us ahead since we'd been given the best arms and ammunition.

We had thought that only combatants were going, but almost all of Managua joined us because the guardia was going to begin their clean-up operation. In other words, they were going to kill all those who collaborated with the Frente. If we in the Pérez Cassar Squad had to fight the guardia on the way, it'd be dangerous because there were more than 15,000 people with us and we were in the front. We'd be the ones to face the guardia. So we all thought that by going to Masaya, we'd die.

We left from the bridge about six in the afternoon.[16] The walk began slowly because some wounded soldiers went with us. We walked behind the Augusto César Sandino airport—it used to be Las Mercedes airport—but we didn't know the territory well and almost went straight into the airport where the guardia was. We got close, but one of the compañeros detoured us so that we didn't walk directly into death. For two days, we walked alongside the road. The guardia set ambushes, but we kept on advancing.

We rested for a while to wait for the other people who hadn't left Managua. The mission was to arrive in a single day, but this way, waiting for wounded, we arrived late. After we started again, the air force shot rockets at us and wounded several civilians. We got to a house with one of the wounded, but the guardia came out and shot at us. We had to eliminate all the guardia there.

Once, near Piedra Quemada, in the jurisdiction of Masaya, we took a white jeep, a bus, and several trucks in order to move the old people, women, and children toward Masaya. We were on the road in the jeep with eight compañeros when we saw Somoza's planes—"push-and-pulls"[17]—coming towards us. We managed to get out of the jeep just in time, but three compañeros were caught and couldn't get out. They died.

We were the first to arrive in Masaya. The people received us well, but there were thousands of us and not much food. We stayed in a house that belonged to a [political] minister of Somoza's, and it became our commando base. The guardia was on a hill near Masaya called Coyotepe and began to mortar the town. Our column had been separated—we weren't all together—so Commander Rolando Orozco looked for everyone in order to form the column again and attack the guardia. The day after the retreat from Managua to Masaya, they sent us into combat. We eliminated many guardia near the Cerro Coyotepe and after that, our insurrection went in different directions. There weren't many people responsible for directing the actions within Masaya, so Orozco took the best combatants and named them chiefs of the squad. At that point, I was the second-in-charge. We were sent to fight near the train station tracks. The guardia had come into Masaya and climbed the Cerro del Coyotepe, but now they came down to get us out of Masaya and attacked our positions from Coyotepe. When the guardia came down, some mercenaries came with them from Israel and Honduras.[18] There were a lot of them, better trained than we were. And our column still wasn't united; it was dispersed throughout Masaya.

The fight began in the Hielera, a place where they make ice, and it was there that the one in charge died. It was my turn to assume the responsibility for the squad. We advanced and cleared the guardia out of the Hielera. We eliminated three mercenaries, captured five guardia, and wounded the rest. After the guardia withdrew, Rolando Orozco and Commander Hilario Sánchez arrived; they saw what we had accomplished and named me chief of the squad for the whole zone. The guardia withdrew from Coyotepe and fled. We had liberated Masaya.

The military staff sent us to Jinotepe, again under the command of Rolando Orozco, whom we called "Stained Face" because he had a red birthmark. Rolando died when we were taking the communications building.[19] I was the chief of the squad of forty people, and we continued until four days of combat liberated Jinotepe.[20] After that, they sent the squad under the command of someone else to Granada. I stayed behind and was in charge of training militiamen and sending them as reinforcements to Jinotepe or Granada. Then I went to Granada and fought for three days, until it was liberated.

At the final triumph, I was still in Masaya with the Oscar Pérez Cassar Squad. I was the head of a company that trained almost a hundred people in guerrilla warfare at a school near the cemetery. We all intended to go to Managua for the first ceremony on July 19, but they told us we couldn't; we had to stay in Masaya until July 23 or 24. Then I went to Managua.

At the time of the triumph, we were poorly organized and poorly dressed guerrilleros who had to be turned into a uniformed and disciplined army. To do that, a training school was needed that had military people with more experience than we had. Within the guerrilla were members of the guardia who had left and joined the Frente, and they helped. Before the triumph, military people from other countries like Cuba and Viet Nam came to Nicaragua in solidarity with us, and they taught us how to fight as army soldiers, not as guerrilleros. One difference between the guerrilla and the army was that as guerrilleros, we withdrew after we attacked the enemy, but as soldiers, we attack the enemy and keep going; we don't withdraw. We needed to be taught these things after the triumph, and that's why we went to a training school. It was set up five days after the victory.

By July 23, I hadn't heard anything about my family. I thought they were all dead, but that day, I saw Leticia and Marta at the school's entrance. I hugged them and cried. The first thing I asked them was about my mother. "Is she alive?" They said she was alive but thin. That was my happiest moment. I had a friend who used to travel from Estelí to the school in Managua, and I had told him, "If you see my mother or my sisters, tell them I'm at Casa Carlos Agüero." So he told them, and they found me. I hadn't seen Leticia in months, and maybe it had been a year since I had seen Marta. But there were other moments of pain. I loved Irene's mother a lot so asked about her. They told me that the guardia had killed her. I cried because that woman looked after me and loved me. Somoza's air force dropped a bomb on her house, killing her and leaving small children. The house was totally destroyed. So I had some of the happiest and some of my saddest moments on that day.

I think I miss the life of the guerrillero. It was a good experience for me. I don't regret it. Just the opposite. I feel proud of having been on the mountain, proud of having shared my life, proud of seeing the suffering of the campesino, of knowing those who died. It gives me great satisfaction to have supported the people who wanted to be liberated and who supported the Frente and the cause of Nicaragua.

4

The Postrevolutionary Years: 1979–1984

The family members proudly assessed the successes of the revolution, often as seen in their personal lives or in their hopes for the future.

Doña María

My life has improved since Marta took charge of me. She works a lot, she takes risks, and I worry about her and the child. It seems to me that something is going to happen to her out there in the war zone. What frightens me most is when she leaves. There are ambushes, and she's in the military. If the contra put themselves on either side of the road, and if a state car comes along, they grab the people in it and kill them. They burn them. It's always dangerous, especially in the north until the November elections.[1] The people who join the contra think they're going to make money. They don't think they're going to die. They've been deceived.

The campesinos used to sell beans and corn at the door. Now they don't. It isn't the government's fault; it's the aggression.[2] There are people who don't believe that; they keep their eyes closed and think it's the government's fault. It isn't. If there were no aggression, we'd be happy. The government has fought for us to have peace in Nicaragua and in all Central America. Not a lot of people believe that. They say the government sends things to Cuba when Cuba has no need. Not true. Cuba has helped us.

Marta works and gives me the money. I do the shopping. She doesn't have to worry that I'll be hungry. I'd worry less if she stayed home, but she doesn't want to leave that work [with AMNLAE].

Right now, she's in Jalapa. That's the most dangerous zone at this moment. I worry, and she tells me not to. It seems to me that they'll take the house away from me. She says they won't.[3] I feel alone. Alone with the child. Sad. Without anyone in the house with me. Leticia's working. Omar's working. The child is nervous because he already knows a lot about war. Everything frightens him. It's terrible.

Marta is a good person. She helps me—not in the kitchen, though. She'd hurt herself if she did! Omar is good, too, and humble. He makes more money than Marta but not more than Leticia. I know he's supporting all those people, but he's a fool. So young to take charge of all that, knowing that he has no money. And he doesn't help me.

I'm at peace when there are people—a lot of friends—in the house. I'm proud when they like the food and don't criticize me. I don't like it when people who aren't friends come by. As a child, I was never permitted to have friends; I was kept locked up. My own daughters have changed me. They have friends, and their friends love me.

I have not lived well. I have no dreams. I'm only waiting to die. I think only about that. But I don't want to die and leave the child because he loves me a lot. I feel old and sick. I think too much, and it seems that I'll die of that. The aggressions have made me nervous. I'm afraid of everything, just like the child is.

Leticia

When we returned to Estelí in 1981, it was difficult to find a house to rent because many of them had been destroyed by the war. A woman rented us a little room, but we had to share everything—the patio and the bath—with her. She had many children, and there were problems. Sergio's mother owned a house on the riverbank that had been destroyed by the river about a year before and even again that year. Sergio told his mother that we were going to fix up the house; we put up the walls, installed plumbing, and changed the roof so that we could move there. I put my salon in the house and continued sewing. I had a muchacha who helped me; I cut, she fit it together, and we sewed. I almost spent more time sewing than working in the salon.

At this time, Sergio was still working for the Ministry of (Agricultural) Development and Agrarian Reform Institute in Managua.[4] I was pregnant with my last daughter, the little one. I was in poor health, thin, and nervous as a result of everything that had happened in the war. I began to feel bad with the pregnancy. The days were all right because I was distracted, but when night came I got very sad and afraid. I went to bed and was frightened by anything. I woke up scared, and the tachycardia would begin. I went to the doctor, but he didn't want to give me a tranquilizer because it might affect my child. I couldn't stand it any longer. The nights were terrible, and I didn't sleep much. I felt as if I were drowning and had to sit up in bed. I put a pillow behind me and slept almost sitting up. I felt so bad.

Then one day Sergio was transferred to Jinotega. It was then I decided to go to Jinotega to see a Cuban doctor whose wife worked with my husband. I told him the other doctors didn't want to give me any treatment, but I also told him I couldn't take it any longer. When I have an attack, my heart beats rapidly, and I wake up with a start. In front of my eyes, I see yellow things, like lights in my eyes. When this happens, I'm afraid I'm dying. When I went to the doctor, I saw he was interested in my case. I told him that the doctor in Matagalpa had told me not to take any kind of treatment, but this doctor told me that I had to take pills up to the moment I was going to give birth, even the day I went to the hospital. From that time on I began to have a little more peace because I was sleeping, and such terrible things didn't happen to me anymore.

Sergio was the one who told the Cuban doctor that I had to be operated on for the second time in order to have my child.[5] The doctor in Matagalpa had told Sergio that the operation was going to cost 10,000 córdobas. We didn't have that much money. I was afraid to go the hospital in Matagalpa, afraid of the trauma of seeing the coarse things they do to you there, afraid of what my heart was doing, afraid they'd give me a total anaesthetic, afraid I'd die. My children were little, and they needed me. To be a mother is a serious thing. Only when you are one do you understand your own mother. That's what happened to me. Thank God there already were international doctors working in Nicaragua. I went every two weeks to

Jinotega for a checkup and to get the medicine, and it didn't cost me a penny. When I started going there, I was four months pregnant. The same doctor who looked after my heart problem talked with another Cuban doctor who was a gynecologist, and they both took care of me. I slept better, had more energy, and gained a little weight.

I began to work for AMNLAE, the national women's association, two years ago, in 1982. I began by attending meetings to clarify for myself what this organization was, and then I joined. I worked for them in publicity and by doing some tasks, always as a volunteer. They named me coordinator of AMNLAE for my barrio. A coordinator gets orientations from AMNLAE or the Frente; there's one for each barrio, and there are probably sixteen barrios in Estelí. We meet, then go to our barrios and meet with the women to give them the same orientations that AMNLAE or the Frente gave us.

I belong to the Sandinista Party.[6] I belong, not because my neighbor does, but because I feel that I should. I don't belong because they told me to or because the Frente convinced me. The deeds, the real actions, convinced me. I began with the organization immediately after the triumph of the revolution by working with the Sandinista Defense Committees. I still work with them. I stand watch over the barrio at night once a week by keeping the door open all night. If something suspicious happens in the street, I tell the armed watchmen when they come by, but only if I see something suspicious; otherwise I say nothing.

The Defense Committees supply the provisions. At the beginning it felt strange because we weren't used to using ration cards or standing in line. It was irritating, uncomfortable; we were used to buying. Perhaps the poor weren't, but the rich were because they had money and could buy what they wanted. They hoarded things so that they did not have to waste time or stand in line. We were happy with that system, but we didn't realize the cost: there were compesinos who couldn't even get a ham taco and children who didn't have sugar. This matter of the food ration cards was a great thing.[7]

I can't explain to myself why Somoza was so brutal. If he had been more intelligent, he would have supported the campesinos. They would have kept him in power if he had just fed them better. Nevertheless, he didn't do it. He didn't remember that the campesinos had to eat and had to dress, just as other people do. I have the idea that he looked at them as powerless people without guns, as somehow made of a different material and not the same as the rest of us. They were robots he had molded. When he talked to them, he convinced them to pay homage to him.

The campesino always felt apart and marginal. Today we often see that the campesinos are [better off]. In their cooperatives they learn how to work and how to express themselves. It began with the literacy campaign, when the muchachos from the city went to the mountains to teach them to read. The families of those muchachos came to see the campesinos and brought them presents and food, and the campesinos got used to seeing more city people. But even today, five years after the revolution, one meets people who talk with city people with difficulty. It's hard for them, so they hide. They always feel that they—even in the way they dress—are somehow less than everyone else.

There are provisions that cost the government more than they charge us. It seems absurd, but it's true. I suppose that there is a way that the government can do that because in some cases like liquor—*guaro* isn't a necessity—the price is raised, and the price of food is lowered. For example, corn costs the State three córdobas. The State sells it to someone for two córdobas and makes up the difference with the one córdoba from the increase in the price of liquor.

One time last year, the government paid the campesino 1.60 córdobas for a pound of corn. The campesino sold all the corn to the State. But the State then sold it to the public for one córdoba. This cost the State sixty cents [.60 córdoba]. Then the campesino sold all his corn and afterwards came to the city to buy it at one córdoba. He bought it for less than he sold it to the State! There came the time that the campesino wasn't clear about what was happening and didn't want to plant crops. The campesino said, "It's better that we buy it from the State because it's cheaper." To solve this problem and to encourage the campesino to plant, the State came and paid him three córdobas for the corn. The State came here and sold it at two; the campesino says that's better. The government gives talks to the campesinos so that they realize what the situation is. And the farmer is now planting a lot.[8]

I've always admired my little sister Marta. She has been completely dedicated to her work, especially since she began to work for the revolution through her work with AMNLAE. My work has been different from hers. I've never taken a gun to go to the mountain; perhaps I haven't had the opportunity or enough courage, but because I haven't done it doesn't mean that I wouldn't if I had to. I admire her for her generosity and unselfishness in anything material. She never keeps anything. She's always thinking about what someone else needs. She matured young because she suffered a lot. She's always for the people. Always. If she has to work from dawn until midnight, she'll do it.

I'm happy now because there are many causes to undertake for the sake of others. I've always liked that. Without being asked, I'm always ready to serve anyone within my reach, even if I don't have any money. For example, when I accepted the work in the Defense Committees, I became more aware of people's problems and how I could help. That made me feel better.

And as a woman I feel better, too, because now I've learned that I have my own rights and that I'm more protected than I used to be. Before, I wasn't so sure that anyone could protect me if I had a problem with my husband. In the best of homes there is, at times, a problem with the husband. Now, he realizes that he can't mistreat me because he knows there are laws that protect me. In the past, he treated me badly when he drank a lot and when I told him his living alone in Managua made me think he no longer loved me. Sometimes he hit me. We women didn't have a place to go and say, "I have this problem" and get protection. We saw the mistreatment as a custom where the woman had to be dominated by the man and always had to be lower then he was. Sergio believed all that. When I got married, I couldn't understand that I was to let someone dominate me. I had always been able to help my family; I felt I was of value and I could share my life with him, but not be dominated. I wasn't one of the women who lowered her head when he hit me. I could have attacked his face and left a scar, but it wouldn't have been the right action to take, and afterwards I would have been sorry. So I didn't do it. But Sergio realized I wasn't ready to let him flatten me.

At the same time I began to be free in the sense that I knew what my rights were and that he had no right to lay a hand on me. I was a compañera in his life, not his daughter nor his slave. So I told him that the next time it happened, we were going to have serious problems because the law that existed was going to be applied. I was already so bored with it all, so tired of that much suffering, that I said to myself, "That's enough. I can support my daughters; I don't need to be with him." I didn't even work or sleep in peace because he was likely to show up at any time, drinking and bothering me.

So things went on; we were having lots of problems, and by coincidence, in 1983, he was offered the scholarship to go to Cuba.[9] When he left, our relationship was tense. After he returned, it became apparent that while he was in Cuba, he analyzed the situation and appreciated it, or he appreciated me and our earlier relationship. He realized the mistake he had made. He told me in letters that he wasn't going to demand anything from me and that I could decide my own life, if I wanted to get back together with him or not. What I wanted was that he change and accept my conditions. He understood that I was just asking to have the liberty to develop as a woman should. He saw how men treated women in Cuba and how women developed. His studies helped him, and he understands me now. I just wanted to work with the revolution. Now if I want to go to a meeting, it doesn't bother him. Before it did; now it doesn't. We speak the same language now and understand each other better. When he's going to do something, he asks if we should. I tell him yes or no, and we come to an agreement. We would have separated if he hadn't gone to Cuba. I wasn't ready to continue the way we were living. There were arguments in front of the children, and they were old enough to understand. I had made the decision that living alone with the children would have been better than living with him.

Clearly, especially in countries that are a little backwards, one does not stop having problems when one is alone, especially when you're a woman. There is still a little ignorance, a lack of culture. People wonder what the woman does, where she goes, with whom she goes. They think that maybe she'll go out with someone else while her husband is gone.

It has been backwards here in Nicaragua, but the revolution is changing the *machismo* of the earlier system. The woman stayed at home before, and the man left her with the children. He'd say that he had children, but he'd give them nothing economically, and no one could get it from him. No one. If a man mistreated a woman and they came to put him in prison, he'd say, "I'm going to join the guardia; then they can no longer do anything to me." They made their salary, and no one got any money from them. There was no welfare, as there is now. Today, if a man leaves a woman who has his children—even if he marries another woman—money goes to the woman with children even though they haven't been married. But there are men who still hit women because they know that even now there are women who will be quiet and not say anything.

My life has been different from that of my daughters because it has been easier for them to study and easier to get food. They haven't had to work because their father and I haven't stopped working. I had the advantage that my mother didn't have in that I was trained. My work was easier, even though it was hard, and it was better paid than washing and ironing. My mother couldn't give us anything. No one worried about children studying or wandering around the streets. Now if a child has no mother or father, there's a place where a child goes and where they give him food and make him study. [If we had grown up in today's situation], we'd have been sent to a day-care center, where we would have had food, milk, and medical help. Now, for example, if the salon I have, small as it is, were to end up in the hands of the State, I know that the State wouldn't leave me empty-handed. I'll always have my work, and my daughters will have their studies. We're going to be better off. I'm going to have a fixed salary, an income I'll receive monthly, and then I won't have any problems. I suppose everything will be the State's. It will be better than it is now because the State will be in charge of a work center where there'll be supplies. Then I'll work for the State and not have to worry about looking for permanents and dyes, as I do now.

Today the salon is mine. It's small, but it's mine. We have so few supplies, but we still work. I work more than I used to because [in the past] the rich gave their children air-conditioned salons, and they bought what they wanted and stored supplies. Those of us with small salons and with no money had trouble buying and storing supplies. We ended up working less. Right now, the State has a warehouse in Managua where they distribute the same amount of supplies to all of Nicaragua. If a hundred hair dyes come, then those hundred are divided among the salons. But the rich still have the advantage because they can go to Miami and buy everything. They want to go, and they go. And they bring back piles of stuff.

I dream that my daughters will have professions. I ask God that He give them a place to work so that they can get their professional titles. Then they can be what they want to be. Certainly they always have to focus on what's needed for the development of the country, but I can't tell them what to study. I can only say, "I'd like you to study such-and-such a thing because the people need it. Be a doctor, for example, not to be a millionaire but to improve your life and help others."

Some people are indifferent to the problems of others, but I am by nature sensitive to people. Never have I been able to see someone with a problem without having to get myself involved and say to them, "How can I help?" Right now there's a muchacha I'm helping. I went to a poor barrio called Camino Segundo. Before the revolution, it was just called Pobre. I was taking a Christian *cursillo* at the time, and we formed a group of special Christian base communities and visited Camino Segundo.[10] Then one day, walking alone, I visited a small and humble little house, so poor, made of wood with a dirt floor.[11] I met the woman who lived there; I asked for water. Then I saw that she was sick. She told me that she had cancer in her abdomen, in her uterus.

I asked, "Is there no cure?"

"No, it's hopeless. I no longer want to live; I'm only waiting for my turn. But what bothers me the most," she said, "are my children."

The oldest, Yamara, is thirteen, as is my daughter. The mother was young, more or less my age. There were other children, a two-year-old and a seven-year-old. I asked her how she got food, and she said that some charitable people helped her. I told her there was a Soviet hospital in Chinandega and maybe the doctors there could do something for her. She said she was already in agreement with what God had decided for her. But I insisted and told her that I was going to get a car because I knew she couldn't endure a bus ride. She got sicker, though, and they had to take her to the hospital in Estelí instead. She got an injection, came back home, and I stayed to visit. Then I went to my barrio; with my friends, I got together some food and money for the woman and took it to her. The time came when she went to the hospital for two months. I helped, with the little I had, to feed the children. She died about a month ago. The small children went to the orphanage. Yamara was to stay with an aunt but told me yesterday that she wanted to live with a girlfriend in the little house where she had lived with her mother. However, the father of the younger children said he wanted to live there with his wife. He was going to kick Yamara out, and she wondered if AMNLAE could help. She didn't want the house to end up in the hands of the other woman. I told her I'd help, but she'd have to study and also look for a way to make a living. I offered to teach her how to work in the salon. "Within a year," I told her, "you're going to know how to work and get along in life. And you're going to be able to pay for your studies." She agreed and started yesterday.[12]

I meet with Christian base communities, groups that work together in the community, once a week; then we talk, and groups of two or three people leave to work in the barrios and form other groups. Later we invite the people we work with to take a Christian *cursillo* outside Estelí. Then these people return and work with other people who form another group, and so it continues growing and growing. It isn't that we have drawn away from the church, but the idea is to see instead a church in each person, to see a living temple, to see God in every person. The Bible asked us for a live temple, not a dead temple. We read the Bible, analyze life in the Bible, and compare it with the times we are living in.

It's difficult to understand the problems the church has here. Even for me it's difficult. But as a Christian, you have to be in favor of the poor. If Cardinal Obando y Bravo[13] doesn't tend to the needs of the poor, then we don't have the same ideas as he has. But if he works for the just cause of the poor, then we'll go with him. My personal opinion—I've never had the opportunity to talk about this with the Frente—is that if the Cardinal were to leave his comfortable place and get involved with the poor communities like Estelí or Matagalpa, he'd see what the revolution has done for the poor. But since he doesn't leave, he won't know. He continues celebrating the word of God in the same way that he has always lived it. He says that the government wants to introduce communism in Nicaragua, but I sincerely think that we have a long way to go before we become communists.

There are some priests who agree with the people, like Father Augustín Toranzo, who's a Spanish priest, a humble man who had his comfortable family in Spain and could have stayed peacefully there with them. If all the priests realized what was happening, the struggle would be easier for Nicaragua. Some Christians still have the idea that going to Mass is enough to save them. If the priests were to work with those people, or if everyone in Nicaragua were to work with them, this struggle would be easier. The contra would have no power because everyone would be conscious of what it is to truly be Christian, which is to put yourself at the level of the poor, to live with the pain of others, to realize that their problem is yours.

I can't be indifferent to the pain of my brothers who've had children killed by the contra. At the same time, we have neighbors who don't go to the night vigil.[14] The dead person is there, but they don't go. The next day, they're in church, beating their breasts and saying they are Christians. For example, if a woman came to me right now and said, "Leticia, my mother's very sick, and I need to take her to the hospital. I don't have the money to pay the taxi, and there's no one to take me." If I say, "I can't do it right now because I'm going to Mass," you have to think about what it is that I should do first. My duty is not Mass. Instead I should go where they need me. That's how we are little by little clarifying what it is to truly be a Christian. For example, in the salon, I've had the opportunity to be friends with almost all the doctors in the hospital. They all come to the salon to have their hair cut. Most are Cubans—there's one Bolivian—and their [monthly] salary from the Cuban government is 500 córdobas, which is nothing.[15] They do get a bonus when they return to their country. I can't charge them to cut their hair. Not a cent. They're doing more for us and for Nicaragua, even if they aren't doing it just for me. We have a good friendship. People say to me, "Leticia, my mother—or my father or my brother—is sick." They want me to take them to the hospital in La Trinidad because I'm familiar with it and the Cuban doctors. Whatever the reason, it isn't important to me if I close my salon, if I lose work, if I don't make money; it satisfies me more to do that favor than to earn the money I'd make. We obtain more through our friendships than through money. In the war, money had no value. We had money and there was nothing to buy, no food. That's just the way it was.

The revolution has given Omar the opportunity to improve himself, but he worries about all those people he has to support. He should have studied more; he'd be making more if he had. He's behind, spinning his wheels, but the army still gives him opportunities to get military rank. Those who want to get it, do. He says he doesn't want to have a rank because if he did, he'd have to stay at his post. Without a rank he can often stay home with his wife Irene. She gets angry and wants him to be at home. He thinks people change with ranks. He has always been a humble person and has never wanted fame. When he worked clandestinely, he'd come to my house and never brag about what he did. He was always quiet about that. He spoke with measured words. Once after he had been beaten by the guardia, a Managua doctor who worked secretly with the Frente came at night to treat Omar but had to take him to the hospital. So that the hospital guard wouldn't ask Omar questions, the doctor said that Omar was mute. He's a quiet person, but he analyzes everything. He has two things on his mind: work and home. He thinks about his work, which is where he should be, but he also has to worry about his home and what will happen if he isn't there. He worries about what they'll eat. They have their food card; he can get food for only four people but has to share it with the others who aren't his children.

He looks older than he is. He has suffered a lot. When children aren't well-fed during their childhood, they're weak and can't endure what others can who were well-fed. So it is with Omar. Both Omar and Pedro were so young to be so courageous. I know that if Pedro had lived, he'd stand out because he had the ability to improve himself.[16]

I hope that, in spite of the aggressions and the life of "today we have it, tomorrow we don't," my family and I won't be abandoned, no matter what the reason may be. Compañero Tomás Borge always says the revolution was for the children. He doesn't want children to live the way we did. There are many things that the government has done, and we'd be blind not to see it.

But when there are selfish people, and if the government doesn't do for them exactly what those people want, then it doesn't matter if the government has done something for others. But I think that we as Christians—the majority of Nicaraguans are Christians—have to realize that what we do for everyone is what interests us as a people. It isn't what is done for just one person. Before it was sad to see children who didn't even have the energy to play; they just sat in a chair with a big belly full of parasites. You could always see a sadness in them. The government doesn't want children to grow up sick because that brings consequences.

Nicaragua was called the hacienda of Somoza. Today's govern-

ment [leaders] don't want Nicaragua to be anyone's hacienda. Instead they want us to be free people with rights to [make] our own
decisions and [to] our own liberty. If a person doesn't develop with
the process, then that person becomes stagnant, stays behind. But
by following the revolution, we can achieve our goals. There are still
people who say, "I'm not going to get involved. It doesn't interest
me." I can't explain to myself why it doesn't interest them. We have
to work with these people; we have to insist and tell them again and
again until they're convinced.

Marta

After having gone through so many hard times, any small detail or
nice thing that we weren't accustomed to made us happy, like getting my first wages of 800 córdobas. That was 1982. I was about
twenty-two or so, and it was the first time I received a large sum. I
cleaned offices in the building project; they didn't know me well,
but when Dr. González, the manager, got to know me and heard
how I had worked, he gave me the job of paying all the workers. I
was happy because they trusted me; they handed me a lot of money
to pay those people, knowing I wouldn't steal a cent and I'd return
any remaining money.

I started volunteering for AMNLAE, the national women's association, in 1981. Since I worked well in a neighborhood, they told
me that for excelling I was going to get a four-month trip to Cuba to
learn about women's organizations. That was at the end of 1982.
People who went to study went for one or two years, but I just went
to visit, to see how they worked, and to learn about their struggle.
They had meetings to explain how the revolution came about and
what's going on there now. I liked Cuba. The people are friendly and
understand the difficulties our country is going through because
they also have lived through a similar situation. They've had short-
ages, too, as we have. And they like our people.

When I returned, I started working at the AMNLAE office for
pay. They told me I was going to work in Estelí, cover five neigh-
borhoods in town and five to seven smaller communities outside

Estelí. After supervising my work with people and their problems, they realized that I did a good job. If people have housing problems, for example, we try to get them zinc planks [for roofing] through the organization. We take it to the regional level and say, "We need help for these people." Then they say, "Okay, we haven't got much now, but we can give this so that you can help them." So they give us something. There isn't much.

Now I'm working for the regional board in publicity. A region is big. There are only eight in Nicaragua, and ours is Region One, Segovia. It's a more important job where I have more responsibility than before, so they're paying me more, 2000 córdobas every month.[17] It helps. We know our government would like to give us more.

When I arrive in a town, I meet with the women leaders in AMNLAE, and we discuss the work that needs to be done. For example, there's this friend in Santa Clara who told me about a family that needs a wheel chair. They are poor and needy, and now we're trying to find a wheel chair [for them]. Another example is that a short time ago, we had a meeting with women farmers who had expressed a desire to support the soldiers; they collected money, cigarettes, matches, and candy that they gave to us, and then we in turn distributed their collection to the soldiers.

In some cases, we've come up with solutions to their problems, but other times, our program has been deficient because we're short of trained people. When help hasn't reached the families affected, we've had to find out why that happened and solve it. I'm frightened when I can't say, "I'll help you" to people who have a serious problem. It's not for my own satisfaction that I help them, but it does make me happy. I don't solve their problems alone; the whole community does, through my work.

I rarely pray. Sometimes. The role of the church, for me, has been good because from the beginning of the struggle, the church has helped the revolution. It was through the church that the Frente was able to grow. When there's time, I attend Mass, and I always do when a compañero has been killed. I don't belong to the Christian base communities because the work I do is the sort of work they do. They go to different places to see the necessities of their brothers and to help them; that's what I do through AMNLAE.

I'm much happier now than I was before the revolution; I'm succeeding as a person and helping other people through my work in support of the revolution. In spite of the problems, we've kept going. We're eating. We're living. During my childhood I never thought I'd be able to study and become useful at something; it never crossed my mind. I spent all my time working for someone else. It was only after the revolutionary triumph that I realized we can all do something. We can advance, learn, and be useful. We can be helpful to the whole population.

Another happy moment was when we got the house.[18] The one we had before had cracked walls and was going to collapse. My biggest dream was to own a house that no one could kick us out of, to live where we couldn't be evicted. Part of the revolutionary triumph was to take steps for the people with scarce resources, and we were beneficiaries of housing. Not just our family, but others, too. There's a monthly payment that I haven't been able to pay this year due to our economic problems, but we know that it isn't exactly a payment; instead it enables the government to help other families who still don't have housing. There's no danger, as there was in the past, that they'll take away our house if we don't pay for one or two months. The house will always be ours.

The saddest times were when I lost Antonio, the father of my son, and when I lost my brother Pedro. These are things one never forgets. My mother and the father of my son greatly influenced my life. So has my brother Omar. I admire him a lot for his courage and his decision. It must have been hard being sick on the mountain without medicine, going about in ragged clothes, being hungry, having a lung disease, being transferred from one place to another. I admire him because in spite of all those difficulties—eating raw corn and raw vegetables, or whatever they could find—he never gave up.

I don't know that our family isn't special. There must be other families like ours, families that are united, yet share problems and numerous things that happen in a home. In spite of these little problems, we've never argued. We have discussions—in every family there are discussions—but we've never had the problem of arguing. We're always eating and happy, without arguing.

My dream for the future is that all this aggression come to an end so that we can live a quiet life and enjoy all these things we've achieved, so that people can plant their crops, study, and work in peace. But I know that we'll have more violence at any moment, and

I know that many of us probably are going to die. What all Nicaraguans want is that our children not go through these difficulties. We want them to be qualified people who can do something. That's what will benefit the country. As for my son, his studies will probably be interrupted because we're going through times that don't let us predict what we'll be doing tomorrow. Life is hard here now, and it's difficult to plan for the future.

I saw death during the insurrections. Even a little while ago I saw the death of three little girls. Less than a month ago, August 29, 1984, I was transferred to the Santa Clara zone to help the women since they were going to honor the Sandinista Popular Army, and AMNLAE was going to celebrate with them.[19] We began the work, and everyone was happy. The women bought cigarettes, matches and made a cloth banner with a greeting on it for the army.

On Saturday, September 1, we were preparing for this activity that would take place on Sunday, but that day the militia in Santa Clara asked the women to celebrate by putting on a ceremony. We began to make the preparations, about twelve-thirty or one-thirty in the afternoon. When it got close to two, two-fifteen maybe, we were painting a banner with marking pens when the alert siren sounded, warning us that there were planes above and that everyone should get in a trench. When the first bombs dropped, the children yelled, and the women cried. Children in these zones get nervous because the aggressions are constant and serious; however, they're usually not by air but on the ground. Eight people in this tiny town had already been victims of the contra. We were told to get the mothers and children to shelters. Those who had guns had to get them ready, and the rest of the women had to protect the others. I was given a gun.

There were three planes and two helicopters. The three airplanes, called "push-and-pulls," are small but fast planes that can drop a lot of bombs, and they attacked while the helicopters shot at the ground with machine guns. The object was to attack the city, but the artillery of the [Nicaraguan] army and the people's militia didn't allow them to bomb the center of the town.

The bombs fell near the town in an area where some children had gone to sell bread. One compañero was milking his cow, and the children were walking down the road when the bombs fell on them.

Three children from twelve to fourteen years old were killed, and another was seriously wounded. The children were innocent, not fighting in a war but just enjoying themselves. Those of us in the trenches know that the enemy can attack anytime and we can die, but these were children who had stopped to knock fruit down from a tree with a stick.

We saw one of the helicopters come toward the people, flying with black smoke. It was just a miracle that it didn't fall on the town. The plane of the mercenaries was shot down by the artillery of the Sandinista Popular Army. We would have preferred to shoot down a "push-and-pull" but were excited enough to get an enemy helicopter. We didn't know then that this helicopter was the one that guided the others. It carried so many munitions that when it fell and burned, the fire set off explosions.

The compañeros from the army went to the spot to see if they could get the bodies out before they burned. We wanted to know who the dead were because our government wants to give back the bodies of these fallen mercenaries to their families. We know that the families aren't to blame for what these people do, and we hope that when the contra kidnaps and kills our people on the other side of the Honduran border that, even if it's just bodies, they return them. But the government of Honduras doesn't do that. We aren't going to do what they do. We're going to do everything to give the bodies back.[20]

The other planes left, fleeing in fear that they were going to be shot down. The compañeros of the army told us the planes were going to return again and the contra would return by land. We had to stay alert, so no one slept for two nights. We had seen planes nearby and had to expect anything to happen at whatever time of the day or night.

Afterwards we had to inform the families of the deaths and organize the vigils for the victims. AMNLAE is good at taking care of things at the very moment of need, like helping the wounded and sending the seriously injured to the hospital. It turned out that the father of one of the girls who was killed was a counter-revolutionary imprisoned in Estelí. He was told that his daughter died in the counter-revolutionary attack; he was taken to Santa Clara to attend her vigil and funeral. Afterwards he was taken back to prison because he hadn't completed his sentence.

The men don't like the changes in the women's role. We know that this is an ideological struggle. We have to make the men understand that at no time are we trying to be *the* authority in a home, but that when they go to the war front, the woman has to take charge of the situation in the home. We want them to understand that we can keep on going, whether the men are in the trenches or not. We've shown that a woman can develop in any role. Anything you put in front of her, she can do.

Before the triumph, a lot of women worked secretly for the Frente, and many lost their husbands because the men thought that the women were going out with other men. The husbands didn't know, and neither did the children, what work the women were really doing.

We have here what we call *machismo*. Men had to have five or more women or a lot of children to feel like men. But now it isn't so much that; instead it's that they don't accept women working in agriculture, in construction, working in any direction, regardless of the organization. They don't accept that a woman can give them orders and that she can be a leader in the workplace. Men don't want to understand that women have the same right as men have to participate in the numerous jobs in this revolution, in this country, or in whatever country. We're part of this country and want them to realize that.

My best friends are those who are in solidarity with our struggle, the compañeras of AMNLAE. There are compañeros in the army and in the barrios who are good friends, but when I have a problem, I talk with Maricruz, a friend from AMNLAE, who's a humble compañera with a simple way about her. She knows how to gain affection within the family just by her way of being. She's single, without children, and doesn't have a compañero. She's a secretary at AMNLAE and does some accounting: how much we receive, how much we sell, all that. She's short, just as I am, and plump. She has glasses and curly hair. A little fat and brown-skinned with very white teeth and black hair. All of us usually wear pants—dresses are for special activities—because we always have to be ready to mobilize, to leave for some place. We have travel problems because we have to get a ride, generally with people we know because these days it could be too dangerous to get a ride with just anyone. The enemy could be anywhere.

I have no prospects [for another man], but I could go to the door and grab someone! [Laughter] Every second there are possibilities of something.

Omar

Before joining the Frente Sandinista, we took an oath promising to defend the revolution even at the expense of our lives if necessary. If I were to drop out of the Frente, then those 50,000 deaths would be in vain, and I'd be a traitor. I took part in the revolutionary fight and will continue to do so until I fall in action. Now that the aggression is at its strongest, those of us who are really aware of the fight the Frente is waging in support of the revolution will defend it until we achieve the peace we want.

Our big obstacle is that the Reagan administration and the CIA tell these counter-revolutionary forces to fight our people. If it weren't for the help that Yankee imperialism provides these mercenaries, we could have defeated the counter-revolution. But Ronald Reagan, the CIA, and the Pentagon don't let us live in peace. Those of us who are in the armed forces and who belong to mass organizations will keep going until we obtain the peace that children hope for, that the elderly long for, that the whole population wishes for.

We have the patriotism that characterized this nation during Sandino's time. Sandino never gave up; he never sold himself. We're called the Frente Sandinista because we follow in Sandino's footsteps; he passed that spirit on to Carlos Fonseca, who taught us that we were fighting for peace. Not the peace of the dead as Ronald Reagan wants, but the peace that will allow us to provide the people with what they need. The revolution had many heroes. Thousands. It isn't that we want to have only heroes or only martyrs, but we want peace, and we want to have it for a long time. Not the peace of the dead. The dead are the only ones who have peace now.

The revolution has also cost us. I've had to give up working and studying. I wasn't able to have fun, and I lost my youth. We still don't go to parties or movies or on trips; we can't be with our families and children. We're going through violent times. But I know that in the end, we'll get our reward. We pray to God. We'll have to do without many things; we'll be poor, but we'll keep going.

This whole business cost my mother the loss of her son. That was what hurt her most, and us too. It cost us 50,000 dead people, and more compañeros keep dying. People are kidnapped, the Miskitos[21] are carried off to Honduras, children are killed. We don't want that. Instead of fighting in the mountains, we'd like to be in our homes. The money that the government invests in the mobilization of battalions could be invested in medicines, in children's studies, in housing for the needy. In Nicaragua there's a scarcity of all those things, and it's the fault of imperialism. Our government isn't to blame. They subsidize food the little they can so that the people can eat. I don't say this because I'm a revolutionary; I say it because I see the true situation that we have today in Nicaragua.

The advantages have been that I've learned to express myself better. I've improved my vocabulary, and I can read better. I've learned that one gets ahead by studying and that studies help the revolution. The revolution has given everyone the opportunity to study. If you don't make the most of it, it's because you don't want to do so. I'm working on my own self-improvement. I'm not hoping to be someone important but that in the future I'll be of service not to just one person, but to many. We won't be in the military force forever. One day there'll be peace, and each one of us will look for a job. I don't really enjoy being in the army, but I'm a soldier because Nicaragua needs us to defend it. My goal always has been to become a bricklayer again, but we're in such a difficult situation now that it's hard to go back to where you began. I'd like to be at home with my family all the time—go to work and return in the afternoon—but instead I have to stay in the military. We, the veterans of the guerrilla, have to make an effort to defend what we fought for after all we went through.

I don't have a military rank. I wouldn't like it because it represents too much responsibility. Ranks make people change. It's nicer to be humble rather than have a title. One eats by having friends rather than by having titles.

I haven't got a house. The house we live in belongs to Irene's niece. Ten of us live there. It's a small house, smaller than my sisters' houses. It's made with wooden planks and has holes everywhere, even in the roof. We get wet. It really is horrible. I may be able to get a better house in time. The Frente said they'd help us, maybe in four years, but they face a big demand because people need housing. The Frente is using all their money in defense, so even if they wanted to give a house to all those who need one, they couldn't. All they can do is give sections of land where people can build their own houses, even if they are built of cardboard. Still my dream is to have a house, not a large one, but a decent house. And to educate my children. I'd like one to be an engineer, or a builder, a nurse. I also want my wife to have a degree and study. My wife Irene has finished the fourth grade and goes to a school for adults that's run by the Frente.

I support everyone in the house on my salary. Four of the girls are children of Irene's mother, who was killed by the guardia. Their father is alive, but he doesn't help them. Irene has two children from an earlier marriage, and she and I have two children. I make 2000 córdobas a month.[22] It's not much for so many people.

I've believed in God since I was a child. My family taught me [to believe], and I've never stopped because whenever I've had problems, I've asked God to help me, and He always has. But I do have fears. I'm afraid of rats and of blood from battles. It gives me nightmares. I don't sleep when I see a lot of blood. I've been left with a psychosis. I think too much about the war.

This matter of the aggression is what keeps us constantly moving. As we finished off the guardia in little time, we'd finish them off again if we could fight them alone.[23] But then they receive a refinancing from the CIA. They receive better armaments, perhaps better than ours. This puts off the peace we long for. Children die every day, like the children in Santa Clara, like the seventy-three children in Ayapal.[24]

The contra kill in the name of Christ, in the name of God. Their slogan is, "With God and Patriotism, we are going to overthrow Communism." The government permits everyone the right to whatever religion without placing any obstacles in their way. In Nicaragua there's no communism, no Marxism; there's just a different system from what we had before.

As we say in the military, our lives are lost. Our lives are a loan. Today we walk through life; tomorrow we cannot. The bullets of the enemy carry a name, even a last name, and if the bullet doesn't arrive this day, it will another day.

I've admired not only one person but several, among them commander Ernesto "Che" Guevara and Commander Omar Cabezas.[25] Cabezas used to be a student leader in the city of León. When he went to the mountain, he had a lot to learn, as I did. He'd get through to the farmers because he's a person who speaks like the campesinos. If one speaks too scientifically, the campesino doesn't understand. Omar Cabezas spoke a simple language, and that's why people still like him.

We used to admire Edén Pastora because we saw him as a person who could relate to the people. After he took over the National Palace on August 22, 1978, people admired him even more because he was the highest ranking leader when the Palace was taken. But afterwards, he made a declaration that wasn't in line with the doctrine and guidelines of the Frente. He disagreed with them because they changed their course of action and had different objectives. The Frente gave Pastora the opportunity to resolve the differences, but he didn't want that. He wanted to be more powerful than the leaders themselves, and that led to his resignation from the Frente. He left with the excuse that he was going to fight in El Salvador or Guatemala with the guerrilla, but that wasn't really the case. He was searching for more fame, more money. Here in Nicaragua he had the fame but not the money, and that was what he went looking for in other countries. He sold himself to the CIA for dollars and fame. That's why people consider him a traitor. When he organized the Democratic Revolutionary Alliance[26] in Costa Rica, the people thought of him as an enemy just like a guardia since he was killing people of the southern Frente, the people of Rivas. From then on people started to hate Edén Pastora. There are many who still follow him, but they're mistaken. He goes around with some guardia now, the same people he fought against in 1978 and 1977.[27] Those of us who know Edén Pastora realize that he doesn't act in the best interests of the people, but in the interests of one person: himself.

There are three Ortega brothers: Daniel, Humberto, and the one who died in 1978 in Masaya, Camilo. They defend the interests of the people. They mingle and have direct contact with people; they don't go around lying. Almost all Nicaragua admires Daniel the most. Somoza couldn't reach the people in the same way that Daniel Ortega has. Ortega is the result of a struggle that forced him to suffer hunger, so he knows the suffering of the people, while Somoza, who ruled the country for fifty years, always had enough food. He never went to the mountain like Daniel Ortega and Humberto did. The people realize that Daniel doesn't lie to them because he himself has experienced, in his own flesh, what it's like to feel the cold and hunger. Some people criticize the fact that Daniel lives in a big house while we live in small houses, but we're aware that he's there not because he wanted it, but because he earned it with his efforts during the fight.

5

A Threatened Family and City: 1984–1985

These interviews took place just after a major contra offensive that threatened Estelí. The attack had made some family members stronger and others weaker. I arrived, frightened, and they were eager to tell me what they had gone through. Doña María was the exception; they asked me not to ask her about it, so I didn't. Oddly enough, she seemed more peaceful that year.

Doña María

I usually get up between four and five in the morning. I can't sleep longer than that. It seems that my body frightens me. The latest I get up is five-thirty. I go to the kitchen to light the fire, make coffee, and put on the beans. Then I go to the mill with the corn, bring back the flour, and make the tortillas. I cook corn for the following day. That way I economize on the fire, save my time, and allow myself to lie down in the afternoon. I cook until twelve and then have lunch. I'm in the kitchen all morning. There are times I can't stand it. I'm exhausted, and I don't want to do anything. But since Marta is working, I have to be with the child, or there's something else I have to do. I get Miguel ready for school and give him something to eat if Marta isn't here. Marta cleans the house before she goes to work.

I usually make soup. We buy a rib of beef and vegetables like squash and a smooth colored yucca called *quiquisque*. We buy whatever vegetable there is, but we always buy chicory to flavor the soup, along with onion, garlic, cabbage. No recipes. It's all in my head. Sheer ideas. The soup changes a little every day. Sometimes

we buy chicken. Or beans with cream and an egg, or pig crack-
lings—whatever can go into soup—or rice.

With a refrigerator, I buy things and save them. For example, a
tomato vendor came by today. Tomorrow he won't, and I'll have
some tomatoes saved. Otherwise, I'd have to send a young fellow, at
the cost of ten córdobas, to buy some because there's no place to buy
vegetables around here. Or the vendors don't come by, or they come
by late, and I'm used to making the food early. By twelve I'm waiting for people to come to eat. I don't like to be late. I lie down and
rest in the afternoon. When I get up, if I have to sew, I do. I make
purses with thread. I have less to do in the afternoon. I sit by the
door. I like sitting there for lots of reasons: I like the breeze that
comes through [the house], and I like fresh air. People come by and
ask for something or where they can find someone. But there are
men who come by who have had too much to drink, and you have to
be careful if they try to grab you. They can't work, so they try to sell
things. But I'm careful. If I'm alone when I lie down, I close the
door.[1]

We eat about five or five-thirty. We have beans and *cuajada* or an
egg. Bananas, if there are any. Not rice, only eggs. Or *chorizo*[2] with
eggs instead of beans. I often eat alone. Marta doesn't come until
seven or eight. Miguel sometimes wants to eat early, before she
comes, but he rarely feels like eating. He's so skinny. I wash the
dishes in the morning. At night I just pick them up and wash the
corn, get things ready. I rest after dinner. Sit at the door. Peacefully.
Until it's time to go to bed, eight-thirty or nine. If I go to bed later, I
get insomnia. People usually don't come by at night. My schedule is
the same every day of the week. The only change is if there's a
meeting of the Mothers[3] at two o'clock on Saturdays.

It has been a good year. I feel more peaceful, more confident in
Leticia and Marta. They worry about me. I still do nothing for them,
but they're good with me.

I've been quite sick. At three o'clock one morning I couldn't talk.
I was bathed in sweat and couldn't speak. Miguel ran without shoes
and just in his pajamas to get Leticia. She came with Florencia's
husband who has a vehicle, and he took me to the hospital. I've
gotten better. Leticia got lots of pills for me, and I've been able to
rest.

Marta was in the north a lot this year; I was worried, but she has a lot of courage and confidence. Now I'm more accustomed to her being gone. Miguel doesn't worry much, either, because we don't tell him when she leaves. Later at night, after she has left, he'll say, "I'm going to where Marta is."

"She's not there; she's at a meeting, in a seminar." We keep him occupied so that he doesn't realize that she isn't here.

Later he'll say, "She didn't come back."

I say, "Ah, she must have left."

Then he goes to where she works and asks, "Where's Marta?"

"She's not here, but she will be." That's how we entertain him.

He doesn't like to see her get in the vehicle and leave. He cries a lot. If she's in Jalapa, we tell him she's closer, in San Juan. It's better for everyone. He doesn't cry much this way. He waits. "Is she coming back now?" he'll ask.

"Yes, I think so. If not now, in the morning. Let's go to bed." He sleeps alone but is very nervous; if he hears shots, he gets up and comes to my bed. When I got sick, I just had to touch him and say, "Miguelito, Miguelito." He looked at me and knew.

"What's happening, Mamita?[4] Have some water."

"I can't," I said. "Talk to the neighbor, and tell her to get Leticia." And he went.

Sometimes Miguel says, "Don't do this; I'll do it for you. You'll hurt yourself." He's different with me. He's more obedient. If you treat him with sweetness, that's what you get; if not, then no sweetness. If I tell him, "You're going to do this," that's what he does; I don't have to ask him. With Marta, he plays and gets angry. It hurts him when she goes, so she's indulgent. When she isn't in Estelí, then I'm lenient with him. He rarely eats and then asks me for sweets, like bananas or papaya. I give them to him to make us both peaceful.

I hope I stay that peaceful in the coming year, if I'm not dead!

Leticia

When the trouble started in Estelí, I felt the need to protect my family. I warned my children that we might be attacked and at no time were they to go out in the street, but I was ready to leave the house if necessary. I wasn't just thinking of myself; you had to leave behind the sense of "I" and think about what people needed. I was told where to go to pick up whatever medicine, antibiotics, syringes, cotton, pills that people could give me. My mission was to set up a medicine supply in my barrio.

There were moments, at the beginning, when everyone kept their doors open at night and practically no one slept, only some old people, but even they were waiting and worrying. We heard planes and helicopters we hadn't seen before, and it frightened people because they thought [the contra had attacked]. Then they attacked La Trinidad bridge, and fifteen people died. Six on the bridge and ten in the town. The six were soldiers going on a mission to Managua. The contra burned the soldiers' car and the soldiers, too. The only one alive is in the military clinic with five bullets in his stomach. When we knew that La Trinidad was being attacked, people got together in their homes to talk about what we were going to do. The men went to a command post in the barrio to get their guns and patrol the city. There was a call for volunteers who were ready for combat. Everyone—the men and the women who could go—went; some stayed taking care of things, and others went to protect places that were economic targets, like the granary and the bank. Or they went to places where the contra planned to enter, places that had been detected beforehand. Everyone worried that we were in a war situation. I admire the people because they stayed calm. They didn't run through the streets; the only ones who did run were going to get guns or were picking up things for the combatants who needed medicine. I didn't see the kind of nervousness that would make people flee or say, "I'm going to Managua," or "I'm leaving." No one. On the contrary, I heard comments from some people who said they weren't moving from Estelí. Of course, some said, "It might be better if we left," but others said, "The best thing is to stay here." In spite of the fact that we saw dead being brought in every day—one day there were ten dead—everyone still had confidence. Many compañeros from the *cursillos* were killed in the town of La Trinidad. The bus that was burned was full of people going to Guatemala on an evangelical mission; they all managed to get out.

The attack on La Trinidad clarified exactly who is against the [revolutionary] process and who's in favor. We now have proof that the majority are with the process because they did get the contra out of here. Those who were against the process stayed in their homes, and that told us who they supported. Now we know who's who, and so does the Frente. It's easier now to organize the city because we know who should administer the state enterprises, and who shouldn't. I've heard people talk about only one person by name who is against the process, and that person has a lot of money. We know we don't have one hundred percent support.

Even the evangelist churches[5] and the Adventists helped. Maybe they didn't take up arms, but they gave their support by making coffee, bringing bread, and standing watch. We want them to feel part of it, and it seems that they're learning. We're called communists, but it's just a word; it would take a long road and a lot of courage to call ourselves that. It seems to me that to be a communist is to learn to live in a community. That's what the word means. And that's what we're trying to do; we're trying to live in a community. We've achieved a lot, and for that they call us communists. The word doesn't offend us.

Marta and Omar belong to the Frente. To belong to the *militancia* of the Frente, [which both Marta and Omar do], you have to earn it through your work, by being responsible and actively involved for a cause. If a person works in a store, for example, and if that person is politically conscious and works in a political direction, he can belong to the Frente. It's possible to refuse it, too, if you wish. No one in our family has been opposed to the Frente, but there are people— not our close relatives—who are indifferent. They don't have any problems as a result; they live their lives normally. I don't know their reason for not being in agreement. It's not that they're afraid that something will be taken away from them; in the case of my relatives, they don't have anything that could be taken away.

I know there has been criticism of how the Sandinista Defense Committees distribute food ration cards, but I also know for a fact that those criticisms aren't right. A census was taken right after the revolution triumphed; when they came to our house, they didn't ask our ideology. They only asked how many were in our family and our names. It had nothing to do with politics and nothing to do with belonging to the Frente. The cards are for beans, rice, corn, sugar, toothpaste, eggs. Not milk because any little grocery store or farm sells unprocessed milk. Powdered milk, though, can be bought with the food cards. Everyone, rich as well as poor, has these cards.

We use them to buy those items at a store called an *expendio de comida*.[6] There are two or three of these in each barrio.

Of my children, only the youngest one was afraid. She said to me, "Mama, the war is here. Let's go to Matagalpa to Grandmother's."[7] But it was just for a moment when she saw something on television; afterwards she forgot. There were four days when, as a security measure, there was no school. The rest of the days, the children went as usual to their classes, more than anything so that the parents had some peace. That's also where they get their orientation about what they should do in case of an attack.

I think that, in spite of our illnesses, all the things we've lived through have made us strong. One thing more isn't much for us. Life has made us strong and maybe a little hard, which is how we see each other sometimes. But really, it isn't that we're hard; it's life that's hard. Sometimes we can't contain the tears of so much suffering, but there are moments when we have to be strong in order to give courage to others. That's when one becomes stronger. Our souls feel the death of the other compañeros—even though they might not be our relatives, they are still our people who are dying—but we can't cry. Instead, we have to act. In this last emergency, a mother's three children died [all] at once. We have to pretend to be strong in order to give the mother and the relatives moral support.

Even last night there were shots. Some muchachos who had been drinking rum went to bother the military delegation. The drunk muchachos were armed; that's unusual. The people in the military shot in the air so that a reinforcement of police would come to help; the military couldn't leave their emergency posts. The police came right away and caught one. The others hid in a house, and the police will investigate today.

You can't drive a vehicle after ten o'clock at night, but you can walk. When those who are standing watch, the men of the barrio, see a suspicious car, they make it stop. If the car doesn't stop, the men shoot in the air to make it stop. It isn't normal for a car not to obey the signal of the person standing watch. These rules exist as a result of the state of emergency. But always, when there's a suspicious car, the person standing watch makes them stop. Last night I stood watch until two in the morning. I slept for two hours and got up at four to take the morning shift.

I usually get up at six in the morning. I bathe, dress, and go to the kitchen to make my husband's breakfast. I make fried beans and eggs and cheese, but when there are no eggs, it's cream with beans. Not mixed. They're separate. When there's cooked rice left over, we make *gallo pinto* in the morning along with eggs. At eight o'clock I go to work. The children get up at five, before I do. They have to be at school at six-thirty. They make their own breakfast—only coffee and bread—then they go to school and return at noon. They never eat with me; in the morning they don't feel like eating anything heavy. There are three shifts at school: one lasts until twelve, then from twelve to five, and one at night.[8] Marta's son Miguel goes in the afternoon, but my daughters go in the morning. We fought about this because I wanted them to stay at home in the morning, but they convinced me that they would do less well in their classes. They say they're sleepy and tired at that time of day. The children who have to work in the day are the ones who go to school at night, but nowadays the majority of those who study at night are adults. Before, when I studied, almost all of [those who studied at night] were children. You still see children selling food in the street as I used to do, but they sell for their mother who makes the food, not for another person, and the mothers send them out when the children aren't in school. I don't think there are children who work all day the way we used to. The mothers have heard talks—I've seen AMNLAE promote this—about the importance of children studying. Of course, there are mothers who aren't convinced, but little by little they realize that the child has to study. If the mothers haven't studied, though, it's hard for them to understand.

The children come home for lunch. They help by cleaning the house and taking care of some details that have to be done. Marisa, the oldest, is taking an embroidery class. The other two take typing classes from my sister-in-law, who teaches them at her home. It's necessary in Nicaragua because there are jobs that people lose because of not knowing how to type. Marisa is going to study bookkeeping so that she can support her studies. An accountant is necessary in the businesses here, and it pays well. She could work during the day, finish high school at night, and take university classes in Estelí on Saturdays. She'd eventually like to study Business Administration, as her father did, in Managua. They're all good students and study without my having to tell them. I know that some parents have problems and have to always remind the children, or the teacher has to call the parents and tell them, "Your child doesn't do her homework." In this, there has been a big change from the earlier situation. The government wants the best for the children and always thinks about their future. The best present I can leave my children is their education. I'm not concerned about leaving them a house or money; that would only cause disagreements: "I want more" or "You got everything."

In Nicaragua, children have always had to help the household economically. Starting from the time I had the use of reason, I knew I had to help. So did everyone else. My children don't sell food on the street, but they have other ways of making money. They make popsicles in the refrigerator and sell them. That money pays our electric bill. They sell ice and sometimes make *chicha rosada*[9] from corn and sell it in glasses. They buy little candies and sell them at school. Sofía, who is thirteen, cuts hair in the salon; she even has her own clients.

I go to work about eight in the morning, return at twelve to have lunch, and go back to work again at one. I don't return home at a set time, sometimes at eight at night, other times at nine; it depends on how much work there is. When I get to the salon [in the morning], I clean it. If someone's there, I ask them to wait until I clean the floor. I ask the client if she wants a haircut, and when we have supplies, [I ask if she wants] a tint or permanent. Sometimes they come to have their nails or feet done. There are no appointments. They show up, and I take care of the one who comes first. On some occasions, when the people have limited time, they ask for appointments. I sometimes have five clients a day, sometimes eight or ten, and there are days when there's no one. Then I wait all day. I write some letters or do some work that's been assigned to me as a project, or I spend it cleaning.

I almost never go to a party. Only on Sundays do we all go out together, sometimes to the river with the children or to see his family. That's all I do. There are times that I'm tired and bored to be leading such a routine life. All the years have been the same. The only year when I felt a big change was when Sergio was in Cuba; I had more opportunities to have friends. There was a group of Cuban doctors working here who visited me a lot and invited me to a birthday for one of them. I felt better that year.

The only change I have now is on Wednesdays when the *cursillo* group shares a sherbet at the meeting and exchange ideas. That's therapy for me. The difference between *cursillo* and base community is in the name, nothing more. They are two groups formed by different priests but they have the same ideals, the same ideologies. We work together and get along well. In our group there are three of us who belong to both groups. The bishop is in charge of the diocese of Estelí; when we want to have a *cursillo,* we consult with him, and he gives permission. I *think* he gives permission because he agrees with us; but in reality, he's a little reserved with his words.

What we do is always the same: we take roles from the Bible, but we bring the roles up to date. We relate the Bible to the life we're living so that people realize what it is to be Christian. Not just to pray without seeing what our brothers need, but to see how they can rescue someone who has a problem, or has bad habits like drinking too much rum, or having a lot of women. We help form communities where people acquire more knowledge and find moral support from their brothers and, at times, economic support. Almost all the people here are poor, but they can still see the needs of others.

Father Miguel D'Escoto started his fast but suspended it because of the situation and his health.[10] For the last four Fridays, since his fast began, we've held The Way of the Cross in the streets of Estelí to demonstrate support for the pueblo on the part of the Christians of Estelí.[11] It's beautiful. We walk through the streets with torches. Four or five blocks of people go with us. First we have Mass in the cathedral. It's a new way of asking for peace in Nicaragua; we want the enemy to understand that the Christian community is alert and is asking God for peace. The children go with me. They go with me to Mass on Sunday afternoons, too.

Other evenings, I go to a meeting of AMNLAE or the barrio, if there is one. Otherwise I stay at home. There are weeks when there are no meetings in the barrios, but right now in the state of emergency and all of Nicaragua living like this, there's always work to do. We plan projects for the barrio, like picking up groceries for the combatants, or we visit the Mothers of Heroes and Martyrs. Or we make plans for the communal house that each barrio has; it's used for meetings and to stand watch. For refugees, too. It's for whatever the pueblo needs, and it's maintained by the barrio.

Omar is one who needs our help now; he broke his leg in an

accident at work. Thanks to God it was only his leg. But now he's quite sick, psychologically. For us it has been difficult because we've spoiled him. He's the only brother we have, and we worry about what he needs. His wife Irene isn't a good woman. She seems to want to see him destroyed. He has come to me many times because he has confidence in me; he tells me that he feels nervous, as if someone were following him and was going to grab him from behind. He's afraid and doesn't sleep well. Sometimes I use tranquilizers, so I've given him mine. He thinks we don't agree with him; we do, but we don't agree with the life he's leading with that woman, because she's destroying him. She made him leave the school where he was studying and is using him as someone to dominate. She says to him, "You stay here," and there he stays. He cannot free himself and continues to be used and manipulated at her whim. I don't think he'll be able to free himself from his sickness either. He's locked inside himself. He doesn't talk. I also don't think it's normal for a man to live with a woman knowing that she has another man. She has one, and Omar knows it. He has seen her. The last time he saw her they fought, and he came to Mother's house. Later he got desperate and tried to make trouble here, with us and with our mother, but we aren't going to fight with him, and we didn't. He had been at our mother's for two weeks but sneaked away by saying, "I'm going to the movies," and went back to her. When she knew he was going to get paid, she went to look for him. He gives everything to her, which doesn't leave a cent for my mother. He'll do anything to get along with his wife. For us, it's unexplainable that she doesn't say, "Omar, go to your class." Instead, she leaves the house and says, "You have to stay here and take care of the house and the children." That's what the neighbors—serious people—tell us. She treats him badly with crude words, like *hijo de puta* or *cabrón*.[12]

The person in charge at Omar's work told me that Omar was a great man who had always been outstanding in his work, and that's why they wanted to help him. We went to where he works because we couldn't figure out what to do with him. They had a private investigation because they had noticed his absences from classes, and they discovered the problem is his wife. They found out that what we said is true. They wanted to see if we agreed that he should be sent out of the country to see a psychologist and study. Omar doesn't know about it; they wanted to know what we thought first.

I hope Omar can get a leave for an indefinite period—he's in no condition to work in the mountains—and maybe work in Sergio's office where he could feel useful. He and Sergio get along well together. Sergio loves him. If Omar comes over, Sergio says, "Let's go for a walk and have a drink." They understand each other's character because both are reserved. Omar doesn't say much to our mother. If she wants to know something or sees that he has trouble, she tells him to go to my house, and he and I sit down and talk. If his problem is economic, he tells me or sends a note with Miguel asking me to give him some money. He has more confidence in me [than in Marta]. She's a good sister, but she wants things to be very upright. Sometimes she doesn't understand certain things, like the problems of a married couple, because she hasn't been married. [Since I'm married] it's easier for me to understand Omar and his wife.

Sergio isn't expressive. He never says anything. In little ways, I used to notice that he didn't agree with everything in the revolutionary process, but he didn't ever say it. But he has changed. His mother is indifferent to the process, but now I hear him defend the revolution when she says something against it. I don't know what caused the change, maybe his compañeros from work. Or maybe he has seen the integration of humble compañeros in the workplace. The revolution itself has convinced him. He does things in his work to benefit his compañeros. For example, in Estelí, firewood for cooking is expensive, so he always says, "I'm going with the truck to buy firewood; I'll split the cost with the compañeros at work." He does the same with oranges and beans. He has improved the business, and it earns more now. He just bought some land for four million córdobas [for the business] that agronomists will fertilize and plant. This will benefit the country's economy. Going to Cuba helped him. He earned the trip because he had been so good at his job; he wasn't sent to be convinced of anything. The Frente didn't know if he agreed or didn't agree because he hadn't done anything against the Frente. In his work, he was fair and honest. He never missed work. And he never robbed the State. For that he earned the grant. When he arrived in Cuba, he saw how things were; he had thought that they lived worse than we did in Nicaragua, but much to his surprise he saw that they lived better. Everyone has a house, small though it might be. And no matter how modest the house, people have a refrigerator and necessities.

Sergio, after so many years of studying, had dreamed of having a lot of money. When he saw the change in Nicaragua, he thought that all his determination was for nothing. He heard that everyone was going to be equal, but he didn't understand in what way people would be equal. In truth, we can be treated equally and have the same rights, but at the same time there are differences between an educated person and one who's not educated. They aren't equal. He didn't understand that. He thought that he was going to be sent out to work with a machete. Now he realizes that his profession and sense of responsibility have been appreciated. He has become the director of a company. I don't know how, and I don't know when I've been an example, [but maybe I have]. He has said that he likes the way I treat people, but even so, he can't be expressive. Deep down, he's a good man, but he isn't one of the people who can say, "I'm going to help others." But if I tell him to go, he goes. He has the idea, but he doesn't make the decision to do it. Sometimes I think it's because he's a little proud.

I've thought about having another man, but I always think of the children: what they'd say and what they'd feel. I'm not interested in any man in particular, but I do need to have someone who loves me and whom I also love. Perhaps not exactly for sex but for affection. All women want to have someone to love them. That's why I have tried to maintain the situation between my husband and me, but I worry that the love between us won't grow again or won't be reborn. When I'm alone, I ask God [to help] me to love Sergio as I loved him before. So I've thought about the possibility of another man, but more often I've thought about being old and Sergio and I finishing our years together. That would be best. Sometimes one must sacrifice a little in order to be able to achieve the best in later years. When a woman is alone, it isn't the same.

The lack of liberation is a problem we in Nicaragua have. It has changed a lot. Before it was worse. Women are more liberated—not libertines—but liberated indeed. Before, the woman was a slave in the house; now she has her own rights as a woman: the right to study, to belong to society as does the man, to carry out the same work as the man. Now it's against the law for a man to hit a woman.

A man could go to jail for six months if the woman has proof on the part of honest witnesses or has marks where she was beaten. If a neighbor says, "It's true," the man is put in prison.

My mother hit us when we were little. I was afraid of the punishment because it was very hard. We had to be perfect, and any errors were paid for with a punishment. She forgave us one, two, or three times; then she punished us. It might have been because we were late getting back from an errand we were sent to do, mistakes that didn't seem important to us but were to her. We might have taken five pennies from money she gave us when we were sent to buy something. I know that what we did wasn't right, but we certainly got a thrashing. I remember it without rancor; she did it because that's how she was brought up. For example, the couple who brought up my mother hit her a lot. It was the custom. After that, [when she got married] her husband beat her. All that changed after the triumph.

I almost never beat my own children. Sometimes, yes, when it's necessary, but not hard. Not out of rancor or rage. Only when they no longer understand with words. Less with the oldest one now. What I do with her is talk, and maybe give her a punishment that hurts her even more, like denying her permission to do something. It's a crime now to severely beat children. A mother could go to jail.

Even though our mother was beaten by her parents and husbands, she isn't bitter. I've seen bitter mothers who treat even their grown children badly. We're fortunate because we have a united family and no problems. We get along well. When I come over at night, we talk and laugh. We make chile and play with our mother.

It's always difficult for her when Marta leaves. She thinks something will happen. Anytime she hears news and Marta hasn't returned, she thinks they're going to bring her back dead. My mother isn't at peace until Marta returns. She has been affected by the past; she's insecure and thinks that she can't do anything by herself. If I'm not here, she misses me. If Marta is here and I'm not, my mother asks why I'm not here. There are things she talks about with me with more confidence than she does with Marta, and things she talks about with Marta with more confidence than she does with me. She misses us both in different ways. Sometimes two days go by without my coming by here, and my mother wonders what has happened to me, where I am, why I haven't come to eat. That's just the way it is.

The same thing happens with Omar. She wants him here. She wants all of her children here. I think she was even happy that Omar broke his foot because it meant that he stayed at her house. She wants to see him every day; she says he needs to eat well, so she fusses over him when he comes and gives him an egg or something. When he isn't here, she says, "Where's Omar? What could have happened to him?" To me it seems logical that if my mother got along better with Irene, she'd see more of Omar. I mean, we all have to hide what we feel toward my sister-in-law. If someone doesn't understand us, we have to understand them; that's why I'm always talking with Irene. I told her that I'm going to help them, that I am going to arrange a vegetable *ventecita* for them.[13] Where they live is far away, and people can't get to the market to buy a tomato or anything. She told me she didn't have any work and how difficult things were. I said, "For some time, I've had a project that would help you, but you haven't come by and seem to be separated from us." I was going to talk with the man who had the vegetables and see if he'd give us credit. We could pay him back with the money Omar made from selling the vegetables from the *ventecita*. I have a table that they can put their things on. I said, "I promise you, and I always do what I promise. If you're interested, I'm ready to help."

There's going to be a three-day *cursillo* in September, and I'm going to invite Omar and Irene because I want them to improve their lives. I've no interest in their being separated. She's his wife, and they're his children. My mother won't agree with my inviting them. She loves her son and wants the best for him, so I have to do things [for Omar and Irene] in such a way as not to hurt my mother, out of respect for her and concern for her illness. I have an advantage in that my mother does whatever I tell her is the best to do. She's always asking me, "What do you think of such-and-such a thing?" She doesn't sleep well and wakes up thinking about Omar, wondering if he'll come here to eat. When she's worried like that, she gets tired and depressed. I'm afraid I've inherited the same sickness. I have some of the same symptoms of tiredness. It's hard for me to breathe and my heart beats rapidly, but I dismiss the idea in order not to have any more worries; I already have enough. Everything bothers me, even if the problems aren't mine.

When our mother got sick, the doctor told me that when she got like this, we should bring her to the hospital immediately because she could die. I don't know exactly what it's called, but there's a part that's inflamed inside, and this restricts [the blood flow in] the arteries. My mother knows she has that illness, but she doesn't know she could die from it. She gradually gets more and more tired. There are times [when] she tries to breathe, but the air doesn't reach her lungs. When she takes pills to sleep, she feels better. But when she doesn't sleep, she says, "Ay, I spent such a night." Right now, with the problem of Omar, his broken leg, and everything else, she has gotten worse.

With this last emergency, I forgot about my problems. Before, I was worried about the situation with my house, and now I'm starting to worry about it again. The man who owns the house I live in wants it back because it's his only house, and he lives in a rented one. I could move to a house just across the street from my mother's, but I'd need to buy that house, not rent it. My brother Raúl has promised to lend me the money.[14] Sergio and I have saved a little, but right now houses are expensive, even the most modest ones. There's no opportunity to get a house through the government because the housing priority is for those displaced by the war and living in the *asentamientos*.[15] Their need is greater. I asked the owner of the house I'm renting if he could wait a little longer for me to solve this problem. He's a difficult person. He hired a lawyer in order to get me out, but there's a law protecting renters if they are legally in the house. Even though Sergio is the boss at his work, he doesn't make much more than the other compañeros. These problems concerning the house don't interest him. I don't think that's right; the duty is both of ours. If I were alone, I could live anywhere. I could live with my mother. But there are five of us, plus Sergio, so I think the worry should be both of ours.

And now, my work isn't going well. Not many people come when there's war. Also I can't get beauty products. They sell some things at the pharmacy, but it's very little. Sometimes people bring products from Guatemala or Mexico and charge dollars for them. The State sells me a few products monthly, sometimes four dyes to last for a whole month. That's all. We've gone almost a year without permanents. The best months for work are November, December, and January because the crops come in. Everyone earns more. That's also the time when people receive their *aguinaldos*, their Christmas bonuses. At the end of the year the government pays each one of the employees a month's salary as a present. Business is good then because people have both their salary and their *aguinaldo*.[16] This year, there was an unevenness when the prices rose and the salaries didn't. Later there was a salary increase, and things leveled out and became almost the same. The prices rose, the salaries rose, and I had to raise the price of my work, too.

La Purísima is celebrated during the first days of December in almost all the homes.[17] In Nicaragua we pray the novena from November 26 to December 7, when we celebrate *la gritería*.[18] That last day is the happiest. We make offerings to hand out, packages of candy and honey with pumpkin. We also make *chicha rosada*. People go through the streets singing and calling, "Long live the Virgin!" Then people leave in groups with their sacks to pick up the packages of oranges and sugar cane and some packages with sweets. The biggest day is Christmas. The family shares dinner on Christmas Eve. We have presents for the children, but they're little presents; it's the idea that's important. We have a Christmas tree and put the children's presents under it. The tree is a dry branch of any sort of tree that we wrap in cotton or paint with white paint and then hang things we make on it. The tree goes in a jar of dirt to stabilize it; then we put it in a visible corner of the house, with little toys below it and the kings and donkey. We don't put the baby Jesus out until midnight on the twenty-fourth. That night most people go to Mass and then home for dinner. We also give presents on birthdays and saint's days. Some people were born the same day as their saint. Others weren't. We celebrate my mother's birthday on Mother's Day because she doesn't know when her birthday is.

In Nicaragua we also celebrate the day of the Virgin of Carmen. The people have faith in her because she liberated the people from Purgatory. In her novena, she says that if people wear a scapular,[19] she'll intercede for them when they die so that God will free them from their sins. [You can see paintings] of dead people in the flames of a fire; they're raising their hands to the Virgin of Carmen who offers them the scapular. Especially now, with the triumph, we celebrate it with more reason to do so. Her day is July 16, the day in 1979 that Estelí was liberated.

I have an invitation from my cousin in Nevada who knows I've been sick and nervous. He has a friend who goes back and forth from Nicaragua to the United States. It's not expensive because it's by land. It'd be just to visit, not to stay. I'm not prepared to leave. My duty is to be here; I have a commitment [to stay in Nicaragua], but he has been inviting me for a year, and I've been turning it over in my mind. I wonder if it's risky in the United States, and I worry about the children and my mother. I know it would be good for me because I've had so many conflicts for so many years. I need a way to relax so that I can continue.

Marta

The military called an alert. It was a Tuesday or a Wednesday. The leaders of the Frente had a general meeting for all the organizations in the city and leaders of all the barrios—maybe 150 or 200 people came—and they said, "The enemy is approaching, and they want to take Estelí. We have to alert the people to get ready for combat, and we have to organize meetings in the barrios to explain the situation." We left immediately to warn the people. We knew the enemy wanted to take Estelí and La Trinidad by surprise, so we organized each position and put someone in charge.[20] We put on our uniforms and got our rifles [ready] because at any time from morning to night it was possible that the contra could surprise the city. The contra wanted to blow up a bridge over the Río Viejo near Estelí in order to cut communications and prevent, or at least delay, reinforcements and vehicles that were coming to help us. Our leadership had thought about that ahead of time and had plans to prevent it.[21]

I wasn't frightened; I was confident. We're used to these things. It would have frightened me if there had been an open invasion on the part of imperialism; then innocent people and those who don't like war or anything that's going on would perish.[22]

The contra entered La Trinidad from the highway dressed as if they were in the military service. They said, "Here we are, the *cachorros*." When the people in La Trinidad realized that they were the contra dressed as *cachorros*, they began to shoot. Then the contra ran to the mountains, where we caught many of them and where others died.[23]

We organized women volunteers—armed them and put them in

uniforms—to watch over the places that were the military targets of the contra. Other women helped the fire brigades and cared for children and old people. Each barrio knew what it had to do. We knew that three regional contra commandos were coming determined to take Estelí, but we also knew that they wouldn't be able to do it. The men were mobilized to the battle front outside the city, leaving the women as the rear guard. Because we didn't want innocent people to perish, we asked people not to go out in the street after one o'clock at night and to stay home until five in the morning, no matter what happened. In Nicaragua people get up early to work. Nothing goes on at night. Places like the movie theater get out early. As a result, it's easy to detect the enemy within the city. During the day people went about their regular work. But the people guarding the places that were the contra targets always had to be ready. Women, along with some men who hadn't been mobilized, were in trenches surrounding places where we store basic grains, or the electrical plant, or our potable water supply. The women who didn't want to use a gun brought food or coffee to the compañeros. The defense of Estelí was almost totally in the hands of women.

Shots came from the east, west, and south because that's where the enemy came from. Soldiers, the militia, and volunteers with combat experience formed a cordon around the city. When the enemy soldiers drew near, they ran into this cordon. Our people shot and pushed the enemy back toward the mountains. Then planes were brought in; if ever there are campesinos in the area, the army goes in, not the air force, so that campesinos aren't killed.[24]

During the emergency, I made rounds throughout the city supervising strategic contra targets. I checked to see if anyone needed anything, like ammunition, and found out if they had seen the enemy and how the situation was. I went on foot or in a vehicle, day and night, day and night. If there was a vehicle, we used it because it was faster, but if we had to walk, that's what we did, at midnight or any hour. We finished at five in the morning. Every day for eight days. We had to stay on alert because we couldn't be sure that the enemy had gone. We couldn't say to the people, "Go to sleep now," because there could have been a small contra group that had stayed behind. We spent all that time without sleep, tense but ready to face any situation.

In Estelí and La Trinidad, we've buried seventeen civilians and soldiers from this area in the last two weeks. Seven civilians, men and women, were killed on the road. They had been kidnapped by the contra. About ten compañeros died in the army. In an ambush, about thirty. I really don't know the total. The contra are artists when it comes to ambushes. But if they have to come face-to-face with our armed forces, they run. They aren't able to confront their enemy. If they feel so confident, let them try to take Nicaragua, especially Estelí.[25]

There are people who thought the contra would win, but now they realize that the contra forces can't even take a city. Those people have to decide if they want to stay in the revolutionary process, or if they'll have to leave. But they can see that the contra can no longer win. I've heard them comment, "The contra forces said they were going to take Estelí, and they didn't do anything."

At times like this emergency, the people who don't agree with the revolution stay in their houses, quietly, waiting to see what the contra does. They do nothing. Neither do those of us who know that they're doing nothing. If they're ready to do something, they'll participate. But if they want to do nothing, there's no problem. They can stay home, hide, rest, whatever. If the contra were to invade Estelí, these people would be sheltered so that nothing would happen to them. Their children would be watched over so that they don't perish. Conscious of the revolution or not, the protection of the people is the same.

The past year has been hectic, not just with this emergency. I worked with people who have been displaced by the war in the zones of Jalapa, Quilalí, and San Juan del Río Coco. You have to pay special attention to those people since they came from areas where the enemy penetrated and then kidnapped and killed them. We had to get the people out of there to a secure place. Then we had to teach them about matters of health, sanitation, and numerous things they didn't know. As a result, the days were full of excitement and work. I spent a month in each place and didn't come home during March, April, and May.

My son Miguel cries a lot when I leave. That's why I sneak away. He wakes up and asks where I am, and they tell him that I'm out working. He gets sad, but afterwards with his school friends, he forgets. When he goes to bed he remembers again, and sometimes he cries. He says he's afraid to be alone and afraid my mother will get sick. When she did, I didn't know about it because there's no way of communicating with the places where I work. We know she could die at any time. She isn't supposed to have any surprises and should stay calm, so we try to be happy with her and talk with her whenever we have free time. It isn't good to have her remember unhappy things from the past. She doesn't know how sick she is. We can't tell her anything.

I'm in charge of the Regional Commission of Publicity for AMNLAE. I advertise what women are doing. If women in a barrio are in charge of food production in five orchards, I spread the information throughout the region by mimeographing and distributing a sheet about it. This motivates and stimulates women because they know what other women are doing. Some women take care of the children of the women who work in [food] production, and they feel good because it isn't only those working in production who are taken into account, but the others as well. If women in Limay make some decorations made of stone, then I take a photograph or do a drawing and make a small poster to be distributed in the region. I write, "The women in Limay are making decorations for the house. They'll sell them at a low price wherever women are or wherever women want them to be sold."

I have several jobs within AMNLAE, and one is to count how many women we have organized: how many in work committees, how many in neighborhood watch committees, how many in the militia, how many armed, how many not, how many protecting the sites the contra want to attack. It's bookkeeping. I've also harvested coffee crops with the women, gone on food-production brigades, and done what we call a *rojo y negro*, which is when we go on Sundays to plant or pull up beans, or work in the tobacco fields. When the compañeros have been mobilized, we have to redouble our forces. We women have to finish what the compañeros can't do. Some women take letters to the *cachorros* or bring back letters to the soldiers' families. Sometimes we do solidarity work for the fighters. With the Mothers of the Martyrs we have a *jornada*; that's when we have activities and raffles in August and September to collect money, uniforms, boots, medicines—everything a soldier needs—which we send to them. We don't feel it's important that women are organized [as members of] AMNLAE, but it's important that they do some task within the revolutionary process.

A lot of people visit Nicaragua, especially this region, and want to know about the work we've accomplished. Sometimes I take care of them, and sometimes another compañera does it. They come to see with their own eyes what we've done. A group of Spaniards—students and professional people—just came. They want to see the work in the countryside and city and the work of the women in our office. Some are workers and want to see how our revolution functions. Groups come from the United States with the same purpose. All of them want to know if abortion is permitted, if there are contraceptives, if men beat women, if men give money to support their children, and what AMNLAE does about all those things.[26]

I get up every day at five-thirty in the morning and help my mother prepare the firewood so that we can have a fire. After that I wash some clothes; then I clean the house with water and a mop. I bathe, dress, and get myself ready. Miguel gets up around six or six-thirty. Around seven I go to buy meat, if there is any, or buy beans. I also get bread to go with our coffee for breakfast. Sometimes we have leftover bread, but I always buy the beans in the morning or some little piece of meat.

At 7:35, or sometimes at 7:45, I go to work. We don't do the same things every day at AMNLAE; it depends on the situation. There are days that we have meetings, and sometimes they're emergency meetings. Or maybe I have to go to Quilalí, or San Juan, or perhaps Jícaro or Jalapa. Sometimes I know before I go to work that I might have to go somewhere. At other times things come up suddenly. Another day I might mimeograph something, do a drawing—I draw well—or take information to the radio about what a cooperative is doing or what women are doing in tobacco. There isn't a set hour for our work to be over. Last night I finished at seven. There are days when it's midnight, other times I don't finish until morning. In this last emergency we worked all the time. There are only ten of us in the office, but many women in the barrio—more than before—work with us.

I eat whenever I get home; my mother prepares the food for my son and me. When I come home tired, I lie down. I always get up early, so I go to sleep early. When I have a chance to sleep, I sleep. But there's no possibility of that when it's my turn to stand watch, which I do weekly from six in the afternoon to six in the morning. I watch over the business district, so the watch period is longer. In the barrio the shifts are shorter, two or three hours, and they start at ten at night and last until two or three in the morning.

To have fun, I sleep, or listen to music with friends, or spend time alone with my son; we go to bed to listen to music. I almost never go to a party. If I do go, it's only to those parties that the compañeras from AMNLAE have. I go for a short time, one hour. I like parties, but not much. It's the time of day to be at home. I have too much work to do to have a man. The only ones I know are just friends. As women, we know that we can like a certain man as long as the ideology is within the revolutionary process. That's to say that I could like a man and live with him, provided that we both understood that I have to work and that I'm not going to be at home all the time.

Everything is more expensive this year. We buy only the essentials. We're aware that we are in this situation not because the government wants it, but because it's caused by the war, by the economic blockade.

We have a new refrigerator. The government lets us make monthly payments when we can, but this month I've had a lot of expenses, so I haven't paid. I make 6000 córdobas a month. It's not much, but we get along. Overall things are better because we have more than we had before. In spite of the difficulties and the fix the country is in, things are always distributed well. For example, if there are beans this month, we buy them, and at the end of the month, we buy something else. It balances out. There are times when things are scarce, but there are other times when they aren't. My sister Leticia watches over us. When I have no money, she gives me some even though she has economic problems in the salon. We take all our troubles to her, and she says, "This is what we're going to do." She's mature and experienced in making decisions.

We'd like Omar to go to a hospital in Managua where there are specialists, or to a medical *pensión*[27] outside the home. It's a war psychosis that has made him afraid to go out. He thinks he's being followed and will be killed. This is how war leaves children and adults. Children are afraid to play because they think the contra will kill them. The leaders and workers of the State, and even those who aren't leaders and workers, are afraid that at any moment the contra will come to their houses and kill them.

Omar was different last year. He was happier, more playful, more active. In the last year there were a lot of enemy raids, and he had to work in the mountains. Things got worse there. The military didn't tell him that the reason he can't have his gun is that he's sick; instead they said that another person would have it while Omar's on leave. It's a dangerous situation, and it's better that he rest. He's afraid to leave the house. He has never been like that before. He's a guerrillero. He has never been afraid of anyone. He worries me, and my mother worries me, too.

Omar

The truth is that I'm in serious trouble. My health is bothering me as a result of what I've lived through. I've had problems with my mind and my nerves. Even more now that the war has begun again. Seeing these planes and bombs day and night brings back memories. I can't sleep. It seems as if everything is as it was before the triumph. Four days ago I had a nervous fit, and they had to take me to a clinic. I don't want to talk with anyone, and that bothers and disturbs me. I hate everything. I have no happiness. All I do is sob every couple of minutes. They were going to keep me in the clinic, but since they had many wounded compañeros, they couldn't. Instead they gave me some medicine. But I still have the same nervous problems. The war psychosis affects me way too much. The doctors say that they can't cure me right now because there's no treatment in Nicaragua to help me. They can only give me tranquilizers, pills to help me sleep at night, and vitamins. But it doesn't help. There are psychologists, but they haven't much time and can take care of only a few. For me, it'd have to be a special psychologist who could spend time talking with me all day in order to get to the problem I have. A consultation with a doctor is just for a minute, and you can't tell him what's wrong with you in that time. You have to spend more time on it because, as the doctor said, it won't be cured today and not tomorrow, either.

I've tried in my own way to conquer this, but I have other troubles, too. One of my daughters has a bronchial-pulmonary problem, and they say there's no cure. Just tranquilizers. Last night her nerves attacked her, and she didn't recognize anyone. This bothers me. When I'm at work, I can't concentrate since I'm worrying about her. I've asked for help at work, but the help has been very little. The problem is that the war is very close. I'd like to work, but they won't let me now. Well, they let me work, but very little. Not like before.

I've really had this problem since I went to the mountain and after the war of liberation. It began four months after the triumph. After seeing the dead, the wounded, the air force, mortars, I ended up with this. When I'm lying down, it seems to me that the guardia, the very same guardia as before the triumph, is coming to attack me. I wake up frightened. My whole body is shaking. At times I don't know the person who tries to control me, and I hit her,[28] until it all passes, until I can recognize the person.

I used to drink a lot of liquor, but I don't drink now. I thought that by drinking I could forget things, but it isn't that way. On the contrary, I was bothered more. I've gone three months without drinking. I've been able to control it myself. Drinking doesn't give me a good future, just the opposite. I haven't been a good example to my children, nor to my wife. My brother Pedro drank too much. If he had money he drank every day, but I drank only when there was a special occasion. My problem started after the triumph; I looked for a way to cure the problems in my head by drinking, thinking it would cure me. When I drank, I wasn't afraid. I didn't feel anything. I felt like a man.

Now with the war so close, it makes it worse for me. And my work never stops. I have to go out looking for the contra all the time. I'm either in combat or in an office where the guardia (contra) are imprisoned. I have to see them all the time. I wish I had a different job [that would allow more time for] sleep. The work often lasts until one or three in the morning. I work all week, day and night for seven days, and then get twenty-four hours rest. The lack of sleep and the amount of military action bother me. In my work, I have to go where the counter-revolutionaries are, and I've had too much of that this past year. The contra attacks have been constant in the north, and I've been there for one month, then two months, and then back again. Until this leave I got as a result of my broken foot, there had been no rest. I'm taking advantage of the leave to get treatment. Even though I have this mental problem, I haven't said that I wouldn't go to battle because of it. Just the opposite, I say I want to go. One day the doctor said I could no longer go to the war front, that I had to rest. I didn't accept that. I said I wanted to be there. But a month or so ago, I did ask to get out of the army. I had medical documentation of my mental problems. The army said they'd look for a solution that would allow me to leave. But when they were about to solve it, I broke my foot, and we haven't talked about it since. Anyhow, right now with the war so bad, there's no way to get out.

I don't go out much now. When I'm shut up in the house, I get nervous when I hear the planes. I'm too afraid to leave. When I do leave, it seems that someone is behind me, following me. So I stay in the house or in the patio; I seldom go out in the street. Certainly not unless I've taken a lot of pills. Then I feel strong and can go. I take pills even to come to my mother's house. That's why I don't come very often. I haven't come for a month.

I had the cast taken off yesterday. I could walk, but I needed a crutch. But the cast isn't what made it hard for me to go any place. What makes it hard is my head.

I hope when all of this is over that my bosses understand my situation and let me work as a bricklayer; but even if they allowed that, I'd have to defend Nicaragua when the aggression increases. It wouldn't be hard for me to find bricklaying work again because I still have a lot of friends who do it. Even now, since I've been at home, bricklayer friends have come by asking if I can work. I tell them no. Even though I want to help them, I just can't do it right now.

I broke my foot here in Estelí. I was working in the office when an alarm sounded. We could hear shots outside our base. We all left with guns in our hands. I went down the stairs—it was raining and dark—I slid first, then spun around and fell, hurting my shoulder and elbow. I landed on my foot in such a way that it broke. I tried to move but couldn't. They had to carry me upstairs. The doctor said I had to go to the hospital at La Trinidad to have a cast put on. I had that on for a month, and then they put another one on. The first one was small and short and served to stabilize the foot. The second one went up farther.

I stayed with my mother for a month because Irene was in Managua with all the children, visiting her grandmother. I felt better in my mother's house with the music and the television. I was more peaceful. I also had a lot of pills.

When Irene and the children returned, I went back to my house. It was harder there with all the worries about the children. Before my radio was stolen, I listened to music. But now I listen to chickens, crickets, and toads. I had trouble with the cast because it itched so much and I couldn't scratch it. I put a little stick between the leg and the cast and stirred up a lot of fleas. Then I put powdered DDT down the cast to kill the fleas. When I had it taken off yesterday at the hospital, there was a pile of dead little animals in there!

The psychologist recommended diversion; I should go to the river or to the park to take my mind off my problems. I've tried, but I end up with the same fear. I intend to go, but it frightens me—until I take the pills. Then I go.[29]

Irene and I have a lot of problems. There are eight children, and I'm the only person who works, so there's no way we can feed everybody. The government pays me 7000 córdobas per month, but every day I spend almost 1000 córdobas, or at least 800 córdobas. At the end of the month, I'm in debt. The problem is that Irene hasn't found work. She went to school [recently] and passed the primary grades. Irene used to have a job, but her boss scolded her; he wanted to use her like a servant. One day Irene got tired of being scolded and when he told her to go get some soda pop, she said she wasn't a servant, she was in charge of the mail. So the argument began, and she quit. That was about three months ago, and now it's just my salary.

The only other work she could get is with the military, but then there's no one to take care of the children, who are all little. I spend my life wondering how we're going to eat tomorrow, how we'll eat the day after that. And the clothes: a pair of shoes for a child is 3000 córdobas. If I buy shoes for one, I can't for the other. If I buy a dress for one, I can't for the other. For us to walk down to my mother's house, neighbors have to lend us shoes for the girls. There are day-care centers, but you have to pay twenty percent of your salary. And the children have to be younger than four or five years. The older one of my two, who are the youngest of the family, is five. The rest aren't mine, but I'm responsible for them. Their fathers don't help; neither do their brothers. The job is mine.[30] Sometimes one accepts this sort of responsibility for love of those who are little, or perhaps the recompense will be when I'm old and they'll work when I can't. They're receiving a good education. Right now, one of the oldest is studying medicine at the university in León. I have this expense, too.

Another reason I have the responsibility is that before my wife's mother died, I promised her I'd take care of her children. I loved Irene's mother very much because we suffered the same repression from the guardia. She suffered because she collaborated [with the Frente Sandinista]. She was older than I and close to Commander Carlos Fonseca and José Benito Escobar, close to all of them. When she worried about what would happen, she said, "Take care of my children. Take care of Irene, too. Never leave them." It has been more than two years since the father, who's not Irene's father, has given them anything for food. We've asked the government to help take care of orphans, but they haven't said they would. There was a time when it might have been possible, but now they've had to cut back due to the economic situation of the country. Since then, I've had responsibility for the house, if that's what you can call it. It's as if we live outside, and that's no way to live. You have to go a long way for water, but there's electricity. There's no bathroom. If I don't die, maybe I'll see a better house.[31]

When the problem gets hold of me, I don't want Irene to get near me, come close to me, or touch me. I don't even want the children near. The noise and the yelling bother me. Irene and I went together to the psychologist, and he explained to her that she had to have patience with me. But right now, the problem has overwhelmed me. We have no food in the house. We always have to go looking for food or for someone to give it to us, to lend it to us, or to give it to us on credit. The little ones don't understand. If we tell them, "Today there's no food," they begin to cry and yell, "Ahhh, food, food!" So we have to go look for something. The two little ones get up early in the morning and come to our bed and say, "I want bread, I want some bread, give me coffee with bread." Maybe there's nothing. So I say, "Wait, I'll go get it."

I have a little hope and faith left that I'll conquer this. I'm not beaten, and this is what keeps me going. Every day I hope that someone will help me. I've always had faith in God. When I have nothing to eat, a friend shows up and I say, "Look, my friend, I have nothing to eat today." And he says, "Okay, man, come to my house to get something." It's like a miracle. At night, before lying down, I think about God and ask him why this is happening to me, why just to me. It seems that God and I have a dialogue, and he tells me, "Tomorrow you're going to eat. Don't worry so much. Go to sleep." So I do, and another day begins. And we begin another struggle for food.

I've never wanted to bother my mother and sisters, so I don't ask them to help us. Really, they need what they have. Marta is the sole support of her house. I don't help because I have my own family. It'd be painful to come to my mother's and take away their food, even though there are only three of them, and we have so many. At times I've come to ask them to give me a little rice, but my mother doesn't get along well with Irene. Because of that, we have many problems. My mother doesn't understand. When I have arguments with Irene, it's due to my mental problems. When I don't want to argue with Irene, I come to my mother's house. Then my mother says that Irene kicked me out of the house. She thinks Irene treats me badly, and that's why I'm sick, but actually, Irene helps me. She has friends who lend her money for food.[32] I've come to my mother's house to talk about my problems, but they just want to tell me what to do. That bothers me a lot.[33]

The government isn't to blame for our problems. On the contrary, we feel we're going to conquer this little by little. This cause has cost us a lot, and now that we're free, we won't abandon it. Even so, many other soldiers have problems similar to mine. We try to bring them up at meetings, but there's no answer, and we resign ourselves. They tell us, "Some day we'll be able to help you." But we don't really believe that. We believe that we're the ones who have to resolve the problems we have. No one is going to come and say, "This is for you; here's your house." The government doesn't have the capacity to worry about all these things. There are many problems with old soldiers and veterans of our war of liberation who smoke marijuana and drink alcohol. The government hasn't worried much about that situation. Even if the government wants to help, it's too poor. For example, there's no center to reactivate veterans. In the combatants' home, there's help for families of people who are in the army right now, but the veterans need help, too. We've asked the soldiers for help and have drawn attention to the situation. They come, never say no, always say yes, and leave.[34]

They go with love for their country and the conviction that they were the only ones who liberated this country.

When I see my friends in the park or in the street who've been on the mountain with me, we talk about memories of the war and how our life was there. "Do you remember this . . .?" Such things. That's all we talk about. We also talk about how there's no help for the combatants and how they just push us to one side. The ones who have the most privileges are the ones who study; they have better jobs than those of us who fought in the war. For example, I didn't learn to write or read very well, but really, I helped in the war a lot. I didn't study these things because there was no interest on the part of my family. Those who did study back then find it easier now to work for the State. The State needs people who have finished the sixth grade, and I finished only the fourth. That's not a lot. But I do have the ability to lead troops, and I showed it back then. They put me in charge of a company. But if I had a job where I sit in an office writing, well . . . , I did take a class in the Frente's school, but the mental problem didn't help. The teacher was writing on the blackboard, and I was somewhere else, thinking about home, worrying if they had food. I mean, I eat well in the army, but at home, it's different. So I couldn't pay attention. I did very poorly in the classes.

At the same time, I had trouble at night because I slept on the top of a bunk-bed at work, and when the nightmare, the psychosis, got hold of me, I fell out of bed, to the floor, and grabbed my gun. So the army took my gun away and kicked me out of the school. I no longer have a gun. They took it away. It's serious.

I do see some of the people who were on the mountain with me. One of them, Lieutenant Rodríguez, died nine days ago in the ambush the guardia (contra) set in La Trinidad. His real name was Ronaldo, but his pseudonym was Aquiles. He was one of the best friends I had in the camp. There are four of those friends in Estelí. We work together in the Ministry, so we always see each other there. Filemón, the one who left Estelí with me, is a captain in Sébaco. Isauro (Cristián Pichardo) is in the Ministry of the Interior. Of the forty who were in that first camp, six have died.

In spite of everything, many complain to me that I should be made a captain or a lieutenant because of the work I did. But I don't want to be a captain or a lieutenant. Six months ago they wanted to give me the rank of lieutenant, but I didn't accept it. There are many soldiers who, when they have a position in charge of something, no longer know their old friends. Many of my friends who are lieutenants or captains—my friends from the cemetery, for example—don't know their old friends anymore.[35] That's why I am happier the way I am without the responsibility of being a lieutenant or captain. With a job like that, they lock you up inside an office, and if a friend comes to look you up, perhaps you have to say, "It's very busy now, so tell him I'm not here and to come back another day."

The friend would say, "He's gotten big now that he's a lieutenant. He no longer loves his friends."

So it's better this way. For example, my friends from the time of the struggle are Walter Ferreti, Carlos Núñez, Commander Pichardo. But if I went right now to look them up, I'd be told that they aren't there. "He's busy," they'd say, and so he can't see me. So I'd think that he won't see me because now he's a commander. That has actually happened. I've gone to look for them to help me, and they've said, "Tell him I'm not here." After being with them for so long in the struggle, it's hard to imagine that this would happen to me.

At work, they celebrated the sixth anniversary of the retreat to Masaya, and it fell to me to talk about it. They admire me for having survived the retreat and wonder how it was possible that I, an Esteliano, was going around fighting everywhere. I told them that it was because, as a Nicaraguan, I knew that I had to be where the country needed me.

But right now, I have to find the solution to my problem. The way it is now, I'm no good to anyone. I have to tell myself that what happened to me was a dream. And none of the dream is left. I went to a movie, that's all, a war movie. I left the theater and told other people about it so that they wouldn't go see it.[36]

I know there are other veterans with the same problems because the day I went to the doctor, one arrived, in worse shape, with a crisis, and they had to leave him at the clinic. They gave him an injection, and he fell asleep. After a while, he woke up, and we talked. "I feel the same as you do," he said. They put him in a mental hospital in Managua. Sometimes I'm afraid I'll end up there. People say to me, "Maybe you're going to go there, too." Then I say, "No!"

Leticia just offered to help me start a vegetable business. If I'm able to sell vegetables, I won't have the problem of worrying about food because I can get food from the business, and I can pay. Before, I had no idea how to do this. Now Leticia is going to see how she can help us, so I hope that at least we have food every day. I'm going to be able to go to work without having to worry about whether Irene and the children eat or not. I already feel happier.[37]

6

Leticia in the United States: February 1986

Late in 1985, Leticia illegally crossed the border between the United States and Mexico. Early in 1986 she visited my home in Corvallis, Oregon, where we conducted the interview.

Leticia

I'll begin when I first wanted to leave. I didn't know where [I wanted to go], but I wanted to leave Estelí and my home. I felt the desire to escape my problems. I wanted to rest my mind. I wanted to go somewhere where I couldn't hear the same things that I heard in Nicaragua and where I could find some peace. I received a letter from my cousin who lives in Carson City, Nevada, at a time when I had bank debts and problems with Sergio. When I answered his letter, I thought that maybe Nevada was the place I wanted to go—not because it was in the United States, but because I'd have my cousin's support. I could be there a while, reflect on my problems, and maybe get some work. By coincidence, my cousin's wife was also going from Nicaragua to the United States, so when my cousin in Nevada got my letter, he called his wife. She came to my house and told me that my cousin said I could go with her; she was going to travel with a person who was coming from the United States and who would return. I wanted to leave, but I was also afraid. As the days passed, deep down I wasn't sure if what I was doing was the best. I made the decision to do it the day before I went.

My three daughters and husband dropped me off, along with my four-year-old daughter Nora, at the Honduran border. It was sad to

154

leave them, but I also felt that I needed to leave. My intention was to recuperate and stay in the United States for a few days, more or less three months. I left, and my family stayed in Nicaragua. It was hard, but the plan was set. I had to leave.

On the Honduran side, we waited two hours for customs to check the vehicle. We took the highway through Honduras and then to San Salvador. I don't know exactly how many people went with me, but some were leaving for quite a while. Some of the women were old. They said they were going to visit relatives. I don't know about the others. I think they were going to the United States to stay. They were all Nicaraguans. We really didn't talk much on the road because the trip was tiring. Some slept almost all the time. When we did talk, we didn't talk about why we left.

In El Salvador, we saw some tanks. There were uniforms of the [Salvadoran] guardia and blood on the road. We didn't know what had happened. We met a man who asked the owner of the van for a ride to Guatemala; he asked if we had seen the battle. We asked him where it was, and he said, "It was back there where you just went through, about fifteen minutes ago." What luck that we passed through after that occurred. We could have been killed. For me it was sad; we Nicaraguans are still traumatized when we see tanks.

On the highway through Guatemala and then Mexico, the driver always asked people how the road was and if there was danger. The people told us to be careful and not to drive at night. There had been a lot of attacks, and it was dangerous. Thank God we didn't meet up with any bad people. We stayed in a small hotel before we left El Salvador. We couldn't cross the border at night, so we slept in the van. There's a park at the border for people who are waiting. That was the only time we stopped. The man drove day and night until we got to the Mexican border. We all had visas for Mexico. Everyone goes to Mexico, so it isn't hard to get visas.

We arrived in Tijuana around five in the morning. We met a man there whom the driver knew. The driver left, and this other man took us to a place where we crossed over a wall and a highway. After that, we were on the other side of Mexico; that is, we were in the United States. I'd known that we were going to enter illegally, but the man told us we'd walk for only ten minutes to cross the border. Instead we walked one and a half hours through mud, and in some areas it was water mixed with mud, like little ponds after a rainfall. I carried only a small suitcase; in Nicaragua they had told us not to bring much on the trip because the van was full. We got to a little house made of wood—it didn't seem to me that anyone lived there—and they told us to wait. About seven o'clock, they moved us by car to another house, where we spent almost the whole day. It was a house that people might live in occasionally, but no one lived there then. There were some household things in the house, but not much. They came for us at about six o'clock in two cars. We hid in the back seat for three hours, and the men hid in the trunk. They took us to a house in Los Angeles, a house where people lived and where we didn't have to hide.

About one in the morning, the owner of the van came to get us; then he dropped each one of us off. I went to the apartment of a cousin, the sister of the cousin in Nevada. She has lived in Los Angeles for four years and is married to a Salvadoran. He's legal, and she has her card. She was good to me and wanted me to stay with her. I wanted to stay—there was someone for my daughter to play with—but I knew that my cousin wouldn't like that. I had to go to Nevada because I had promised I would. My cousin couldn't come to get me for eleven days because he had car trouble. All I did was wait.

When my cousin came, the man who had driven us to the United States came to get the money my cousin had agreed to give him. They talked, and my cousin said, "How much is the bill for Leticia?" The man said it cost U.S. $947 for each one of us—for me and for my daughter. They figured out the bill, and then my cousin said to the driver, "What I owe you is this amount, and that number—U.S. $1894—is what Leticia owes you." There were a lot of people in the house, so I just sat there thinking about it. That was a lot of money. I thought my cousin was going to tell me later, "I just told him that it was your bill, not mine, so that maybe he'd make it less." And in fact, the driver did say that although the bill was almost U.S. $1900, he'd settle for U.S. $1500. I didn't even answer him because I was so confused. I remember that in Tijuana he said to my cousin's wife—not to me because he had never made an arrangement with me at all—"Tell your husband that the bill for Leticia and the child is U.S. $1100." Since they had made their arrangement, I said nothing. But when I arrived in Los Angeles and heard this conversation between the driver and my cousin, I didn't understand. Back in Nicaragua, when I decided to bring the child along, I talked with my cousin's wife and told her that I thought I'd come, but also that I planned to bring Nora. She talked with my cousin by telephone, supposedly, and told him that I was going to bring her. I asked her what he said about the child, and she answered that he said there was no problem, I could bring her. But then in the apartment in Los Angeles, he said that he didn't know the child was coming, and that if I had told him, he would have arranged it beforehand. So I don't understand if his wife lied to me, or if he told her that I could bring the child and forgot that he said it.

The trip to Nevada went well. It had snowed earlier, but the day we went was a good day. I felt the difference between Nevada and Los Angeles: it was very cold there and not that cold in Los Angeles. We went to the apartment where my cousin lived with other people who had come from Nicaragua a year ago. My cousin had been there two or three years. In Nicaragua, he was an agronomist, but from the time he arrived in the United States, he has worked in a factory. When I got there, he had been unemployed for nearly a month. There had been a strike, but later the work started again, and he went back to the same place. He has another job at night cleaning kitchens in homes, but just when they call him. Twenty days after I got there, a muchacho found work for me in a factory— it's like a laundry—and I worked there almost a month.

More than anything, now that I've come to the United States, I feel bad. In reality, I had no need to leave Nicaragua because I didn't really have problems in my country. At this moment, it seems I made a bad decision. But now that everything is done, maybe it's best that I did it. I think God has plans for us. Not even a leaf on a tree moves without His will. My visit to Corvallis and the talks I've had with the students are what I should have done. That's the good that's come from this trip.[1] People are interested in learning about Nicaragua, people who knew little about Nicaragua but now know more about the revolution and the process of our government.

However, I still feel bad. First, I feel bad not to have paid the driver. He's going to tell everyone he knows in Nicaragua that I didn't pay. It has occurred to me that he's not an honest person because he takes advantage of people's situations—or their bad decisions—to charge so much money. In Nicaragua, that's a lot of money. So I think I have to forget about this because I have more important problems in Nicaragua to solve. Every time I hear about the aggressions, I worry because I know that if something happened, my family would feel more secure if I were there. They count on me for everything. And my mother could die at any moment, and I wouldn't like to be away when that happens.

I'll be in Nevada for two weeks before I go to Miami in order to work and save money.[2] I have to help my mother because they can't live on just Marta's salary. I also want to help Omar get his new house. In Nevada, I met many Latinos, and they liked my hair cuts and recommended me to others. Maybe I can do that or work at the same factory.

If things go well for me in Miami, I'll be there less time because I'll be able to quickly save the money I need to buy the ticket to Nicaragua. I'll stay with a childhood friend from Estelí who has lived in Miami for many years. She sews in her own house for a woman who has a shop, so she doesn't have to go out in the streets. I'd like that more than the factory in Nevada; they say Immigration never comes, but any day they could, especially when more and more Latinos are working. Even if the North Americans who work there have no bad feelings toward the Latinos, there might be one of them who does. It's hard to work peacefully in that situation, and I think I can work with my friend. She said I could.

My cousin in Nevada doesn't support the revolution because he's confused by things people say. Nicaraguans come to the United States as a result of personal problems, but after they arrive, they say they came due to economic problems. Even I could say I came for economic reasons because, in reality, I'd like to make some money, but I don't see the necessity, as an honest person, to talk about my country just to get along well with the people in the United States. It's the opposite; people will understand if you tell them how things really are. My cousin stayed with a man who had been here several years, and this man influenced him by telling him things against the [Nicaraguan] government. Now he repeats what the other man says. I said to my cousin, "People say things that aren't true." They talk about the lines that you have to stand in to get things, but I said, "But here, too, I've seen lines to maintain order." I explain that you have to stand in line in Nicaragua so that everyone gets things, but he says that we stand in line as if we were asking for something. I told him that not everything he heard was true. He was told that the sugar they give us is what they used to give to the animals—a black sugar. And it's true that there are times they sell us that, but almost always we have white sugar. He says we don't. These are things that I know aren't true, and I tell him that. His wife doesn't say anything. Once I said to her in front of him, "But you know that what he's saying isn't true." I asked her, "Is it true or not?" She had to say that it wasn't true because I challenged her with the truth. But I think that behind my back, she says the opposite.

Life in Nicaragua has improved for Omar. After Irene got work and I proposed that he could have part of my land to build his house, I could see in his face how happy it made him. That gave me a lot of satisfaction because lately I've seldom seen him happy. He's always worried, sad, nervous. But this time he was happy and asked if I really was going to give him the land. I said that I was, but I told him that just two days before I came here. A piece of land for my children or for my brothers and sisters is like savings. It's the first thing we need because when we were small, we had to go from one place to another renting houses. Land increases in value, but money in a bank doesn't. I bought it because I liked it, but I didn't know what I'd use it for.[3] It's large and pretty because the land is flat, but it has a view. You can see the valley, and you can see the mountains. Estelí is where I like to live. Maybe if we make some arrangement with Sergio, he can go to Estelí on the week-ends. And if I'm in Estelí I can be near my mother, [which is important] especially now that she's sick. Marta always leaves her alone when she goes to work, but if I'm in Estelí, whatever goes wrong during the day or night, Miguel or a neighbor can let me know.

Omar said he had a new job [within the military], but he didn't say specifically what it was. It has always been unusual for him to say much, even though he trusts me. His new job is in the same Ministry of the Interior, but now he has responsibility over other people. Many times I've seen him going to my mother's at night, usually in a military vehicle. She gives him coffee, and he talks with his compañeros. Then they leave again. It looks like a job where you go and return the same day. He comes to see my mother more now, and she's happier because she sees him almost daily. She worries that he doesn't eat enough, so she saves food from lunch for him to eat when he comes at night. He's fatter now, in better health, and more tranquil. I hope that everything has gone well and that he's looking forward to having land for his house. Living in El Rosario barrio, as he does now, is dangerous.[4] I arranged with a woman lawyer to transfer part of the land to him. I hope he has a good head and hasn't done something else, and when I return he has begun to build his house.

Marta's health also worries me. She likes her work, and she's more ready than I am to give her life for it. I've seen her go to work when she should have stayed in bed, times when she was tired and pale with no color in her skin. She's sick more often than she's well. She recuperates quickly because of her enthusiasm for her work, but she's still sick. She has a throbbing pain around her waistline, front and back. The doctors say that it might be a kidney infection, which is followed by what we call pus. We know that kidney illness is dangerous.

She never has a fixed hour for work, but she always goes at seven-thirty in the morning and returns when she returns. If she comes home at six in the afternoon, that's early. If she has a meeting or work to finish in the office, she comes home at ten, eleven, twelve at night. When she stands watch, called *oficialia*, she stays all night. Sometimes they stand watch with guns because those buildings can be attacked or ransacked. Another woman accompanies her when she does that. The women in AMNLAE take turns working in the north, in Jalapa, and Marta regularly goes for a week and sometimes for a month.

Miguel is always asking about her; he's intelligent and mature for his age. He's nervous, too, and for good reason. So many things have happened to him. He has seen the war and saw the guardia hit my mother with a pistol when they were trying to find out where my brothers were. Miguel and my mother were alone, as usual; Marta wasn't there, and the muchachos had gone to the mountain. Miguel remembers everything. He must have been three years old when that happened, and a child at that age can remember things. Today he can't bear to look at people who have had a lot to drink. He says they are dying and they frighten him. I tried to not let my children become afraid during the war. I controlled myself as much as I could so that I wouldn't transmit the fear and terror I felt. When we were in Managua at the time of the triumph, they saw many things—there were dead people in front of my house—that I didn't want them to see because it was terrible.

It bothers me to be so far from home when my mother's health is delicate. The doctors have said that she could die at any time. Every day that goes by is closer to her last one. We try not to let her realize how sick she is, and we don't tell her that she's going to die soon. We just tell her that she has to be treated and it will make her better, but we also know that we are lying to her. I ask God that she not suffer much on the day He wants her to stop living. I know how horrible the sickness is because I have a foreboding that I have the same one. Sometimes I've wanted to be the one to die first, but then I've remembered that my brothers and sisters depend on me as if I were their second mother and that my mother will die peacefully because she knows that she has me. That's why I can't change anything.

I can't decide my own life, if I want to stay here or there or go somewhere else. My life doesn't belong to just me. It belongs to my daughters and my family. I'm sure they know, as I do, that I won't fail them. I'm convinced that the revolution is for us, for the poor, for those of us who have always been marginal. So I have a commitment not just to my family but to other peple I have learned to love. I have to do something in my barrio, in my city, or wherever I am. I don't know why God has chosen me for this. There are people who can live peacefully without problems, but God must have known why He chose for me not to be one of them. Even when I hear someone cry, I go to see what has happened. Sometimes Sergio would tell me, "Leave them alone. They have their own people to take care of them." But I can't be deaf to cries. I've sometimes gone in the middle of the night to see how I can help. Every day I believe in God more than ever. He puts things in front of you and says, "You have to do something."

I've been criticized for many things, even by my own husband. One day I went to the vigil of an old woman's grandchild whom she had brought up as her own son. Earlier in the night there were a lot of people at the vigil, but by dawn everyone had gone. When I saw that she was alone, I couldn't just go home and leave her there. So I stayed. Sergio came to get me. He was angry and told me that everyone else had gone and why hadn't I? I told him I knew that my obligation was to stay with her because she was alone and besides, I wasn't everyone else. He said, "When people see you going down the street toward your house, what are they going to say? Where's she coming from? Maybe she went out looking [for something or someone]." I told him that people could talk about me, and they could say that I was coming back after staying with some man. But I knew what it was that I should do, and my obligation was to stay there. I said to him, "The most important thing is what you think." He didn't answer, but he stayed there with me. I used to think he didn't understand me. He'd criticize me, as do people who think I'm up to something else when they see me out in the street when the rest of the world is sleeping. What I'm really doing is talking with someone who needs my help. One of the most important things in my life has been that he has learned to have confidence in me. I can come home at midnight or one in the morning, and he doesn't lose faith in me. I thought he doubted me; when I went out, he thought I was going out with another man. But he wrote from Cuba that he recognized the good sentiments I had and that he was happy with [the way I treated people]. He'd seen drunks come to the house and say to me, "Leticia, I need a drink," or "I need a glass of water." I never closed the door on them. I bought a bottle to keep in the refrigerator, not for me to drink but for others. Once a drunkard who was dying came while Sergio was here. He was trembling and needed a drink. I put the drink [of water] in his hand, but he couldn't raise it to his lips. I helped him do it, but I thought that when he left, Sergio would criticize me. To my surprise, he said nothing, absolutely nothing. When he wrote me from Cuba, he said he admired me and had become convinced that I could be no other way. He wrote, "I remember your gestures of kindness with the drunk when he came to ask for water." Now I realize that without knowing it, I was making him a more humane person. Before, he was selfish and thought only of himself, but now he thinks of what others need. If he comes here with a sack of oranges, he says to me, "Leticia, send these to such-and-such a woman." I like that.

But at the same time, we've grown apart. Maybe it's his way of treating me as a woman. It's difficult to explain, and I think only women to whom this has happened can understand. At the beginning of the marriage, I didn't feel what I feel now when we're together. I'm speaking of intimate relations. I felt good then. I could respond sexually. But now it's the biggest problem I have with him.

When the time comes to have relations, I can't respond.[5] I don't understand why. He always asks if I'm satisfied or not. But sometimes I wait for him to go to sleep before I go to bed. There's no one for me to talk with about this. I'm not a frigid woman. I'm a normal woman. I feel the desire to share. But when I'm with him, I seldom feel good. We might have relations three times a week but it's because he wants it; I don't want it more than once a month. I don't know if it's because I'm tired. It must be [caused by] my problems making me tired. When I tell him that I don't want to, he gets angry. He says I don't love him. He thinks there might be another man, but he isn't sure.

Now that I've been far away, I think I'll go back to him. Before I was thinking, "I want to leave and never return." But not now. But I don't know if the same problem will happen. When we're separated, I miss him. But when I'm near him, there are times when I can't stand his touching me.

We've talked about this because I want him to understand my problem and know that it isn't that I don't love him. I've tried to explain it to him, but he told me that he thinks I've stopped loving him. I think he's wrong. When someone doesn't love the other, that person also can't stand the marriage in other aspects as well. That person wouldn't want to make plans with and think about the other one. I think I love him because when I'm far away, I make plans for when we are together and with my children. Down deep, I'd be afraid if he were to have another woman. I'm convinced that if I didn't love him, it wouldn't matter to me if he had another woman. I felt that when he was in Cuba, and I feel it now. I don't plan to leave him and find another man. I don't know. I'm more confused than ever.

He warned me he might find another woman. He knows I'm an honest woman; I'm not going to blame him, and I wouldn't tell anyone anything he tells me. He told me that in his office there are women willing to sleep with him. They've insinuated as much. But he hasn't wanted that, as least not in the office. They have rooms there where they spread out mattresses during the rest hours and places in the Estelí office that are occupied by the men who live outside the city—in Managua or other places—and the women go in there and ask him why he doesn't lie down and rest for awhile. But what they really mean is to ask him to sleep with them. It isn't because he isn't man enough—he could do it—but he thinks of the consequences it'd bring. For example, since he's the one in charge, if he slept with a secretary, he'd no longer have authority over her. He doesn't want to have problems like that.

We've never had a total intimacy. There has always been the fear of the children's room being next to ours, and there's no door. But I don't know if that's the problem. What I'm sure of is that I'm always tired, I always want to sleep, and I don't want him to bother me. When he touches me, I can't stand it. That's the problem. I just hope it passes quickly and doesn't last long. I don't think it has to be like this forever. He's indulgent with me and says, "Where do you want us to go? What do you want us to do?" He's not one of those men who just does what he wants to do; instead he does what I want to do. But he doesn't talk much, and that confuses me. I wish there were reasons to justify my feelings, but there aren't. I've analyzed the problem between us, and there isn't any problem. He left behind his family inheritance for me, and he has been a good man.

When I decided to come to the United States, he still hadn't been transferred to Managua. He planned to live in the office and the children would live across the street from our house in Estelí with my sister-in-law, Florencia. She's a good responsible woman. Her husband is my cousin, but he has been like a brother. He's a good person, very Christian and noble. He belongs to the Christian base communities and *cursillos*. She belongs, too. We're like sisters. I told her my problems, and she said, "Perhaps if you change your surroundings, you can better understand your situation. If you want to leave, I can take care of your children." So I talked with Sergio. He said he'd live in the office, come to see the children, and take care of what they needed. But it turned out that two weeks before I left for the United States, they offered him a better position in Managua at a higher salary. I asked him what he intended to do, and he thought he'd take the offer and live in our house in Managua. I told him it'd be better to leave the children in Estelí with Florencia. Everything was arranged; he'd go to Managua, start work December 1, and the children would stay in Estelí. I called Estelí from the United States on December 26 and talked with the children. He was in Matagalpa with his mother. They told me that he had decided to take them to Managua. Their things had already been moved, and they were just spending the holiday with Florencia. Afterwards, they'd go back to

Managua and stay with Sergio's sister because there's no electricity in the house we have in Managua. He made the decision himself to do all this; we hadn't talked about it.

My plan is to go to Miami, where I'll be closer to Nicaragua. I intend to work, save some money, and return as soon as I can. But I don't want to return empty-handed. In the future, I'll have to live in Managua when Marisa goes to the university; I'm not going to let her go there alone. But that's three years away, and I think that Sergio will accept my living in Estelí until then. He can come from Managua on the week-ends, and that will improve relations between us.

Right now he's the person in charge of the Third Region, Managua, in PROAGRO. The company provides all the products and insecticides for the crops in the countryside [as part of a government agency]. He'll be given the opportunity, if he wants it, to be responsible for all Nicaragua. It'd be a big responsibility, but he has earned it by being an honest man. I'd prefer to stay in Estelí because there's more opportunity there [than in Managua] to do something with the people, with my barrio, and with my communities. I know that if I go to Managua, I won't have anyone with whom to make a community because I barely know anyone. The people run around a lot, and there's less opportunity [to help], even if you know people. I spent a long time there, and after the triumph, I organized a primary school so that the children would learn to read and write. We used a big house next to mine that had belonged to the guardia. I got people in the barrio to agree to teach classes. So I know that when someone wants to do something wherever they are, they can. But they need me in Estelí, and that's why I'd like to stay there. My mother is there. In Managua, it's more tranquil [than in Estelí]. It's another world. They don't have as much trouble.[6] People need more help in Estelí. And I have my work established in Estelí; I'd have to start all over in Managua. So it'd be best if Sergio could come on week-ends, but I'd have to see what problems that would bring. During the week he'd have the opportunity to drink and go out with women. Especially in Managua.

7

A Family Growing Apart: 1985–1986

Leticia returned to Nicaragua a month before I arrived. She had spent eight months in the United States and was living in Managua, which is where I interviewed her. I interviewed the rest of the family in Estelí. Her absence had hurt them all.

Doña María

I've been sick for a long time, more or less four years. Only the pills have kept me going. When Leticia left, I was worried because it made me feel alone with just Marta here. It's the same now [even though Leticia has returned]: I'm sick, and Marta is the only one who worries about my being sick. Something might happen [to her] when she leaves, and the child would be left alone. It worries me that there's no family to take him. It seems that Leticia has changed. When she left, she knew that I was gravely sick. My health had failed, and she went and didn't worry. She came to me before she left and said, "I'll bring you some vitamins." Well, I haven't seen them, and she hasn't been in our house, not even for an hour or two, since she returned. She just comes in, sits down a little while, and goes. She's worried about her family, about her husband. He doesn't love us. He doesn't talk with me; we've never even chatted. The only one who watches out for me is Marta. So then I have to worry about myself and look after my own health in order to help Marta. She works so hard that there are times when she doesn't come here to eat. She has lots of aches and pains. I think it's nerves. When she leaves, it makes me nervous, and I pray to God for her because it would be hard for me if she didn't exist. It's only the two of us who support the household and buy food and the medicine. Right now she's revitalized because I'm better. Thanks to God and to Marta, I am up. When they took me to the doctor, I went with little hope of living, and now I'm happy that I'm better.

Omar isn't worried about us. He earns his salary and never says to me, "Take this córdoba." The only thing that interests him is that woman [Irene]. She runs him. We don't even know how much he earns because it's just for her. He doesn't help me in anything. Nothing. Once he got to the point of being so angry that he opposed and belittled me. I couldn't even be around him because it hurt me so. The things he did against me for that woman really hurt me. For my part, I wouldn't even be living if it weren't for Marta. I have another daughter in Managua, Norma, a poor thing who wants to help me, but she has six children and has to work. Sometimes she can't come to Estelí because she doesn't have money for the ticket. It's enough that she has the desire to see me. When she does come, even though it's some little thing, she gives me something. She's more concerned about me than Omar is. He has a salary, and he could come, but instead he first goes to see Irene, and only afterwards does he stop by to see if I'm here. We receive him well; we don't despise him for not being of any use to us. We feel sorry for him because it seems like a sickness, but not a natural sickness; it's because Irene doesn't love him. She just needs money. He has to try to get along with her so that things are good. If he doesn't, things are bad. All this has hurt my health.

I love Miguel a lot. I have twenty grandchildren, but I brought him up from the time he was born. If the child sees that I'm sick, he becomes distressed. If I vomit, he runs to get Marta. When I got sick in the middle of the night, he ran to get help. I told him to go to the neighbor's, but he doesn't like to go there. We taught him to respect the house next door and not just run in. If it's my time to go to the hospital and Marta isn't here, he'd have to take me. The rest of them have never been interested. But thank heavens Marta is interested now, and the doctor has checked me. Before that [checkup], they said I couldn't chat with anyone, get angry, or have any shocks. When I had a nervous attack, I felt I was going to die; I was getting weaker and felt like vomiting. Now I sleep too much, but then I didn't sleep and didn't eat. I had insomnia and had to sit up all night because I couldn't get enough air. I can't stand not doing the work I should do. I'm used to getting up and doing my work, but I can't do it when I'm bent over.

As Leticia and Omar know, I help Marta, but I still receive them all equally. When they're all [in my house] happy, there's peace. It's like medicine. We're talking and happy. Like when Omar's wife kicked him out. He was here; he swept the floor and mopped it, he sang, put on music, and ate. He danced and drank. But when she came back, despair came over him. He left and didn't return. He gives his life to her, and she orders him to wash dishes, to bring the water, to do everything. That makes me miserable. I was happy when she told him that she was going to Managua with the children. He had even gotten a little fatter. Ah, he was so affectionate. He danced with Marta. So happy. Irene had barely returned when he went there [to see her]. And there he stays. He still comes by, but he goes there first, even before he sees if I'm alive or dead. I welcome him with happiness [when he does come] because I don't want him to think that we criticize him. And we don't mention that woman to him. She doesn't come here. Well, one time she came to lie to me, and before that, in May, she was upset and came here to get drunk. He gave her rum and beer, but he wasn't talking with her. Then he started to talk, and they began to dance—happily—and he left with her. That bad woman. Before that, when she lied to me, she had come to say that she was going to Managua. I was so happy, but it was a lie; she's still in Estelí. He's like a child dominated by her, and she does what she wants. We feel sorry for him because we want him to control himself, to see and hear things clearly, and to become a man.

He lost the rank he earned from the army in the war. They wanted to promote him, give him a rank, but he hid. He said that he didn't want a rank, but what he really doesn't want is to be sent to Managua to study. He just wants to stay in Estelí. He was a commander because he had earned it. He's very disciplined, and they liked him in the army because he fulfilled his duties. I grieve over that. When I see him, I feel like crying. I wanted him to become an alert, sharp man like all his friends who are commanders. Omar Cabezas was a compañero of his on the mountain. Germán Pomares was—all of them were—a friend of our Omar. Monterrey was going to take him to work in Managua, but they couldn't get him to leave [Estelí].[1]

And Leticia has grown away from me, now that she has returned changed. She says she has much to do, arranging I-don't-know-what. When she went to the United States, I was sick; she told Marta to take care of me, that the beauty salon would help. I helped Marta. I did some work for people, and they paid me. We ate. We bought water. I bought firewood from a man, then people bought it from me, and we made some money. Marta had no help, only me, so I had to stay healthy. The two of us were happy. We didn't argue about anything. We played, told jokes. The two of us spent the time peacefully.

Leticia and her husband do as they choose because they feel they're owners of their things. It must be that she gave the right to him to do the things he did. He didn't take us into account. To him, I'm an object. He doesn't talk to me. Only "Hello, hello." That's all. When he took the children to Managua and things of Leticia's, we didn't know what was happening. It hurt us. People asked us because no one could believe it. I mean, when Leticia lived here, it was different. Every day, or something like that, she'd come for lunch or something, but after [she came back from the United States], no longer. We find it strange. She came eight days ago and sat down for only a little while. She didn't eat lunch, just talked with the driver who came by, and they left. Marta wanted to get off work and go to Managua with them, but they didn't return. She hasn't called Florencia [who has a telephone] to see if I'm alive, if I'm sick, how I am. She could ask. But no.

Before she left for the United States, she was going to live in the house across the street from us. I was happy because I thought we'd be close. We were going to take care of the children, have fruit trees, have chickens, and be together. Afterwards she said, "I sold it." She bought [a house] somewhere else. Who knows why. Maybe Sergio didn't want to be close [to us]. I don't know what will happen when he goes to Mexico. She'll work; she has always been a hard worker. Certainly I've never helped her learn anything that she knows because I was always off working in the countryside or at the river. An aunt of hers really brought her up, but that doesn't seem to be the reason that she has scorned me so much since her return. Before, I could always say to her, "Give me this," or "Give me that," and she would. She'd drop by and give me some money, or I'd tell her to come for lunch. She'd come, but since she returned, she hasn't had lunch here once. We sit here waiting for her to let us know when she'll be coming. I said, "The best present for Mother's Day would be to have Leticia with us." I waited all that day, but nothing.[2] We've grown apart.

She said she was going back to the United States and would leave the salon for Marta to take care of. I don't know who would take care of her children. Marta can't go to Managua to do that; she has to stay here to take care of me.

When Leticia left for those seven months, she said she was going to help us through the salon, but we didn't even get five córdobas from that. Now that she's back, she has changed. Her friends ask me, "Where's Leticia?" I say, "She's in Managua." People see that she's not here, and it hurts me because they'll say that she's different for having gone to the United States. While she was gone, I was happy when a friend said, "Leticia wrote to me." I thought it was all right for her to write to them and not to me because when she returned from the United States, it wouldn't look as if she had forgotten about her friends.

It's better to have friends and not a cent. If I have money and someone doesn't want to sell something to me because I'm poorly dressed or ill-mannered, they wouldn't sell it to me, and a friend would. We've helped our friends when we see the necessity. It's because we always think about God. We don't expect a recompense from one neighbor or another, only from God. Without Him, we don't exist. Without Him, we don't have life. We don't have anything. I don't visit anybody, but if some neighbor said to me, "Hey, Doña María, do you have such-and-such a thing?" and I had it, I'd say, "Yes." And if I don't have it, I'm annoyed for not being able to help. I can't say, "No, I don't have it," when I really do have it. We aren't like that. What would that accomplish? For that reason God hasn't abandoned us. We get by. I don't know why. When I have some money, I buy some little thing and save it for Omar. I save it for Norma, too, the poor one in Managua, even if it's just a little piece of soap. We don't have bad thoughts toward our fellow man. Leticia has always been good. In the barrio where she lived, they loved her for being like that.

The work is harder in the house without the refrigerator. The motor is broken. There were parts in Managua, but it costs more to take it to Managua than to buy one. When we had a refrigerator, I used to make popsicles and sell them, and Marta had her job; that way the two of us helped the household. I'm happy when I feel good and can help. Marta doesn't have a fixed day to receive her córdobas, her salary. It isn't like other work, where on the twentieth of the month, or the fifteenth, you receive your pay. She has to wait until they can pay her.

My doctor treats me beautifully. He receives the sick people with love. When I first went to him, he said, "Ah, Doña María, how are you?" What did I know? So he said, "Tell me about your sickness."

So I made a joke. I said, "I have all the sicknesses that anyone has had or will have. I'm going to tell them to you one by one."

He was laughing. "Go on," he said. "Do it."

"I suffer," I said. "I'm too tired. My heart, when I lie down, seems like a horse in a race. You know how awful that would be. I can't bend, I can't talk, I can't laugh at anything; when I'm bent over, I can't get up. I can't go to the bank because I almost fall over in the street."

Then he took my blood pressure and told me I was quite sick. He said the tube to the heart was almost closed, and there was no longer any place to breathe [*sic*] through. The arteries to the heart were going to explode. He told Marta to buy me some injections. He asked, "What do you do to lower the pressure?"

"I urinate a lot." At night I get cramps and diarrhea. I stretch and move but have to get up. He gave me the first two injections, and my blood pressure went down by ten. Only one day did I have cramps, another day just a little, and now I don't have them.

"You're going to get better," he said. "Don't worry. Hope is in God and in yourself." He treats me well. The doctor gives me courage and is very affectionate. I don't have anything to pay him with. He said to Marta, "If, within two weeks, she hasn't changed, I'll give you a paper so that you can take her to the hospital in Managua." What about the child [if I have to go]? I suffer a lot for that little boy. But God hears me. I ask Him not to have me go.

Sometimes I sit like a chicken waiting to die, my arms hanging like rags, without the breath to knit or to wash a pair of socks. My arms look like great big rags. A dying old hen! But now I feel good.

This year my daughter Adela died, but that wasn't all that difficult because she had a husband who fulfills his obligations.[3] Their children are working or studying, and they have a new house. The death of María Elena was more difficult; she was so young.[4] To grab a Christian like that and to kill her in such a way. A lot of people died that day, something like thirty-two. There were eight women, eight little girls, and eight males.

We don't know what will come with the next year. It has been good that nothing [bad] happened on the seventh anniversary. It's incredible that we have had a seventh anniversary of the revolution.[5]

Leticia

I left Nevada and went to Miami because I thought I'd find better work, and I had a friend there. I hoped to stay two months, no longer, in order to make a little money. In Miami I stayed in a room with a friend of mine from Estelí. There was a big bed that we slept in, my daughter Nora, my friend, and I. My friend worked and, at first, I stayed there cleaning and embroidering. I worked on little girls' dresses for eight cents a dress; each one took a long time. It wasn't a job you could live on; you could just buy some food with what you made. Then I found work with a *señor* on the beach. We sold things to people from other countries who came in boats. Most of them spoke Spanish, but some didn't. The *señor* spoke English well, even though he isn't North American. If I didn't understand something, I asked him. I worked with him until a few weeks ago when I returned to Nicaragua. During that time, I also worked with Avon. I telephoned them, and they came to see me. They asked me some questions, I filled out some forms, and they accepted me. They gave me a little card which allowed me to enter the shops as a recognized distributor of Avon. Every two weeks new products came out with new folders, so they left me the new folder the day they visited, along with a portfolio and some catalogs. I started that very day with neighbors.[6] There were many Nicaraguans where I lived, and in my free time at night, I visited them.

Nora always went to my cousin's house. I left her there in the morning and picked her up on my way home from work. I helped them with money for taking care of Nora and for food. I usually ate with them, too. I almost never cooked. Sometimes I took Nora with me; the *señor* told me I could, but Nora didn't like to go. It was boring and too sunny and hot; I think she went twice.

The *señor* told me that he didn't want me to leave because I had helped so much. I checked things over for the following day because after we left the beach, we went to shops to get what we were going to sell the next day. People would ask me to get things they needed. Some had credit, and the *señor* would ask, "Leticia, what does that guy owe?" People would pay me, and I'd tell him what they owed or if the bill was paid. That's why he didn't want me to leave. He wasn't all that young; he was tired and needed help, especially to buy things for the next day. No one else had done that for him; they'd go home, and he'd shop alone. He said he had another van that I should learn to drive so that we could take more things to the beach.

I always told him, "I have to go back to Nicaragua."

"What are you going to do in Nicaragua?" he asked.

"All my family is there."

"But you're going to come back here, aren't you? The day you return, even if I have hired another person, you'll have your job. You always will."

The other work I did was in the house. When I had time, I continued the embroidering; sometimes I sewed and watched television until twelve or one in the morning. I had three jobs—the beach, Avon, and embroidering—but I never felt so tired as I do now. I worked at the beach from nine in the morning until six in the afternoon. With Avon, I worked from seven until ten and also anytime during the week when I didn't have to go to the beach. After ten I'd sleep a bit, rest, and then sew. With the problems I had, I didn't sleep well, but I was almost never sleepy. I had headaches, but not a lot—not as many as I have here—even though I was in the sun a lot. Maybe only two or three headaches in all the time I was there. They were serious ones, and I vomited, but I didn't have them often. I don't know why that happened. Maybe it's because I wasn't fighting with Sergio! And I got fat. That I didn't like.

I had a lot of ideas to make money. When I worked with the *señor* on the beach, he paid me weekly; I sold things to my neighbors—stockings, deodorants, brushes—that I bought in the same shop where he bought things. There was a Japanese woman in a shop where he bought clothes who set aside dresses to sell cheaply to me.

I'd sell them to neighbors who didn't have time to go to the stores. Sometimes I earned five dollars, depending on what I sold.

At the same time, I didn't like the life-style. It isn't like it is in Nicaragua where you can talk with people. You can't have a conversation. You can't find out what their problems are or what you can do for them. There are important things to be done, but people don't stop their lives long enough to do them. People live life just for themselves. They don't think about doing something for someone. At least, I didn't see it.

Only once did I have the opportunity to visit a church. It was a Baptist one; they did a lot of things, but always for themselves, for their [church] community. The church was pretty, but I didn't like it because it was just for the people who belonged to that church. What they did seemed little compared to what we do in Nicaragua. We do things with more commitment, possibly even with personal risk.

There's poverty there, too. I knew a woman who reminded me of my mother. She's Cuban, an old woman who lived on the second floor of the building where I lived. She had a daughter, and the daughter had three children. The daughter had to leave Cuba and left a son there whom she'll never get back. The other children— they're little—just wandered around the beaches. The neighbors notified the police, who took the children away and put them in a place like a reformatory. The daughter is about thirty, like Marta. Both mother and daughter reminded me of my family, except the old woman drank every day, and the daughter smoked marijuana. The old woman never had anything to eat. I asked myself how it's possible for such a situation to exist in such a developed country.

The two women would fight. One day I went up to see the old woman because I heard her crying and knew she was alone. She told me that her daughter didn't take care of her and hit her when she complained. The old woman had a husband, but when he came in from the street, he complained that there was no food for him, and then he'd hit her.

So what I did, after everyone left in the morning and before I went to work, was cook and give her some food. I brought her food at night. We talked a lot. That woman was special for me. I learned to love her and felt that she was like my mother. She loved me, too.

She told me that never in her life had she met anyone who worried about her as much as I did.

One of the things that bothered me in the United States is that old people who weren't born there but are naturalized don't have the same rights as others. The old woman is legal because she's one of those who came with El Mariel.[7] The government gave her a pension of $250, but it's only enough to pay for the apartment and maybe a little left over. People in a church give her clothes and shoes. That's just one of the things I saw that didn't seem right. It's not fair that some have so much and others so little.

From the time I left Nicaragua, I planned to return. [Now that I'm back here], I've decided to live forever in Nicaragua. It's my duty to be here; there are important things to do. Above all, my children are here. And maybe I can make a home again with my husband. I thought I'd return with better intentions, better plans [than I had when I left], but unfortunately it hasn't been like that. The most serious problem is with Sergio. Since December, he has had another woman. He wasn't interested in what I had to say on the telephone or in letters. He said he wrote to me, but I didn't receive one single letter in Miami. Not one. I wrote to him almost weekly, and he never answered. When I called him on the telephone, I always asked him what his plans were for the year, what we were going to do. But his plans changed. I suspected that something was wrong, something wasn't working the way it had before. The phone calls were short. He usually hung up before I did. He didn't want to talk with me. I was almost sure there was a woman. I just felt it. No one told me. I sensed it by the way he acted, by the way he talked with me on the phone.

By coincidence, a sister of Sergio's wrote to a friend of mine in Miami and told her about the woman. My friend then called to wish me happy birthday on May 30 and told me that Sergio's sister had written that he was going out with a woman in front of my family, in front of everyone. My family knew but they didn't tell me anything by phone or letter. They thought it was best that I not know, but for me, that was a mistake. They should have told me the truth.

It was hard for me when I returned and realized all these things, although I really knew everything before I arrived. While I was still in Miami, around the middle of June, I called Sergio at work, and a secretary told me he had quit. It was a terrible shock. She said, "He's no longer working here, but if you want to leave a message, I can have the driver take it to him."

So I said to her, "Do you know the house? Do you know the address?"

"I don't know where his house is, but I know the house of the secretary he lives with."

I said, "All right," but I was trying to pull myself together because I felt terrible. "Send the message to the place where you say he can be found. Tell him to call me at this number because I want to talk with him. Thank you." I wanted the secretary to think that everything was normal, that it wasn't important. But that was a lie. I felt as if I were dying. It was a horrible feeling. I had gone to a neighbor's house to call him, and when I got back to my apartment, I couldn't cry because it all seemed impossible, like a nightmare.

He didn't call. Instead his sister in Miami called to tell me he was going to Mexico that week. That was another blow because I still had hopes of seeing him in Managua; maybe it was a passing thing for him, and everything would be as it was before. I was ready to forgive him because I thought he had done it because I wasn't with him. The majority of Latinos are *machistas*, and they say they can't be without a woman. But when she told me he was leaving for Mexico, it meant that it was serious. He hadn't even called to say, "Leticia, I'm going to Mexico; come back because the children will be alone." So I had to hurry however I could, get my things ready, and make the trip back to Nicaragua. I had planned to stay in Miami a couple of months longer to make more money with Avon because I wanted to help my family. I knew I'd have to start over with the salon in Estelí because it had failed with the muchacha I left it with. But I couldn't stay in Miami; instead I had to hurry back to see what I could do.

I found out that he hadn't left for Mexico because I called Florencia [in Estelí] to ask her; I said, "I'm arriving July 10. Ask my brother Raúl or your husband to meet me." I didn't ask her to tell Sergio to come or to tell my children, but she told the children, and then Sergio found out. He meant to leave even sooner when he found out I was coming, maybe out of fear that I'd complain or because he didn't want to see me. But in the end, he waited.

When my daughter Nora and I arrived at the airport, Sergio was there with his sisters and brothers, his mother, and my brother Raúl.[8] The customs officials let Nora leave [the customs area] first because they still had to check my suitcases and could see how anxious she was. She went directly to Sergio. He picked her up, and the two of them began to cry. He asked her what she did in the United States, and she said, "Cried for you." She continued to cry for an hour. She cried with great feeling, and so did he. Customs sent me right out with all my suitcases and packages, and everyone hugged me.[9] Sergio stood a little apart. He was the last to greet and hug me. I hugged him as if everything were normal. I tried to hide how I felt; I didn't want to show anger or anything. We went home. Everyone was happy because I had returned, and we had a party. We talked a lot, and I told them how life was in the United States.

So the first night was normal, as if I didn't know anything and neither did he. We had [sexual] relations, but I felt as if he were a different person, not the same as before. He didn't want me to see that he had changed, but he couldn't even pretend. I don't know why he [made love]. I wasn't obliged to, and if he hadn't wanted to have relations, there wouldn't have been any. When it was over, he was cold, and that made me feel bad.

The following day, we went to Estelí. My brother Raúl—he says that when I'm there, he's complete—invited us to spend the day; he was going to kill a pig at the farm. We went, killed the pig, ate it, and had a good time. We stayed in the house of a cousin of mine, the one I call my sister. She's a daughter of the aunt I spent a lot of time with when I was little. She always gives us a separate room, but even so we didn't have [sexual] relations. That was unusual after so much time; it had been almost eight months that we hadn't seen each other. He was pensive and insisted that he wanted to go to Managua: "Let's go; I want to go today." It was as if he had one woman in Estelí and another in Managua, but the one who attracted him most was in Managua. So we left. We didn't have relations again. One day, he went to get a mattress to sleep in the other room because he was hot. It was a pretext. I stayed in the bed. I didn't say anything; I knew it would be a serious problem if I exploded. But I was reaching my limit.

Then one day his niece Yolanda took me to customs in order to get out the boxes I'd left there. I hadn't directly asked anybody anything [about Sergio] because that's the way I am. I don't like to ask. I feel bad, as if I'm lowering myself. I like to have them tell me without my asking. But she's a good friend of mine and isn't afraid of anything, so I asked, "Do you know the woman your uncle has?" "Yes, he brought her to my house one day. He introduced me." "Aha," I said, "and how did he introduce her? In what way?" " 'I want to introduce a friend,' but I knew," she said, "that she was the woman; I had already heard that he was going out with her and had taken her to Matagalpa where his mother lives. The woman has two children who are big. I don't know what he's thinking. He already has four daughters, and his life is set. Besides, he's old and shouldn't be out looking for women. I told him that. When I did, he got angry with me. I said, 'Sergio, what are you thinking? You already have four daughters! You shouldn't be going around like a young kid, doing things you shouldn't. This woman isn't good. She's a woman who likes a lot of luxury. With what you earn, you aren't going to be able to give her that much luxury, and she'll have to have another man to give her the expensive things she wants.' "

I later learned that he took her to a sister's house one day at lunch time. He introduced her and said, "I want you to meet my family." His sister said, "Sergio, come and eat," but she didn't offer any food to the woman; the sister didn't agree [with what he was doing] and so ignored her.

The woman quit work in July and was working in another place called Alto Grande, but she quit there, too, which is what made me suspicious. I called her at work. I was going to say anything [that came to mind]—not that I was Sergio's wife—I was just going to ask her any old thing. But they said, "She doesn't work here."

"Could you give me her address?"

"Yes," they said, "of course." So they gave me her address, but I haven't seen her. The children have because they went to the office several times and met her there. They say she's more or less my age. She's shorter. I asked if she was pretty, and they said she wasn't. So I asked, "Then why do you think your father went out with her?"

"We don't know," they said, "but you know how men are." That's the only thing they said. They try to say little. They hide things from me so that I don't fight with Sergio.

I hadn't told him that his niece had told me anything about the woman, but I did ask him why he had dared take that woman to his family. He didn't answer me. The only thing he said was to ask who had told me. I said, "Who told me isn't what's important. What is important is that you took her."

That night Ileana, a cousin of his, came and said, "Leticia, I'd like to have a beer."

"Let's send out for one, then," I said.

We were drinking it when he came in—he had spent all day in the streets—and said to her, "Ileana, let's go on an errand."

"All right," she said, still innocent. Then they left. But it had been a pretext. Out in the street, he asked her why she had told me about the woman. He imagined she was the one because he had taken the woman to Ileana's house.

When Sergio and Ileana returned, she said, "Leticia, I'm leaving. Sergio says I'm the one who told you about the woman."

That's when I exploded. I said to him, "You go about creating scenes and disturbances after you've publicly gone out and livened things up for yourself. Now that everyone knows about your woman, you criticize your cousin and try to get her involved. She told me nothing. I realized everything when I was in the United States. You have to ask her forgiveness because what you've done isn't fair. I've been quiet about all these things," I said, "because I didn't want it to come to this. The only guilty one is you, and the only one responsible for everything that's happening is you. Now let's talk and decide what you're going to do. I know your woman quit [work] when you did, and I suspect you're leaving together. You weren't frank on the telephone when I was in the United States. It would have been better to call me and say, 'Leticia, I have another woman. Don't think about me anymore; just think about your daughters and what you'll do with them, whether you'll take them with you or stay here, but I'm going with my woman.' If I'd met another man in the United States, I'd have done that; I would have called you and said, 'Sergio, it's over. I have another man.' You've been a coward; you aren't enough of a man to speak honestly. You didn't have to wait until I came back here. I could have made my own decisions there. Here I don't have money. I'm without work, and so are you. You're leaving me with a bunch of problems, and besides that, you tell me you're giving [legal] control over the house to your nephew. Well, your nephew has nothing to do with this house. This house is my daughters'. Everything I've worked for has been for my children. I haven't worked for me, not for you but for my daughters, and I thought you did the same. If that isn't the case, I'll offer to buy your share. You're not going to kick me out, not you nor your nephew. Even if you do what you want with the house—it's in your name—and your nephew gets control and wants to kick me out, he'll have to kill me first. For so many years, I've fought and worked and helped you, but now you don't remember that. Since you already have another home, leave me my house, and leave me my daughters. No one will kick me out into the street ever again."

"No," he said, "because when I return, you'll throw me out in the street."

"I don't intend to do that," I said, "because I don't have the heart to see you in disgrace. I wouldn't do it, Sergio. Even if I had just a tiny place, I'd make room for you to live the rest of your years. I wouldn't send you running. It has been fifteen years. You know me, and you know how I am. Material things don't interest me, but neither am I going to let someone take away what I've earned. What I want now is that you give me the legal control and leave the house in my daughters' names or in mine." He didn't answer. "And if you don't do it, somehow I'll arrange it. I know I will, no matter what you do. So it's better that we arrange it the best way possible, without arguments and like civilized people. You know what I'm telling you is the truth. I'm within my rights."

"But the only thing I have," he said, "is this house." (The house in Estelí is mine because I bought it with my own efforts, but the house in Managua we bought together.)

I said, "I'm not going to allow anyone to kick me out of my house or tell me when to sell it. They'll have to walk over my dead body."

It's difficult to imagine how horrible it was for me. I'd been humiliated from the time I came from Miami. Everyone was saying to me, "How fat you got!" At the same time, everyone was happy because the time had served as therapy for me. I realized that Sergio and I always argued because we didn't understand each other. We had gotten as far as we had because I had hidden so many things. When he did something [I didn't like], I forgot about it, and we started over the next day.

The day came that we went to the lawyer to arrange [the legal control]. Later that same day he said to me, "Go home, and I'll come later; I have to look for some thyroid medicine." He had been operated on for this and needs to take medicine every day. He didn't return for three days. He spent them with the woman and then, as if nothing happened, came home. For me as a woman, that was horrible. I was so angry. So furious. But I controlled it. I didn't say anything to him.

The children said that when I was in Miami, there were several times when he didn't come home to sleep, even some week-ends. I asked him why he had taken the children from Estelí when they would have been more secure there with their aunt than they were in Managua with him. He didn't answer. He does what he wants but doesn't answer for it.

Last Friday I went to Estelí to see my mother, and that same day, when I wasn't here, he went to sleep with the woman. When I returned, I asked if he had slept here, and the children told me he hadn't. That was the limit. I couldn't stand it any longer and got hysterical. I got his clothes, put them in a bag, and said to him, "Sergio, please, I want you to go. I want you to go with your woman. No one here is going to stop you. Make your life as you wish, but I don't want to see you here one more day."

He said, "Calm down, Leticia, calm down." He saw that I had lost my patience. "What happened to you?" he asked.

"Nothing happened to me. It's simply that I don't want to see you here." I said, "I'm a woman, but I have dignity. And I'm not going to put up with these humiliations. How can we have anything intimate if you don't respect the children and respect me as a woman? You're not going to keep on walking all over me. Why do you stay here? Your woman told you she had a house and didn't need this one. (I told him one day that maybe he wanted to give the house to her, but he said she had a house.) Go there. What is it that keeps you here? You say she loves you." He had told me that the woman loves him and that he wanted to love her, but he didn't. One day I asked, "Do you plan to stay with her?" He said that he didn't intend to because she had two children, and he wasn't going to remake his life with a woman who had children. He told me this before that Friday when he stayed with her. That confused me. I left for Estelí feeling better because we had talked. I sat by his side and asked him what his ideas were, if he was going with the woman to Mexico, or what it was that he was planning.

"No, I'm going alone," he said. "I want to think, figure out what I want to do."

"But your plans with your woman?"

"I never promised anything to her. I'm going alone, and she stays."

"Why?"

"Because I don't love her. Because it's over. Because you don't believe that it hurts me to have everything finished between us. Because we have four daughters. And because, sincerely, the day I tell you that I don't love you, I'm lying. I do love you. And I don't want us to be separated forever, but I do want you to give me time. I want to leave to arrange my thoughts and figure out what I want."

"That's fine, then." I told him, "Go."

"And I'm going to prove to you that I no longer have anything to do with her, that it's finished, that I promised her nothing. I'll show you a letter she sent me." It was a letter where she said goodbye to him and wished him success on his trip and in his plans, success with his wife and children. It was like a farewell. I was more at peace then. I thought it was fine that he went and got his thoughts in order and saw what he wanted to do. I had then—and probably still do—the patience to put up with a lot. I think about the children, and I think about how horrible the separation is for us, for them.

But this was before I left for Estelí. When I returned, what hurt me most was that the children were the ones who told me he hadn't slept at home. He had promised me differently. When I was leaving that day, I asked, "Are you going to stay at home? I need to know if you're going to stay with the children or go to your woman."

"No," he said, "I'm going to stay here." But he went to her place. When I found out, I packed his things, threw them in the hall, and told him to leave. I said it was no use arguing. I was hysterical. I've never been like that. I never wanted to see him again. Every time I looked at him, I felt this anger, this rage.

But he refused to go, saying, "Calm down, Leticia, calm down. I promise you I won't go out again."

I said, "I'm not asking you to promise me anything. Your promises are always false. I just want to be done with this nightmare. I want you to leave. I don't want to see you here again."

He, as the director or PROAGRO in Managua, made the highest salary he could, but it wasn't enough money to live on.[10] It made me feel so sad when I returned and saw his shoes. He was the director of a [government-owned] company, and he went about in broken-down shoes. I don't think Sergio is the most suitable person [to be a director of a company] because he has never been a political man, but he has been honest. He's a man who has given to the revolution what an honest employee should. In this, I've always admired him. There are many companies where there are embezzlements, but Sergio didn't do things that way. I know because he has told me many things about the director before him; he was imprisoned for taking money from the company, for buying things for himself. No one can say that Sergio stole anything. He could have given his own family preference when it came to selling things, but he never even did that.

In spite of everything, the children say they had everything [while I was gone]; he always got them the food they needed, and he bought their clothes. In reality, he did what he should as a father, but certainly he was wrong to leave them alone. The time came when they had a talk with him and complained. I know they did because one day, in front of me, they said to him, "Remember that we told you that if you got another woman, you'd have to leave the house. And if our mother got another man, she'd have to leave." So when he and I had that argument, they said to him, "It's better that you go; that was the arrangement we had. You chose your woman. Go with her."

But lately, he doesn't want to go. It'll be hard for him to find work in Mexico. His brother, who has lived in Mexico for two years, has influenced him and says that they should go, that Sergio will earn a lot there. Sergio is a professional and is used to working as a professional, while his brother works at anything. For someone like that, it's easier to find work than it is for a professional. Sergio isn't used to working at any old thing.

The man I owed U.S. $1500 called me in Miami. He talked with my cousin [in Nevada], still trying to collect from him. I told him that I wasn't working but that I was trying to find something, and little by little I'd pay him back. When I came here, I met him coming down the street. He said, "How are you?"

"I'm fine. And you?"

"Fine," he said. "Listen, your cousin said you were going to pay me the money, said he had nothing to do with it."

"Yes," I said, "I'll pay, but I had to return to Nicaragua; I have problems with my daughters, and my mother is sick. You know I can't pay you now because here we don't earn dollars. But when I return to the United States, then I will."

"That's fine then." This was a Sunday, and he planned to leave on Monday. Immigration caught him that day on a plane in Nicaragua with twenty-four passengers he was taking first to Mexico and then to the United States. They all got on as if they were traveling alone. Someone found out; I think Immigration had followed him for a long time. They all had to get off, and now he's a prisoner. The passengers were young men evading military service. That was the problem. Adults can leave without any problem, but it isn't that way for the young. When they were interrogated, they confessed and said he was taking them to the United States.

When I left Nicaragua [nine months ago], a pound of beans cost around 5 córdobas, and now, in the *expendio*, it costs 300, and 1000 córdobas in the black market. The salaries have gone up, but the moment they do, the prices go up, too. I just don't know what's going to happen. I still can't get products for the salon. That worries me. I intend to ask the Ministry of Commerce if I can go to Mexico every six months to bring back beauty products.[11] I'd prefer to go to Honduras because it's closer, but we don't have relations [with Honduras]. I'll go back to Estelí after the children finish school.[12] Meanwhile I'll work here with the people who know me, but I can't make any money in Managua because I don't have any clientele. As soon as I get back to Estelí, it will be Christmas, and there's always a lot of work then. But not without products.

Marta

Let's start this last year with the turbulent times we had in the region and the work I've just develped in publicity. Both were difficult. The counter-revolutionaries killed people in the cooperatives and ambushed civilians. My job is to send out a call to everyone— not just Estelí, but Ocotal, Somoto, San Juan, all of the region—to help people with food and medicine in the areas where people lost everything. I was sent to some of those territories to help with defense and food production. With each attack or with everything we do here, we and the revolution have become stronger. Everyone, all Nicaragua and especially the committees of solidarity, realizes who our enemy is. This makes us stronger because we're aware that the problems of food production, housing, and health aren't problems of just the government but problems caused by the aggression. My job is to detail and highlight the work the women are doing in defense, in health, and other areas. We've developed all this work in the past year. It's incredible to think that we had our seventh anniversary this year.

Several things made me happy, things that happened in the political and economic field, in the military, in the family. In the political area, we know that we're gaining ground. The visits of the commanders to different places have been positive, and the Court in The Hague condemned the government of the United States for its aggression toward Nicaragua.[13] In the military area, we know that the counter-revolution isn't going to triumph because it hasn't been able to take any town. They have no strength, no morale. They don't even know why they're doing it, except to make money. Another thing is that, in spite of such aggression and in spite of the many trips that my brother and I have made to the far-off places in the region, we're still here alive, this year. And my sister returned. What she went to do was good, and we're happy to have her in Nicaragua with us.

When I have to go to the zone, I worry because the nervous tensions that afflict the people of Nicaragua make my mother sick. It bothers her that her children aren't in their homes but are out there working for the people. Every time we leave, she thinks we won't return and that instead, we'll meet up with the counter-revolution. She understands the work that Omar and I do, but it worries her and makes her sicker.

Leticia had this desire to see how our brothers and sisters live in the United States. We know there are Nicaraguans who support the aggression of the United States without realizing the truth. We, in the family, understand that when she went there, she was going to tell others how we live here. We were sure people would listen to her, pay attention to her, and support the steps toward peace that the people and the government in Nicaragua are taking. But personally, it was difficult because she has been our support and comfort whenever we've had health or money problems. We've always appealed to her, and she knows how to help us. But when we had trouble this year, she wasn't here. I had to face it alone, but I did so with the hope that she was doing good work. I despaired because it seemed to me that she wasn't going to return, that she was going to stay in the United States. People said to me, "Your sister isn't going to return. You'll see; she'll stay there." And I felt even worse because my mother said she was going to die before Leticia came back to see her.

From my point of view, what her husband Sergio did wasn't right; he said he'd help us while Leticia was gone, but he didn't. Instead he ignored us. Not even their children visited us. They came twice. Never did we think it would be so seldom. We didn't know what to think.

We lost a cousin, María Elena, in an attack by the mercenaries.[14] She was one of the compañeras in charge of caring for the happiness of the children in the countryside. She was on her way to fulfill that mission by taking a *piñata*—some happiness—to children of campesinos. The enemy doesn't like it when people bring this joy, so in an atrocious way they killed her in an ambush. They wounded her, and while she was alive, they cut off her breasts and a leg, then burned her.[15] It can happen to any of us, to any Nicaraguan. They killed thirty-two people that day, eight women, eight little girls, and eight young men.

My sister Adela died. Shortly before she got sick, she visited us. She loved the plants outside the house, and my mother always sent some little ones back with her so that she could plant them at her house. While they were chatting, Adela said, "We'll see who dies first, you or me." They were joking, but a week later this thing happened, and she lasted about a week in the hospital. Worries [about the contra attacks] accelerate sickness. That's what happened to her; it made her die. When she got sick, the situation was difficult. The contra had blown up one of the electric plants, and there was no electricity in the whole region.

I'm worried about what will happen when my mother dies. It's really just the three of us, my mother, Miguel, and me, and we don't have anyone to look after us. When she dies, it will be horrible for me. She's my sister and my mother. She's everything to me because she has been more than a mother. She has taken care of my son. I get the doctor, the injections, the pills, everything to keep her in good health. The child cries when he sees that she's sick and runs down the street looking for me. For example, just now he said, "Don't go to work," he said, "because your mother is sick." So I said, "Then I won't." But I exaggerated a little so that he wouldn't take it so seriously; when she's sick, he gets sad, doesn't eat. He despairs.

There might be a man [in my life]. [Laughter] There has been a change, and what good changes! Let's call him David. He has brown skin, the same as my brother has, and he's as tall. Thirty years old. He works in defense and has a lot of responsibility. He doesn't work here in Estelí; he's always mobilized. Some days he can come here, and other times when I'm mobilized, we meet. Sometimes I see him two times a month, sometimes once or twice a week. We met when he was taking families to see their children in the military service in Pantasma. We were going to the same place. We talked, and he came to Estelí to coordinate some things. We visited. We looked at each other. That's how it went. In a simple way. At first we talked mostly about work and the difficulties we have solving some of the problems of the families of the displaced. Things like that. We both were ready at the same time to think about another person. He said, "At this stage, seven years into the revolution, it's time to think about another person rather than be alone, rather than work for other people without having someone special to work for." We understood each other well. I want to say that I never, at any time, have had any ideas about getting married, in the church, outside the church, or any place.

No one knows him here, nor do they know anything about our relationship.[16] My family would have problems if they knew. The child is very attached to me and wants me to be with only him. My mother thinks the same. I want to avoid problems and prevent her health from worsening. My son's old enough [to know] but isn't mature enough. David doesn't like the idea of being secretly in love. That he can't come here isn't an imposition of mine; it's just that there's no other solution.

We're lovers. My friends from the organization help me [find a place]. They see it as normal, so there's no problem with getting a place to stay for the night. When he and I have finished with work or when he has free time, he comes to look for me where I'm working and says, "When will you be free?" And I say something like, "Within a half hour." Then he goes for another walk and returns. Then if we agree, and if he has nothing to do, we go.

The compañeras where I work don't want me to be alone. They've offered to talk with my mother, but I told them that there's no need. It's going to last, provided David and I understand each other. We talked about what would happen if he no longer understands me because of the difficulties we have in sleeping together often, or if in time he gets tired of me, or I tire of him. I told him, "The day that you tire of me, or I tire of you, or we both tire of being in this situation, then we'll finish this peacefully without any problem. We'll be friends." Like mature people, adults. He agrees. He said, "The day you find another man I'll give you the time you need. No problem." He told me that, and so it is. No problem. Really, I can't be with him all the time. Perhaps not in the moments he most needs me, or when I need him.

The male my son models himself after is my brother Omar. That's why he says, "I'm going to be like my uncle." He's proud of what his uncle does and accomplishes. This motivates him to study, be a man, and perhaps join the army. Children do what the parents do. He listens to Omar tell of the attacks, of the capture of so many contra, of the recovering of so many guns. He likes these things. In our situation everyone is in defense or in food production, so Miguel can't even think about anything else. But if we had been students, Miguel would say, "I want to be a student." They begin with what they see. I want him to fulfill his military service but not stay there, to be instead a technician, a trained person. What happened to Omar and to me is that we didn't have time to prepare ourselves. Even though there's opportunity to study now, we can't. If I went to study, there'd be days when I could go and days when I couldn't because I have to work. The same thing happens to Omar. Days when he'd be able to go to class and days when he wouldn't. He has his job, too.

Miguel learns quickly. Leticia tells me, "Give him to me so that he can study in Managua." Or she could take him to Mexico to her husband's family. If he did go, there would be a clash, especially when he'd be told to do something he's not used to. It's better to avoid this. I don't like such problems, and I don't want to have an argument with her. My mother has liked being here, as have we. My son is so used to everything that he knows when she wants to sleep; he closes the door and plays just outside. But to go to Leticia's with her daughters who've never lived with my mother and don't know her way of being and way of thinking—well, it isn't the same to visit as it is to live together.

When people are sick or when they have problems, money isn't the solution—not without affection, attention, and respect. I take care of my mother without money. I'm not paying the doctor. It's a friendship from a long time ago. We met through the work of the Frente Sandinista. I didn't know he was a doctor, but after the triumph I noticed he was in charge of the Regional Ministry of Health. When I saw him, we greeted each other affectionately, and then he said, "Take me to your little old mother, and I'll take care of her for you." He looked after her well, showed affection for me, and gave me medicine for her. It isn't necessarily the medicine that she needed, but it was that attention, someone to say, as he did, "You'll feel better; you're going to dance again." These things help people recuperate. But if I say to her when she's sick, "Here's 5000 córdobas," that won't help her feel better. It's not money she needs. I know my sister loves and respects us, but she has come to the house only two times since she returned to Nicaragua, and those times she didn't stay all day. Once she came for about twenty minutes, the other [time] about half an hour. That's all. I swear that I never thought this would happen. Perhaps it's because of the problems she has. One can resolve a problem with a man by saying, "Are you staying, or are you leaving?" She wouldn't be the first woman to be alone in this country, and it wouldn't be the first divorce.

She left Nicaragua for personal reasons, to rest. But leaving isn't the solution. Facing problems with courage is the solution. Facing them and saying, "I don't want this to continue; we're going to do such-and-such." If people have studied, they should be able to talk. She can say, "Sergio, you go over there; I'll go over here, and the children will go with me." He has another woman! He goes with the other one, and Leticia does nothing. I just can't imagine living with a man in such a situation.

Her husband has never loved us. He's from the middle class, and we had nothing. When he met Leticia, we didn't have a house. We didn't have anything to eat. We ate when there was something, and when there wasn't, we put up with it. And we always worked. He believed that we were going to eat up his money or eat up his food. We're poor but proud. We have dignity, and thanks to God and the revolution, we have a house, a place to sleep, everything that's here. We had none of this before. Nothing. Not even the beds.

I'm not afraid to work. It distresses me when I don't. I want to work, and I work because I feel that the money I make, I make with pleasure. I'm not lying down waiting for them to give money to me. I know I earned it; my mother or my son can spend the money with pride. The refrigerator broke down, but AMNLAE is going to help me get another one. I hope that by the next year, if God wills, I'll have one. All the problems we have in Nicaragua would affect us less if we didn't hide them or decorate them with flowers. If we put everything on the table, we can see them better and say, "This I like, and this I don't." I can't promise Miguel a bicycle because I can't buy it for him. I'm not going to say, "Look, my dear son, would you like to have a bike?" He'd tell me yes and say, "I'll take this one. Won't I look good!" It's better to tell him nothing. We have to start with the reality of what we're able to have, of what we can buy, and not imagine beautiful things that aren't within our reach.

Leticia is hurting herself and her daughters. They don't know who's telling the truth when the fighting goes on. If a woman fights with her husband, the children try to solve it, quietly turning it over in their heads saying, "Mother, who's right?" "Your father." "Yes, he's right." "No, no, no, your mother's right." "Oh yes, she is." The one who's right should be called right.

If we're attacked by the North American government, do we have the right to ask the entire world to help us stop that aggression? Or does the North American government have the right to want us attacked? We're the ones who are dying. We're the ones who have no food production. That's why we can ask that the aggression stop. They're only paying with money, and we're paying with our dead.

I don't think that all the people who leave do so because they don't like the revolution. They do it because they need to look for work, and they think they'll easily earn dollars. It isn't that they don't love the revolution, but they love dollars and want to work. But they aren't paid a pile of dollars just for it being midday; they have to work hard to earn it. They don't realize that until they get there. There are some who return, and others who put up with it.

When Leticia left for the United States, it was about six o'clock in the morning. I was going to drop her off at the border, but I got sick with a [vaginal] hemorrhage and had to return to my aunt's house in Condega. I was bathed in sweat; I don't understand why, but it must have been nerves. Leticia was leaving, and I felt sad. That must have caused the hemorrhage. From the time we said good-bye, I spoke no more about her because she didn't write to me, except for one letter where she said she sent me something. Whatever she sent me, I didn't receive it. I was sad because people asked me, "When is Leticia returning?" I told them she was just spending time with friends; for us that was the idea. Leticia said that was what she was going to do, not that she was going to work or stay there. My mother got sad; she said that she wasn't going to have anyone with her when she died other than me and that Leticia wasn't going to return. My mother watched the dates with anxiety. Another date would come and go—nothing, no Leticia. Finally she said, "I'm not going to wait any longer. I'm going to die, but don't let her know. Don't tell her that I died."

I think that Leticia has forgotten about us and that she thinks only about the United States. I can think this, but that doesn't mean it's true. It just means that this is what I think. We, as human beings, are very sentimental and subjective because we think of things that it might be better not to think about. We'd feel more satisfied if she came for a whole day, chatted, teased, and told us about her trip to the United States—the difficulties, the happiness, the sadness, all those things—but it never happens. She went and she returned, nothing more. We don't know what happened there.

I think Sergio is going to the United States instead of going to Mexico, as he tells everyone. He can't tell anyone that he's going to the United States because that would create political problems. You can't get a visa to the United States, so he has to say he's going to Mexico. When Leticia left she said she was going to visit Sergio's family in Mexico; she didn't say she was going to the United States. She told us the truth but to the others, she didn't.

Sergio is an individualist and *machista*. He thinks he can have many women and dominate anything because he's a man. He took care of the children while she was in the United States, but he did it just because those were the circumstances, not because it was his work. When the two of them are here, he doesn't do those things. If a man isn't macho, he shares the household duties. Her husband doesn't wash, iron, cook, mop, or do anything around the house. His daughters or his wife do everything.

A person with a petit-bourgeois or bourgeois mentality like Sergio's can have difficulties finding work in any country, but especially in the United States since he isn't accustomed to doing things that poor people do, like washing, ironing, [or] cleaning. Life is more difficult elsewhere because what people like Sergio know isn't what's important to know in those places. He'll have problems because he doesn't even clean his own shoes, but that's one of the things he'll have to do there to survive. He'll have to wash cars and clothes. We'll see how long he'll be able to stand it. He has studied and been a professional, but in another country it's difficult, different. Perhaps he'll have to find a woman with money, marry her, live well, and not have to work washing cars and clothes.

Leticia wants to return to the United States and leave her children with me. It wouldn't help me at all to take care of the girls, even though it's work I can do at home. It seems like a lie; she'd get to the United States, dedicate herself to something else, and maybe not send money here as she says she would. Then I'd be in bigger trouble because I wouldn't have enough food for her children. I'd have to run around to Sergio's family and ask them for food for the girls. She can't be sure that she can find a job and right away send me money. No one is there waiting to give her a secure job or money. She has to do it all. Sergio made enough money in Nicaragua. It depends on the way you plan. If I want to live like a king, I'll never earn enough.

Machismo is when the true man is thought to be the one who has many women. The ideology is wrong and has a cure, but we're still looking for the medicine. The majority of women are without compañeros because they're afraid that the same thing will happen to them as happened before. But to not have a man ever again isn't the solution. Before you have a compañero, you talk to him. If I'm clear myself that *machismo* isn't correct, then I have to put the idea in his head. In Nicaragua we know the majority of men have several women, and we didn't think that would suddenly change on July 19, 1979.

Many women who have children are alone, not because the men died but because the men live with other women. These women have eight, seven, twelve, five children. Men have to be told that they can't trample on the dignity of women. In Nicaragua we have several laws to protect women, but laws don't educate, nor do they solve the problem. It's the consciousness of the people that will change things. Thousands of laws can exist in Nicaragua, but if people don't ensure that the laws are complied with, we can't educate other people.

I don't agree with a law that allows abortion. But when a woman has been raped by counter-revolutionary bands, which happens a lot in our region, or there's a rapist on the corner and the woman ends up pregnant, or if a pregnant woman gets sick with something that threatened the fetus, or the child is going to be retarded, then these cases should be considered and, yes, they should be aborted. If a counter-revolutionary took me by force and from this I had a child, having that child would be such a trauma for me, for everyone. But I don't agree with abortion without having educated the people about sexual relations. In our country to talk about sexual relations shows, for the older people, a lack of respect or something lacking in that person's religion. If school-age children took the pill, or if they had a checkup, if they knew what sex was and understood well the bodies of men and women, if they talked openly about sexual relations, I'm sure there would be fewer pregnancies. In Nicaragua it's a sin to talk about sex. That's why we have so many cases of young girls walking around with big bellies whose fathers have run them out of their homes. In the time of Somoza, they didn't let them continue studying in the schools. They were told rude things because they had become interested in sex. There was no support from the family or from society. But even now, it's difficult to talk about something that has been taboo.

Years ago, in Somoza's time, a certain person asked me to live with him. He'd buy me a house, and I'd have everything in exchange for sleeping with him. Today that doesn't happen. I don't mean to say that it never happens, but if I'm going to have relations with an important man, I know it's a passing matter rather than a stable one; he isn't going to devote himself to me. Women used to have children and hope the man would take care of them. The justification was that we lived in a difficult situation, and for a poor person, it was hard to get a house. Now we're able to study, develop within the society, have social relations with many people. But there are always women who go along with such fantasies in their heads. But it wouldn't occur to me that if I had sexual relations with a man, someone important in charge of the region, for example, he'd take me to live in his house, or I'd have a car or a farm.

David understands me. He understands the work of women and why they do it. He's from a campesino family, and the campesino people have respected women for a long time—more than the people from the city have.

Omar's not macho; he's a man who, from the time we knew what *machismo* was, fought against it. When he had his first daughter, he washed, ironed, cooked, and still worked at his job. Those are values that not all men have. When he stays here in our house and I come home from work, he has everything clean. He does these things because he knows that the woman shouldn't have to do everything. He doesn't help our mother much now because he thinks he has a family obligation of his own and his obligation to her has finished. This needs to be cleared up, but it, too, is a process. In Nicaragua, the man who marries thinks he no longer has an obligation to his mother. We have to educate the man as well as the woman about this. He loves our mother, but his affection and his love are shown in a different way, and we have to appreciate that also. He's more worried about his daughters and his wife than he is about his mother. They're different things, but one must value both. It would be worth praying about this problem.

Omar's wife Irene is another problem. She does things to him, and my mother knows it. They fight, he comes to our mother's house to sleep, and then he goes back to Irene. These things happen in marriages, but I think he might be immature. He isn't stable and doesn't know what he wants. He doesn't know if Irene is going to continue to be his wife, if she's the one who will make his home. He's clear in his decision to defend the revolution, but in this, he isn't. And Irene doesn't help him make more mature decisions.

Omar's friends come here without him and have a few drinks or beers, listen to music, and leave. They like to come and chat with my mother and make her happy for a little while. She loves it and says to them, "And my son, how is he? Take care of him because if you don't, I won't give you soup. No cool drinks, no beer."

"Ah, little old lady," they say to her, "of course we're going to take care of him."

They feel happy. They come here as if it were their house; they come to see her. "Grandma! Isn't there anything to drink around here?"

"Yes, *hombre*, let's look for it."

"We want something to eat, Grandma; we haven't eaten." It makes her happy because they seem like her children.

I'd like life to be different for my son. But if we don't defend ourselves, they'll kill us. So it is. I'd like to take Miguel with me when I go to San Juan, Quilalí, Jícaro, Jalapa, Limay, Somoto, Ocotal. I'd like him to see [how those areas are different from Estelí], but I'm afraid he'd be killed. When I leave, I have to leave secretly; he cries because I don't take him. Every time I leave, he's psychologically hurt. That's worse than sending him away to study.

I think I'm going to die before everyone. The contra can find us at any moment. We don't know how they'll look for us. We don't know who they are. We don't know who they'll use. Maybe they'll make use of friends at a party, I don't know. Everything is possible for the contra forces; they pay them well. I live in more danger than the others in my family; right now Omar doesn't go to the battle zone, and I do. The counter-revolutionaries say that AMNLAE is changing women into something that's incorrect. It's my work in AMNLAE and also [my brother's work] in security that puts us in danger. The contra forces also look for regional directors and members of the party. But it's not just if [people are] important that they want to kill them; they also do it because of politics. They want to win territory in the political field, and there they can kill at any moment.

I personally know only two people who've worked with the contra. They are women who believed that the revolution was going to distribute everything without cost to anyone, and so they turned to the counter-revolutionaries. But part of it was because they didn't have the capacity that one needs to be a revolutionary and not ask for anything in exchange. A revolutionary gives rather than receives. These are difficult things for people to do. The women were imprisoned for a few days, nothing more, and then let free to see if they understood the situation. It looks as if they did because they no longer have an antirevolution attitude. Even so, it's hard to give everything without receiving anything in exchange. There are cases of divided families, but they aren't really counter-revolutionaries. It's more that they aren't in agreement with the revolution; that's different from being a counter-revolutionary. I've never seen a family where there are contra and Sandinistas in the same family.

If we had not had to fight this war, the government would have built so many things: recreational places for the children of the people who died in the liberation and centers of technical and athletic preparation for the orphans of the war. Health centers which, instead of defense, would have been the revolution's number one priority. The second priority would have been education: many people would be highly educated, and there would have been no illiterate people. What we're using for defense would have gone to health, to education, and then to housing. There would have been lovely housing—charming places—with parks for the children and good health centers. It would have been delightful. How I would have liked it. The people who are in the war zone now, instead of standing watch twenty-four hours a day, could be at a recreation place with their families, or perhaps sailing. I'd love these families to have healthy children and grow carrots, cabbage, and beets. To have better daycare centers with refrigerators and television sets—places where the children of working people are fed and where the children can enjoy themselves. Dreams that some day can be true. Perhaps I'm not going to see it, but other people will. Maybe Miguel.

The work with AMNLAE has given me satisfaction. I'm doing something good, and it will make me sad to leave it. In another job, I'd feel that I was doing nothing. For the sake of my family, though, it's necessary to look for another job. There's no other work within the government; what does exist is outside the city in a cooperative. The countryside is the government's first priority; that's where most people die. I'm going to look for different work because my mother and son need more attention. With AMNLAE, I get five days off every seven months, when possible. I work every day of the week and every Saturday and Sunday. For me there's no free day. There are moments that I can't bear it due to mental fatigue. When I drink two or three beers, it helps. I want to find a job that allows me to be home Saturday afternoons and Sundays, too, and get home at five in the afternoon. Leticia's brother Raúl has a printing shop. But what happens is that the people who had nothing before and now have something think that when a person of little means comes to talk with them, it isn't to get work but to ask for something. I want to talk directly with him, face to face, and have him tell me yes, there's work; if there isn't, no problem, I'll look elsewhere. I know how to make envelopes. I also worked doing other things in printing, and I'd like to learn more.

I make 15,000 córdobas a month compared to 8,000 last year; prices have increased, so they raised the salaries. Any day now there might be another increase in prices but without the same increase in salaries. I can't eat in a restaurant now because it would cost my entire month's salary. And in addition, I probably would end up owing part of next month's salary![17]

For entertainment, I have a beer and watch the news or a movie on television. That's all the amusement I have because I can't go to large parties—some I can't, others I can—because they recommend we don't; at any moment, something can happen.

You can still belong to the Sandinista party if you work outside the government; you can work for the party in the barrios and in the business district, standing watch, for example. I like to do it; it's important to know what's going on during the day as well as the night in order to be able to make a report.

My work right now is in Quilalí, about five or six hours from here. We say we're going for two days, but if we have problems, we stay longer. The enemy intends to remove the cooperatives from the *asentamientos*.[18] Sometimes there's an ambush waiting for us, or our military is trying to stop an ambush; all these things delay our arrival and departure. Once we're on the road, we have to be prepared for anything. The next time five of us will go, and we have to decide what vehicle to take—some vehicles are recognized by the contra—and if we should have the military accompany us.

Sometimes I have trouble at work. I felt bad yesterday because of the way some of the compañeras acted toward me. When I told them that my mother was sick, I saw that they didn't believe it. These things will resolve themselves when I talk with them about how we misunderstood each other. My way of being is that I can seem to be peaceful, and when some attitudes of my brother and sister give me problems, I never show it to them or my mother. It's worrisome to fulfill my duties at work and at the same time leave her alone in the hands of only Miguel. When I have to leave for several days, I'm tense and worried because the situation on the road is dangerous, and the situation at home . . . well, I have to do so many things.

Each day new things occur, some bad, some more or less bad. It would be a lie to say that only good will happen. The good that happens is a bonus. The bad I see as natural. All I can do is try to keep myself in good health so that I can respond to the troubles I have to confront. I almost don't know how to cry. I do it in silence. Some of my compañeras from work have seen me cry, but I try to hold it in so that they don't, and I mostly have managed to do that.

When my mother got sick, I didn't have anyone near, and I was desperate. There were moments when I lost control, when I yelled at my son, exasperated, and I wanted to hit him. There were times I did hit him, but that isn't right to do. I have to try to keep myself as serene as I can.

When we were little, our mother beat us out of frustration because of the troubles we had getting food. Sometimes one of us would cry because we had nothing to eat. This distressed her, and she hit us. But now I understand her. It doesn't happen as much these days because we, as a people, can face these things. Because I have a job, I can say to a person, "Lend me something until I get paid," but my mother didn't have a profession or a fixed salary. She washed, ironed, and sometimes, when she needed the money to buy food for us, she'd deliver the work and the people would say, "Come back another day because right now I don't have any money."

It has been a difficult year. But we know it will get better.

Omar

This year of our lives, from 1985 to 1986, has just passed. I haven't had the psychosis for six months. I've conquered it. I'm not nervous anymore. My work is different, and my situation at home is even more different. Irene and I have struggled so that our children wouldn't see a husband and wife fight. The only thing that worries me is the health of my children. Dora was in a Managua hospital for several weeks with meningitis, where they took out liquid from her spinal column. After that, the other one got sick from asthma. Right now they are both sick with a cough and cold. We always have problems with their health.

That's more or less what happened during the year. Irene and I understand each other better. She worked for five months in the military, but since she had to be mobilized from one place to another, she couldn't take care of the children. They got so sick that she had to quit work to take care of them.

I take political classes during the day. That's my work. Pure politics, nothing more. I mean, it's still within the military, but it's not the same as before. I learn about Nicaragua and how countries develop. I have classes from eight to ten in the morning, and from one to three in the afternoon. After that I rest, watch television, and listen to music. In part, this has helped my health since I no longer have to be mobilized. The only place I go is from my work to another office to bring magazines or political documents. I don't go to the war front, and that has helped me conquer those war nerves.

At work, I'm being trained to focus on the need for all people in Nicaragua to improve. We have to reach a more developed level, learn who our enemies are, what it is that they claim, and how to face them—not just with guns, but politically, too. That's what our president has done; he has politically defeated imperialism by going himself to talk about the damage done to our people. My work is calling this to the attention of those who don't study. It's easy work, not dangerous. It doesn't wear me out, and that has helped. I'll try to keep on working there because I like it. It's better than the other work. I don't have a gun now. I don't need one.

I cured my psychosis by not having family problems. I mean, if you have problems on one side and problems on the other side, well, I couldn't find an accommodation until Irene and I found an understanding between us. They helped me at work. The medicine they gave me was good, and the new job helped. I don't need to take pills now. There's one tranquilizer I take daily. And sometimes, instead of that pill, I take vitamins. I don't take a pill to sleep as I did before. I no longer have the nightmares.

I still live in the little house on the hill. We're trying to improve it. The bosses at work say they're going to help me get a better house. Leticia talked about giving me a piece of land, but there was a problem while she was gone because her husband got involved. I couldn't build on it because he said he was the owner. He and I are friends, but sometimes it's more self-seeking than friendship. He wanted that piece of land—it's selfishness—and I had no title or paper that said I was the owner. I didn't want any problems and thought it was better to let it go until Leticia returned; let her take care of it.

She left as a result of the hopelessness that people feel when they see themselves pressured and humiliated. They think they can find the answer in another city or place. That's how it looks to me, anyhow. She had problems with her husband and her work, economically, and saw an alternative where she could improve herself and feel more peaceful. She hasn't talked with me about what she did there. I don't know if what she did—leaving her daughters and going to look for something that she couldn't find in Nicaragua— was good or bad. Many people despair when they go through what we're going through here; they think the only alternative is to look for an adventure or to acquire some material thing. This causes them to leave their land, their family problems, their economic problems, the problems of society. That's what I see in her. She told me she had problems with her husband; she was going to take a trip and maybe she'd find there what she couldn't find here.

Another problem we have is that every day our mother gets worse. It's something that those of us who live nearby, as Marta and I do, have to face. We both work all the time, and that doesn't allow us to be at home much. As a result, our mother is alone and doesn't have us around every day. At times, this work separates us for a week or a month, and she lives with this constant worry about us. From one moment to the next, she hears another piece of news that affects her health, especially her heart.

Even though I no longer go to the war zone, I'm still in the military, part of an organization. And if the organization says that today no one can leave, then no one can leave. They pay us by the month, and that means we have to work for the whole month. At times, we have no free day. Other times, whenever we want, we can leave, but for only two hours. If you don't arrive at a certain time, you lose the day's work. He who doesn't work gets no salary.

This year I make enough money. The State has improved a little. At times, as a consquence of the aggression that we live in, the government has to defend us. That hurts all of us because the money we spend on defense could be invested in raising the workers' salaries. An increase in profits favors the working class because we are the workers of the State. The government sometimes sacrifices the construction of a school to support defense. Without defense, we would be again with Somoza, but without Somoza himself. By celebrating one more anniversary we are acquiring more experience, more knowledge of the country's economy. As we say, sometimes it's cheaper to buy a pound of nails than one single nail.

Most of Irene's sisters who were living with us decided to leave. One has a husband and studies in León; the others live with another sister. I no longer have this bunch of people who eat what my children could have eaten. It's Irene and me, her two children, and our two. A pound of beans lasts all day! Our children are five and six; hers are nine and eight.

The separation from Irene was almost natural. We fought constantly. I lived at my mother's house and went home only to get my bags. My boss told us that a revolutionary shouldn't abandon his children and have his wife going around to the office demanding things. Nor should the man hit the woman, and she shouldn't do things to him. She was motivated by the same despair I suffered from, and we made mistakes. But little by little I've improved, thanks to government programs—television and radio programs and political talks that Irene and I hadn't heard before—that guided us in the problems of men and women.

There are a lot of problems like this. It isn't just a problem of war psychosis; many times the problem is that of liquor. People are addicts. Now I might drink beer once a month or so, but not too much. I've conquered it all this year. I'm better than I was last year.

8

Survival: 1986-1987

Leticia was back in Estelí by the time of these interviews. The family's complaints about one another continued as they struggled sorrowfully with the deterioration of their mother's health and the weakening of the economy.

Doña María

When Leticia first went to the United States, I didn't think she was going with the idea of staying there. I thought she'd buy the house across the street from us and we'd have a place for chickens and fruit trees. She sold it cheaply, which she shouldn't have done because it's worth a lot now. She was out of control. I suppose it seems like that to me because the house was my idea; I imagined the salon being there, the room for her daughters, a place in the back for chickens.

She wasn't always as worried as she is now. She isn't peaceful. She worries about the economy, even though she has her work and can buy and sell. We don't have those problems, so we live more peacefully. She worries that her brother, her uncle, her papa, her I-don't-know-who needs something. So she's there for them, and she doesn't have anything herself. Her daughter Marisa understands that her mother causes many of her own problems. If there's a sick person, there she is. If someone dies, she's there. But people are jealous and talk about her. When she has problems, there's no one for her. People say she and Sergio have separated. That he left her. She has had problems ever since she lived in Matagalpa because Sergio's family didn't like her. She never got along with them. Not with him, either. He doesn't speak to me. I don't know why. He

202

doesn't like me. We never chat. Marta, too, is distant from him. Omar is closer.

The thing I have resented most this year is that my compañeras from the Mothers of Heroes and Martyrs have abandoned me. Only two visit me. The other mothers stay away. I'd like them to have a meeting, and I'd tell them directly that these hypocrisies among us shouldn't exist because we're all suffering the same. A friend of ours used to get us together every Saturday, but she retired. She sent us to see the sick people. We had activities and celebrated May 30 for the mothers. We did things, like collecting funds. But she retired, and they no longer think about me. I resent that. After I die, they'll say, "So-and-so died, the mother of such-and-such a person." I want them to know before that time. There was only one happy thing [this year], a trip; my friend was in charge, and they took me to Ocotal. They have meetings because Tomás Borge helped them get a gallery where there are photos [of the dead heroes and where Pedro's photo is displayed]. But they don't tell me about them because I'm sick. I feel no unity. But I don't want them to feel it's important to me. If they come, they can sit down and we'll talk, but that's all. What I'd like to do is ask permission to take my son's photo out of the gallery. But I won't ask them why they don't visit me. We're all equal. When we die, we all go to the same place. Why do some people feel that they're better than others just because they're good, or healthy, or go around with Tomás Borge? I resent it because we were so united before. Every Saturday at two in the afternoon, we'd get together. Sometimes twelve of us, or thirty, or twenty. Now we don't. Now only Doña What's-her-name, who has money in Managua, goes to see Tomás Borge to find out what he has to offer. She comes back and says, "Ah, Tomás Borge gave such-and-such to the Mothers." I don't pay any attention. We're just fine [without them].

Miguel will be a proud person, as I am. So is Omar. He doesn't visit anyone. I don't either. I haven't been in these houses around here. People come here, though. To the kitchen to see if the fire is lit, to see if there's salt, to see if there's coffee, to see what we have. But I don't go there. I know the neighbors because I sit at the door. I wouldn't go in some place and sit down. "Come in, Doña Whoever-you-are." Lies. Afterwards they'd talk about me to another neighbor. One has to avoid these visits, as Omar says. Let them visit you, but you don't return the visit. If you visit them, you bother them. So we don't struggle to keep these relationships going. It bothers people to see the firewood, the salt, the coffee, but if other people have those things, we put up with it quietly. I sit outside the door so that people can come by and say hello to me.[1] There are people I get along with, so I get a chair for them, and we talk. Otherwise, I just say, "Hello, hello." Miguel's the same. If he doesn't like something, he's quiet. After a group goes in a house, people say, "We lost such-and-such a thing," so we don't want them to say he was the one who went in. He has to stay in the door of a neighbor's house. Not in. Only in the door.

When I sit outside, I don't like all the vehicles that come by. Some people I like, so I say, "Hello." Of course I greet the good-looking men, and even those who aren't. [Laughter] I still look at men. A good-looking one is Leticia's father's lawyer. But I don't think I've seen anything really interesting. I sit there because it's cool. There's a breeze that goes [from the *solar* in back, through the house, to the front where I sit outside], and it makes me feel good even when I'm alone. People I know go by. And if I don't want to see them, I bend down and tie my shoe. That way I don't see them. A lot of bicycles and motorcycles come by. A lot of traffic at night. It seems to me that they're going to stop, so I can't sleep. Some vehicles park right out here. Army cars go by, one following the other. There are more now than before; it must be caused by hidden groups around here that are part of the aggression. Right now, I'm not afraid of the contra because they don't want to come face-to-face with the army, and there are lots of army volunteers here. Miguel wants to be in the army some day. He says he wants to be like his uncle Omar. He has seen military people all his life. He's more afraid of drunks [than he is of the military]. If a drunk comes by, he runs in the house and closes the door. But if he sees a group of people in the army, he looks out to see the truck or walks up to see the commanders.[2] A lot of them come through here.

The thing that gave me the most satisfaction this year was the behavior of Marta. And what worried me the most was my sickness, because Marta will be left alone. Leticia's going to leave, and I don't know who Miguel will stay with. So if I could get better, Marta could work without worrying [about me], and Miguel would go to school. I hope that Miguel won't be a bum, that he'll be honest and that no one will be able to say anything bad about him.

Omar is the person who troubles me. The woman dominates him. She orders him about as if he were a child. She has hit him. [I'm his mother, and] I wouldn't do that, but she would. He has come here after he has been beaten. I've asked his daughter, "Does your mother hit Omar?"

"Yes."

"With what?"

"With a stick."

The neighbors tell me that she sends him to make the meal while she does nothing. From the time she was in the military, whenever he was free he had to cook, bring the firewood, and bring the water. And he came here beaten up around his neck and arms. When a child gets sick, the woman tells him to get the medicine. I tell him that I never would have asked a father to go get medicine for the children. We aren't used to women ordering men to do something, so I don't like it.

Marta left work to take care of me because I've been seriously sick for eight months. So many difficulties this year. I'm not hungry. I'm not thirsty. I have no strength in my arms. Like a rag. The doctor once told me that it was high blood pressure; if the treatment didn't work, I'd have to go to Managua. But I told him that I had faith in God and in him, the doctor, that they would get me up. He did it; he gave me pills and got me up. From the bed to the chair. A good doctor. He's the same one I had before. So happy. He took care of me here in the house. He came at night to see me because I told him I didn't have a lot of life left. So he told me, "You're going to recover," and gave me medicine. I'm encouraged by the way he treats me. When I don't have something, Marta goes out looking for it. We have to pay for the medicine. There are some that aren't available here, but I've always had what I needed. The doctor isn't free, either, but he's considerate.[3]

Marta has suffered for my sake. She brought me to this house from the one I was renting. I rented homes for forty years. I'm grateful. I tell that to people. They see that she's a good daughter. She tries to entertain me by chatting, dancing. She doesn't want to annoy me. She doesn't want to make me angry; the doctor doesn't allow that. My arteries were bursting; I could feel it on my shoulder. I slept sitting up with a pile of clothes behind me. When I lay down, I couldn't breathe. The doctor got rid of all that. Now I can sleep lying down.

I don't know what Leticia plans: if she'll stay here and work, if she'll go to the United States and work, if she'll take the children, if she'll sell that house. I tell her, and so does her oldest daughter, not to sell the house. You don't know what's going to happen. If she came back, she might have to end up living squeezed in somewhere with another family. That's why Marta has sacrificed to have this little house. I helped her by making popsicles, but now we can't find the bags, so I no longer help. She wanted to build something for the chickens, but you can't get the material. I used to sell firewood, but the Ministry came and stopped it.[4] There's no consideration for the poor here. You used to be able to buy firewood cheaply from the government. Not any more. Now people buy it wherever they can find it. Costs 500 córdobas for a little stick. The Ministry did a bad thing to the poor. They made it so expensive that I can't buy it and sell it to others; I can only buy what I need. Every day things become more expensive. Friends have been good to us. Sometimes we receive money from Leticia. She doesn't have much either, but it's really more that she just *thinks* she has no money. She wants to sell things and earn more. Sometimes she is paid, sometimes not. She loses. She wants to be good, so people take advantage of her. Leticia thinks her problems will be solved by her father's family, but they're the ones who hurt her, not us. They take her things and say, "I'm going to sell this." Then they give her just half [of what they sold it for]. That family is hypocritical with her. When they have no money, they scorn her. We don't say anything to her about it because she gets irritated.

We can't make ends meet. The aggression causes damage, then the government has to take something from one place to help another. That's how it will be until who knows when. All we have is rice and sugar. There's no corn. You have to go to the north, to Jalapa, to find corn to make tortillas. No meat. First we had to stand in line. Then it got so expensive that the poor were left with bones. Now even the rich people have to look for bones.

I still think it's better to have friends than to have money. A friend helps you every day, and money lasts for only a moment. I've had friends from [the time] when the children were little, friends wherever I lived. If you have to bother someone, it's better to bother a friend. Perhaps without being asked, someone comes by and says, "Take this." I sit at the door, and they see I'm sick and without work. They know I've worked hard, and that's why I'm this way. I worked too much and suffered bringing up the children. People come by and say, "How are you, Doña María?" I tell them I'm in bad shape.

My mother and sisters have never loved me. My mother gave me away at three and didn't recognize me as her daughter. Neither did my sisters. So I don't feel anything for them. I wasn't sad when my mother died. She loved only her son, who had money. She gave him some cows she had, and then he left her. She fell about seven years ago. He didn't even have her operated on so that she could stand up again. When the war started, he went to Honduras. My children all loved my mother. I'm not selfish and didn't instill in my children any resentment toward my mother, even though she didn't love me. Once during the war in April [1979], we lived two blocks apart in Condega—I had taken Pedro there so the guardia wouldn't find him—and I visited my mother early every morning out of obligation.

A year ago I didn't want Marta to notify Leticia if I died. I think that less this year. Anyhow, if she goes to the United States, she couldn't come back, and Marta would have no way to notify her. Marta has no thoughts against anyone. She wants to resolve everything without anyone knowing. Sometimes there are things that she doesn't tell even me. But I figure them out and mention them to her. When you get as old as I am, you understand some of these things. But she wants to solve everything in silence. She has friends who don't talk to her, only Alejandra does. The others have pulled away. Alejandra notices when Marta needs something and sends us milk or potatoes. However she can, she helps. Maricruz doesn't come by anymore. Marta worked so hard at AMNLAE, and now when she's out of work and I'm sick, they don't support her. They don't visit her. They just need her in the work, nothing more. She understands a lot about AMNLAE. They wanted to send her to the north and leave us here. I said to her, "If you go there, I won't send Miguel to school." Miguel said, "I'm not going to school if Marta leaves." He doesn't like her to go because she has been in accidents.[5] The contra places mines and sets ambushes, and that frightens him. AMNLAE wanted her to work in the most dangerous part. My niece died there; they burned her, and she was brought back in a bag. He knows all this. He knows that children die in these ambushes, that children are left without mothers, without fathers, left by themselves. He likes to avoid problems; the neighbor no longer hits him, because Miguel avoids him. If the neighbor does something, he stays quiet so that we don't have trouble. If Miguel doesn't like something, he tells me or Marta, but he doesn't tell the mother or the family of the little boy next door. They don't care if I'm sick, but they let the children come over to watch television.

I don't want to die. I feel bad about Miguel—my dying and his being so little. It's because I love him so much. I love him with compassion and sorrow. It'd make me sad to leave him here where everyone would beat him. I treat him with kindness, and he's obedient. I don't punish him. The punishment that I give is that he can't play until he does such-and-such a thing. Then he obeys. That's the best kind of punishment.

As the doctor said, "You have a bit of spiritual suffering." And that's true. I suffer in silence.

I never thought that Marta would take care of me. It seemed to me that I'd always live as I had lived, renting, and being in charge of the house where I was living. I never thought I'd need taking care of. I just thought I'd live and take care of myself.

She has proved that she loves me. People say to me, "Good daughter, very worried." She doesn't demand that I do anything. I do what I want. Even if she's feeling something, she doesn't show it so that I'm not bothered. She does it in silence. People see the strength she has, how she behaves with me, how she worries about me. I'd like to be in good health so that she can rest and work less.

I cried recently when Irene gave me money[6] because I don't like to receive money from her. She's a hypocrite. She came because he sent her. He thinks I have to get closer to her, but I think not. The obligation is his to say to me, "Take this." Besides, when he gives me nothing, I still welcome him in the same way, with money or without money. I've always helped him when I've had money. I've given him money so that he can have his rum with his friends, so that a friend doesn't humiliate him when his money has run out. I've never asked for anything. He says, when they ask him, "My mother's sick," but he doesn't know what I have. He doesn't know who gets the medicine. He doesn't know if I need shoes, if I need a

dress. Before we got ourselves in this situation, we lined up everything for him to take to his house: the rice, the soap, the corn, the
tortillas, the sugar. It doesn't matter to me that he doesn't give me
anything because I'm used to it.

If I could live my life over again, I think I'd live it the same. If
Marta worked, I'd take care of the house and animals, and we'd
always avoid problems by not visiting our neighbors.

Leticia

Sergio left for Mexico on September 18, 1986. I thought he and the
woman in Managua were making plans to go together, but it turned
out that they weren't. It wasn't until I went to Mexico myself that I
was convinced that they hadn't. Before he left, we barely talked. He
talked only with the children and almost never with me. Whenever
we did talk, we ended up fighting. We spent most of the time angry—
fighting, arguing.

The day he left, he told me that he wanted me to go with him to
the bus station. I told him that the children could go, but I didn't
want to. He pleaded with me to go to the station, so I went, but I
didn't wait until the bus left. In spite of everything, it was hard for
me to see him leave.

Time passed, and I heard nothing about the woman or what had
happened. I was confused and didn't know what to do; should I
finish this once and for all or what?

I had a little money saved from being in the United States and by
selling some things I had brought back, I got together enough money
to go to Mexico. I wanted to buy some supplies for the salon and to
speak with him once and for all. He had been there two months by
that time. I thought that by being so far away for that long, his
thinking would be different, or mine would. And I needed to see
for myself if she was with him.

I stayed with a friend of mine in Mexico, a Nicaraguan nurse, and
didn't have to pay for room or board. While I was there, I met a
muchacho who had a beauty salon and needed someone to manage
it. I wanted to stay there so that I could think better and get a little

rest—I was feeling very nervous—so I accepted the offer to work for him. He gave me fifty percent of what I made. He wanted me to stay forever because he liked my work and liked me, too. I told him that I couldn't because I had to return to Nicaragua. He was good to me, so it distressed me to leave. He was a young muchacho, about twenty-seven years old.

While I was in Mexico, I received the news of my brother Raúl's death—we had the same father but not the same mother. He was killed on November 3, 1986, eight months ago. Sergio's mother and a sister came to Mexico with the news that one of my brothers had been killed, but they didn't know which one. Sergio came to the house where I was staying to give me the message. I was eating with my friend when he came in, so he waited until after I ate to tell me that one of my brothers had been killed. But he didn't know which one. It frightened me. I wanted to run away. I called a cousin in Nicaragua to find out what had happened and who had died. She told me it had been Raúl. They had waited three days to see if they could find me, but by the time I heard and called Nicaragua, they had already buried him. It was terrible; I felt so far away, and I couldn't do anything. I wanted to have wings to fly back to Nicaragua.

A man killed him, but we still don't know the reason. Raúl had no enemies; he never fought with anyone. I don't say that just because he was my brother but because everyone loved him. He was poor, but he worked, struggled, and always tried to improve himself. He began his print shop before the war but also went to the mountain and worked for the Frente. The man who killed him is in jail, but Raúl's death is confusing because the one who killed him was supposedly a friend of his. The day before he died was a Sunday, and on Sundays all the avid fans go to the cock fights. Raúl has a cock pit, and they all say he was there singing—he liked to sing Mexican songs—and he went around serenading some of his girlfriends. He had another woman besides the one he had in the house; he also had a woman with whom he had lived for a long time, fifteen years, whom he serenaded that night with mariachis, too. He wasn't married to any of them. He must have had a lot to drink.

The next day, Monday, this muchacho came—it was a young muchacho who killed him—to Raúl's house and invited him to have a beer with him and another friend of my brother's. So the three of them went to a restaurant located on the road to Condega and drank beer. They say that my brother had not drunk much. He usually didn't drink on Mondays because he was almost always at work. The owner of the restaurant says that he had one or two beers.

The other two men began to argue, and my brother stood up and said, "What's going on with you two? Why are you arguing? Stop it. There's no reason to fight; forget about it."

At that point, the muchacho got out a pistol and said, "You've no reason to get involved; this is our problem." He shot immediately after he pulled out the pistol.

They've come to the conclusion that it was a plan; the day before, my brother had lent the other man—[not the one who killed him]— 300,000 córdobas. The moment my brother was shot, this man fled. The one who shot him was immediately grabbed by another friend of my brother's who happened to be in the restaurant. The muchacho is still a prisoner, but things aren't clear, because the other one ran away. Supposedly he hadn't committed a crime and had no reason to run.

Raúl died immediately. The bullet entered either the right or left nipple. It was a bullet from a .22, but explosive. It exploded inside and destroyed him. He was still talking when they got him to the hospital. On the road from the restaurant to the hospital he said, "Don't let me die; I don't want to die. My children and family need me." But they couldn't do anything for him.

Raúl had two women, and right away they began to fight over the things he left. The one he was with for fifteen years and had five children with trusts me and kept saying, "If Leticia were here, things wouldn't be like this. She would have arranged things better." But the other one—she had two children—found a lawyer, so the problems began.

I tried to return to Nicaragua as soon as I heard, but my friend took me to a doctor friend of hers because I got very sick. My head hurt, and I was nervous, I cried all the time. I didn't want to eat. The doctor told me that it'd be better to wait and have treatment before returning. I don't know why, but he said it'd be dangerous to go by plane. Sergio was good to me. He told me to be brave and strong. He knew that my brother and I loved each other, that we had always gotten along well together.

I know my brother missed me when I went to the United States, because he came to me a day before I left for Mexico and asked me not to go. He said he'd help me in anything—economically or spiritually—that I needed. He said, "We always take care of each other's problems. I need you and don't want you to go." But I lied to him. I said, "I'll return in a week. I'm just going to Guatemala. I'll buy some beauty products and return." But that wasn't true. I wanted to talk with Sergio in Mexico so that I could make a decision once and for all. So I went.

His death was the hardest thing this year. It's true that the problems I had with Sergio were also difficult, but the death of my brother is something I can't forget. We shared so many things from the time we were little. Our lives were so similar. He sacrificed as much as I have to get what he had, and now all of it is in the hands of lawyers who, instead of Raúl's children, are going to end up with his money. It hurts not to be able to do anything for them; I still remember Raúl's telling me that if something happened to him, I shouldn't let his children be left in the streets without money. But the problem is that I can't do anything. There was no will, no paper to support that, no legal authority. Raúl had recognized all of them as his children. Once, after I returned from the United States, I asked him if the boy was his, because I had heard some comments that the woman had gone off with another man. Raúl said the child was, but when he went to establish that at the Registry, he used one of his two signatures; on everything he signed, we could see that he had two different signatures. Even knowing that, they didn't recognize the child. Then the Nicaraguan Institute of Social Security and Welfare intervened, and the lawyer.[7] Part of the money belonged to my father, according to the law. My father has been sick, and Raúl helped him. Now that Raúl has died, I help my father however I can. He's another person who has been left alone by my brother's death. Raúl gave him the house he lives in, and my father depended on him. A lawyer said he had a right to some of the money, but the other woman is fighting that. Eight months later, no one has received a penny; it will all go to the lawyers. Everyone says the lawyers are Raúl's heirs.

They say that at the funeral even the men cried. Raúl had many friends. He was well known in Estelí. He was a good-natured man with a heart of gold who helped everyone, and that's why they all loved him. No one imagined that he'd die this way, that someone would kill him for his money. He never had any enemies; even the one who killed him was a friend, supposedly. It was all very difficult for me.

It was also hard when I got to Mexico. Sergio didn't know we were coming. I waited to see what he'd say. He was living with a niece of his, and I went there along with his nephew who had gone with me to Mexico. We knocked on the door. When he opened the door, he was surprised to see me. He turned pale. Pale! He couldn't find anything to say or do, only, "Come in; come in." Nothing more. He talked with the nephew, not with me. While they talked, I talked with the niece. She told me the other woman wrote to him often, and he wrote back to her. Meanwhile we, his family, had received only one letter, plus a telegram telling us that he had arrived. The niece said it seemed that he was in love with the woman and missed her. That was what I wanted to know. Whatever the truth was, I wanted to know.

I went to my friend's place, and Sergio came over that night. I didn't tell him what his niece had told me. He talked with my friend and her husband, and then told me he was going. "Okay. Well, good-bye." And he left. He came back the next morning. He asked me how the children were. I told him they were fine but missed him. The days passed. We didn't talk about much of anything. One day he stayed for lunch and asked me what I was thinking. I said, "I always think the same thing; it's that you have to tell me what you think. More than anything, I came so that we can make a decision. I know that when you left, you were in love with that muchacha. I thought that maybe you had brought her here. But I want to know, since you have been here two months, if you've made a decision. I want to tell my daughters once and for all what our situation is."

He said he had never intended to bring the woman to Mexico. It was true that she had been good to him, but she had two children from another man; he wasn't going to pick up with a woman who had two children who weren't his when he had a wife who had his children. It would seem absurd, he said. I was so sad when he told me all that. He said he got along well with the woman and she loved him, but he had no intention of staying with her because he loved his own children and wanted to be with us. I spoke to him in a straightforward way and said, "I know you love your children, but I'm not going to live with you just for their sake. We'd live without loving each other, and you'd want to be with the other woman. We wouldn't be happy, neither one of us. The love the children have for you won't disappear; they're your children and will always love you. So we have to make a decision. It's true that they need me, and they need you; for that reason, it might be worth it to sacrifice ourselves. But in another way, it's just the contrary: being together would hurt them more. If we were separated and didn't hurt each other, letting the children keep a good image of you and of me, it might be better for them. Sometimes when we argue, they hear things they shouldn't. They're getting a terrible idea of matrimony."

Sergio is too proud to say, "I love you." I don't know if it's like that for all women, but he's too proud to tell me that he loves me. He says it only when he has been drinking. Then he says, "Yes, I love you, and I could never love another woman as I love you." I mean, he's either too proud or too timid; I don't know which. But on this occasion, he did say, "I love all of you. I love you, and I love my daughters."

Then he wanted to know what I was thinking. I told him I loved him, too, and that's why I had come to Mexico. I didn't want to destroy my home without first talking with him. I could remake my life, but if I were still thinking about him, it'd be difficult trying to love someone else. He told me to be patient because he was in a bad economic situation, but he did love us. He said he had to work longer; he didn't want to return without money and be as poor as when he left. His job is with an advertising business; he takes orders from commercial businesses and then delivers them. He doesn't earn much because it depends on how much he sells, but they're going to give him a basic salary plus a commission. In the beginning it's like that, especially in other countries. It's harder.

After I returned to Nicaragua, he talked with us by phone; he said he missed us and wanted us to come to Mexico. He thinks he isn't going to be able to work in Nicaragua as he had before. He was disillusioned in his work even before I went to the United States, and that's why he decided to leave. He was very responsible in his work here, as he has always been. He's honest and capable. After a year at government-owned PROAGRO, they sent him to Cuba to work with technology. Before going, he had been named deputy director. They removed the director, who wasn't honest; he wanted to take advantage of the company, so business declined. When Sergio returned, even better trained than before, he was made director, and the other one was transferred to Matagalpa. Later Sergio realized that PROAGRO was almost bankrupt. He began to work closely with the people. It's not just that he told me that, but so did his compañeros from work when they came to my house for meetings. They said PROAGRO had improved. Sergio bought a large farm that produced coffee, corn, beans, and vegetables. He formed the employees into groups to work the land—one day for each group— so that they didn't have to pay a lot for food. He did lots of things, like putting several tanks of molasses in places like Santa Cruz and La Trinidad. When they crush the sugar cane, a juice comes out and becomes molasses; it's stored in those enormous tanks. PROAGRO was growing. In the two years that he was director, it had changed. Everyone agreed.

But the regional director of the Ministry of Development and Agrarian Reform, which PROAGRO belongs to, had a friend he wanted to place in Sergio's company. It wasn't because the person was qualified; it was because he was a friend. The regional director sent a letter to Sergio telling him to accept this man as the one in charge of sales. Sergio answered that he had already chosen a person for this position, someone who lived in Jalapa, and he didn't want to go back on his word. The man in Jalapa thought that since Sergio was the director, he could hire people for the position. But the regional director was Sergio's superior, and when Sergio said he wasn't going to accept the friend, the regional director felt that Sergio wasn't being obedient. Suddenly a letter came from Managua transferring Sergio to a better job in Managua to work with administration on the national level. It said, "Because you're so capable, we want to move you to Managua," but Sergio knew that wasn't true. Even though they had given him something better, he didn't like what had been done. They offered him his choice of the Managua region or administration on the national level, where he'd have to visit all Nicaragua. He said, "Okay, I'll accept the one in Managua." But he really didn't agree; he had affection for his company, and besides, all of us were here. This meant that the family would have to move again to Managua, but there was no alternative. He said, "It's fine; I'll go."

But one day when he had something to drink—it was at a reception they had for him in Managua—and he and another friend were there with the general director, Sergio said, "I want you to tell me something. I know you didn't move me from Estelí to Managua to improve my situation. My opinion is that it was because I wouldn't accept that person in my company, but now I want to know your side."

The general director answered, "Look, Sergio, I'm going to tell you the truth. We took you from there because we needed a political person in that company. And you aren't political." Sergio didn't like that. He told them even though he wasn't political, he had always done his work and his duty. I, as a revolutionary, think that at times he has acted better than some of those who say they're revolutionaries but who don't act honestly. That's a mistaken idea that will take years to correct. Some things aren't good here. Mistakes are committed by people in those companies. Maybe the government mistakenly thinks those people are capable, or if not capable, at least honest, but sometimes they aren't. This is why the revolution doesn't advance as it should. They put people in a position only because they go around in an olive green uniform and carry a gun, but they need, in my way of thinking, a capable person or someone who's honest. When Sergio told me about it, he cried. He felt cheated. He said he'd work for a while in Managua, but that later, he'd leave.

Now he's in Mexico. I don't think he'll be there forever because I think that in his heart he's most interested in his family. Many times he told me that there are moments when he wants to grab his suitcases and return, moments when he despairs and wants to run away. But he has to give it another try in a different job and see what happens. It's hard for him to make enough money to help us. He still hasn't sent us any, but supposedly he's saving some to send us. Or he's waiting to see if we're going to leave or stay here. It's hard to decide what to do. It's another country, and we're used to living here. At the moment, I don't intend to go. I want to save some money—and maybe he can send some—to buy a little farm where he can come and work for himself. That's what a lot of people do now; they sell their homes in the city and buy a little farm. They work and plant. It's not much, just corn and beans, and you can have a cow. I can't tell Sergio to come now, though, because the situation is too difficult.

We made love in Mexico. I felt good [about it] and felt he had changed; he wasn't the same person I'd been with here in Nicaragua. I don't know if this was just because he'd been alone or what, but it was different. He treated me differently, and I felt better with him. I tried to forget what he had done, and he tried to be considerate of me. At the end of my time there, we lived in the same house; he came to live at my friend's. Things went well. I had thought that maybe I didn't love him anymore, [but even before I went to Mexico] I thought about him often, and at times, wanted us to be together. In every respect, I miss him because I feel alone with the children; when I have problems, I need someone to tell them to. Even though Sergio isn't very communicative, a person has to have someone. I don't have anyone; I'm practically alone.

Before I went to the United States, I left my salon with Lola, a friend of mine, and told her to take care of it until I returned. I also told her that when I came back, I'd help her get her own salon with money I made in the United States. I left the salon with confidence, just like the muchacho in Mexico who handed his salon over to me. The salon had a glass case full of beauty products, the mirror and the table from years ago, the drier, everything she needed to do the work. Lola gave the money to Sergio weekly so that he could give Marta and my mother what they needed. There was a set amount for him and a set amount for them. I knew his salary wasn't much to live on; we've lived mostly on my salary. So she started turning money over to him, but each day it was less, and the products were disappearing from the salon. It seems to me that she sold them, maybe along with driers and tweezers from the salon. When Sergio realized this, he immediately closed the salon and took what was left to Managua.

When I returned, I asked Sergio what happened to my license. In order to work, I had to have a license from the Ministry of Domestic Commerce. He said Lola had it; she hadn't wanted to give it to him. I went to her, but I didn't complain about what happened; I just asked her to do me the favor of returning my license. She told me that she had taken it to the Ministry because they had asked for it. So I went there, and they said they didn't have it. I went back to Lola and told her to go with me to the Ministry and point out the person to whom she had given my license. She went with me, looked at all the desks and the people who were there, and told me that the person she had given my license to wasn't there. I talked with the person in charge of receiving licenses and told him to look for my license.

"But you," said the man, "weren't here. You were out of the country."

"And how do you know that I was out of the country?"

"I don't know [how I know], but I do know that you were gone for almost a year," he said, "and other people who were gone aren't given licenses to work in a salon or anywhere."

"Are you doing this with an order from the director general of the Ministry or personally?"

"No," he said, "I'm just explaining it to you."

"But you have to have a basis upon which to tell me what you're telling me. Do you have an order from the director that I can't be given a license because I left the country and that it's a crime?"

"No," he said, "what's happened is that there's a woman who has her salon here and lives in the United States."

"I didn't come to talk about her. I came to talk about me and my license. It's mine, and you have to return it. I've worked for twenty years in the salon. That's how I make my living. You're pushing me to return to the United States when I want to work in my country. If that's what you want, I'll leave."

"No, we're going to fix this somehow. Come back on such-and-such a date."

"Look," I said. "Let's not waste time. My license isn't here. I know it isn't, so there's no reason to look for it. I'm going to talk with the director."

This man told Lola what he had said to me and then said to her, "Don't worry; yours is all arranged, and no one will take it from you." They had given her a license. She already had her own salon when I returned.

I went to talk with the director of the Ministry, but he wasn't there; his assistant, a woman, was. That woman's secretary knows me well because we worked together in the barrio with the Sandinista Defense Committees. She greeted me and then asked, "What are you doing here?"

"I'm looking for my license because Lola (who hadn't even tried to go with me to this office) says that she turned it over to the Ministry, and it's not there. She says you have it. Lola has a license now, and there's a law that says there are no licenses for people with new salons, only for those who have had salons for many years. And there are no licenses for people who have another profession;

she already has a profession as a secretary, yet she got a license. They're taking away my profession just for having left the country. I want this investigated."

"We'll check it for you."

"I suggest that you don't waste time looking in another place. Look in Lola's papers. My license will be there."

"How do you know?"

"If it isn't there, do what you want with me."

"Let's see," and they began to look through the papers. The license was there.

"What I don't understand," I said, "is that I don't look like Lola. My name is very different from hers. She's white, and I'm black. I'm brown and she's very white. We're not alike, and we don't look like each other in the photo." The license had to have a photo.

It seems that Lola had been helped by that first man who had treated me so badly there. He'd helped her get a license by using mine. She told them I wasn't going to return to Nicaragua because I was a reactionary. Neither the director of the Ministry nor anyone else knew this. When these papers got there, they had a lot of work in the office—a pile of licenses to arrange—so they checked the papers but didn't notice the photo or the name on the license. So she took in my license, along with other papers that had her name on them. This whole thing took six months for me to solve. I started working on it in December, immediately after I got back from Mexico.

My children talk about leaving. They say they want to go because they miss their father. I talked with Marisa about it, and she thinks I shouldn't leave because I have my work, but she'd like to go, alone, to help him work and to help us. It's just an idea, nothing more. She sees my difficulties; at times the work isn't good, and now that Marta doesn't work, I have to help everyone even more than before. Marta and my mother are my responsibility because I told Marta that she had to leave work to take care of my mother. If I took care of my mother instead of working, we wouldn't eat. We couldn't have lived with what Marta made. With my work, I help more than Marta could have.

Right now I have work, but I don't have any beauty products. There are excursions to Guatemala where you can buy products with U.S. $250 and bring back enough to last for a while. I'm thinking about going myself because those who go charge me three times what they paid. They also don't know what I need. If I go, I can bring back products to last for at least six months. I did bring products back from Mexico, but I had to leave them at customs; I didn't have enough money to get them out because [Nicaraguan customs] charged me 850,000 córdobas [as a tax on the products]. At that time, in December, the dollar in the black market was at 2,000 or 3,000 córdobas, so 850,000 córdobas was a lot of money. The products went up for sale. They have a shop where they sell whatever people can't get out of customs. I came back by plane and thought they wouldn't take things away from me because when I came back from the United States, I entered with fourteen boxes and had no problems. But this time, it wasn't like that. I had only one box and one suitcase, and those two ended up being left at customs. The box was full of paper products. A person in Mexico had given me credit of U.S. $150 to bring back greeting cards. In a large suitcase I had rollers for permanents, shampoo, face cream, cutting scissors, and curlers. I went last week because I was going to borrow the money to get them out. Customs told me the suitcase had already been sold, but the box of cards is still there. I don't know how much they're going to charge me. I think half. But I don't know if they'll value the money at the rate it is now.

Lately we eat just twice a day; the price of food has risen too much. Five pounds of beans was 5 córdobas in 1985; in 1986 it was 300 córdobas and 1,000 on the black market; and now in 1987 on the black market—that's the only place where they're available—they cost 15,000 córdobas, equivalent to U.S. $3.00. There are no beans in stores; people have hoarded them.

I don't know how much I make a month, but there are days I make 20,000 córdobas, days I make 10,000, and others when I make nothing. I have to pay a tax. It's not a percentage; it's a fixed quota. Work or no work. The taxes are collected by Revenue and by the Administrative Board of National Reconstruction.[8] One tax is on income and the other on the rebuilding of the city, so I pay a tax on the house where I live, on the salon where I work, and on my income: it comes to 55,000 a month, equal to U.S. $11.00. A man comes by with receipts and papers to collect it. Marta has to pay, too. I have to help her. Even when she was working, she was behind. She didn't tell me; my mother has to tell me when they need something.

I've had to sell things to help my situation. The fourteen boxes I brought from the United States, for example, weren't all mine. Some were things that other people asked me to bring back.[9] Just a couple were for me. Since I know that the money will always be devalued, I have to invest what I have. I don't like to have money here in Nicaragua. If I can buy something, I do. Then I save what I buy—I don't use it—because I know it will cost more later. I brought back a television, a stove, and a sewing machine that I sold. At times we don't know what to do because each day the situation gets worse, more hopeless. A lot of people have left Nicaragua lately. Quite a few have sold their homes. They're not leaving because they're reactionaries; they leave because they can't endure this situation. They have to survive. It's especially sad after the struggle we went through.

Omar is another problem. Not for me, though. For me, he's like a son. But he's another worry because I know he trusts me. I want to do something for him, but the problem is that he won't leave his job. I imagine he'll put up with living here for who-knows-how-long because he likes his work. But I also know that he and Irene have difficulties. As a result, he suffers and needs help. Sometimes he comes and says, "Leticia, lend me money," and I have to do it. He hides that from my mother and Marta so that my mother doesn't think he's bad or in a bad situation. He can't help my mother in any way. His salary is small. It isn't enough for his family because he, for all practical purposes, has four children; two are his and two are hers. At times I think my mother is right when she says that Irene influences him too much. I have nothing against her, but she does dominate him. My mother doesn't want Irene to come to the house, but she did come on May 30. We were with my mother—it was Mother's Day—and we had a party for her. We had a good time, danced, ate a chicken, and made a soup. Omar was here, but I could see he was worried; I asked him why he didn't go get Irene. I said I'd talk with my mother so that she wouldn't say anything. He went for Irene, and I said, "Look, mama, Irene is going to come. You have to accept that he loves her. You can't take that away from him." Nonetheless, I was afraid that when they came, my mother would say something to her. But Irene greeted my mother, and my mother greeted her and told her to come in. We ate and had a good time. We had some drinks with her and nothing happened. There were no problems, and she left.

But my mother still doesn't get along with Irene. I know my mother is right; she wants Omar to have a better position. After all his struggles in life and in the revolution, he should be in a good economic situation and have a good military rank. But he hasn't succeeded because of Irene. She always makes him miss work; she wants him to be at home. He has been disciplined for that and hasn't managed to get the rank he deserves. Omar was a compañero of Omar Cabezas and other great men who now have good positions, and Omar is nothing. He's improving, though; I think they just gave him a different position. He earns a little more, or so I think, but we don't really know how much he makes. He never says anything. But no matter what he makes, he always has economic problems, always. Just a little while ago I gave him a broken television set. He told me it bothered him that his children went to the neighbor's house to watch television because they were often kicked out. I had a television set at home that was missing a few pieces, and he said he had a friend in the Ministry who could fix it. So he took it, and afterwards I bought another old television set—same kind—and gave it to him to take out the pieces to fix the first one. I don't know what happened, whether he got it fixed or not, but he didn't tell his wife that I gave them to him. Instead, he said he bought it. I really don't understand why he did that. It isn't important to me, but I do wonder why he says and does those things. I don't know why he comes to my house and not to my mother's. I've analyzed myself, and I can't maintain any resentment or rancor toward anyone. Not anyone. Even though Sergio has done the worst thing in the world, I can't do anything to get even with him. Even though some little things have happened between Omar and me, we haven't had many problems.

But it's different between him and Marta. The other day he told her he wasn't ever going to come back to the house because Marta felt proud of living there and having that television set. It seems as if he has a complex about not having anything, but the reason is that he hasn't found how to improve himself. Marta worked for years to have that house and still hasn't paid for it. About three days ago Marta and I were eating, and she cried when she told me what he said to her. She almost never cries because she's very strong. But this time she was crying. He humiliated her.

Now that Omar is earning more, Irene told my mother they were going to help her. They gave her 10,000 córdobas, but then Omar came with a woman friend—after they had given my mother 10,000 córdobas—and told my mother to send out for a half bottle of rum. He knew she didn't have any money; but with the same 10,000 córdobas that he'd given her, he sent out for rum. To me, that's living only for the moment. You enjoy the money at the moment you have it, and tomorrow is another day.

There's no law that says a man who's married no longer has an obligation to his mother, but the custom is that when sons get married, they think their obligation is only to their wives and their children. There are sons who always look after their mothers; however, the majority don't. Sergio, for example, thought his obligation was only to me and the children, not to his mother. I told him it was true that his mother had money and didn't need him, but he still should help her, even if he takes her just a small thing. Maybe it's because the wives of the sons think that the men no longer have an obligation toward the mothers. I know women who get angry and fight with their husbands if they give anything to their mothers.

Marta is a realist; she knows she has to take care of our mother and she can't have a steady job. My mother agrees. She's aware of some of my problems, and told Marta, "I'll miss Leticia, but I want her to go because I know she suffers." I don't ever tell her about my problems because I don't want her to worry, but sometimes when Marta and I talk, we try to hide what we're saying—we're always trying to figure out how to improve things—and my mother will say, "Why are you talking so much and talking alone? Why don't you ever tell me anything?" We say, "We aren't talking about anything in particular, just little problems, nothing serious."

It makes me sad to have to go, but here I don't have the moral support of anyone but my family, no one but Marta, my mother, and Omar. The person I confide in is Marta. I don't know why, but Florencia isn't the same as she was before. Maybe it's because we live farther away from each other, and before we were neighbors. And maybe it's because she has a lot of work, and so do I, and we don't have time to visit each other. When I returned from the United States, I realized exactly who was a friend and who wasn't. I was confident that Florencia would help my children [while I was gone], but no one in my family helped them. The only one who did was my father. And Marta was concerned about them. And Raúl always went to Managua and brought them beans, oil, rice—things they couldn't get there. He was the only person who visited them. So I had a lot of disappointments. That's when I realized that the only person my children have is me. And their father.

I don't know what I'll do when my mother dies. Sometimes I think that the only thing that keeps me here is her. Since my brother died, I've felt so alone. I wish I knew how much time my mother had left. If it's a year, I could go [to the United States] and come back. But if it's less time, it'd be hard for me because I don't know if I'd have enough money to return.

Sergio recently told me, "If you decide to leave, maybe we should go to the United States." He has a sister who lives there, and she told him there was work for him. But going to the United States makes it a question of conscience. I feel bad inside. And it isn't all that easy. I didn't like the life in Miami. I don't know if I didn't see it right, but I noticed the people in Miami were different from those in Los Angeles and the other states I went to. There was more corruption in Miami. Los Angeles was less dangerous. Nevada is a healthy place— even though there's gambling, it didn't seem dangerous—and people worked normally. But I didn't like Miami. The only thing that kept me there was the language and that I easily found work. I think I'll leave Nicaragua for just a little while, and if we—the children and Sergio—are all together, we'll stay longer to help Marta, my mother, and particularly Omar. I especially want him to improve. I know it'd be difficult to return [to Nicaragua]; maybe the children would marry and stay there, but Sergio and I would return when we're old. None of us knows what to do, and things arrange themselves along the way. But returning is what I have in mind. One time out of your country is enough. And when you get older, it's worse. If you save and leave a house [in Nicaragua] to return to, you can come back and live on what you saved—that's how it looks to me now—and when the children are older, maybe they can help us.

The situation confuses most of the people. The majority of us feel, above all, cheated and disappointed by everything that has happened. You see it in your family, in your work, and in the things that happen to you personally; you realize you're alone. More than anything else, that's what has made me feel sad.

I know that my personal problems will go with me, but now the biggest problem is economic. And I have to help my daughters.

Even though I haven't wanted to, I've shared my problems with Marisa. I have to talk about what I feel, and she's the one who's there. She just turned sixteen, and I'm thirty-nine, more or less. Two years ago they still played with dolls. Not now. Their attitude toward me hasn't changed, but Marisa told me that she thinks her father should concern himself with them more and send money to help us. She said to me, "You shouldn't be the only one who has this obligation," and said she's going to send him a letter telling him that. It has been eight months since they've seen Sergio, but they felt more alone during the time I was gone because Sergio spent a lot of time with the [other] woman.

I don't know if he still writes to the woman, but I don't think so. When I was in Mexico, I found some letters she sent him. From the time I arrived in Mexico, I looked everywhere for those letters. Eventually he got careless and forgot about them. He had them in a portfolio. When I saw the envelopes—three or four letters she had sent—I ran out with them. He followed me, but I hid them well. He grabbed me and said, "Don't read them; please don't read them." I said, "I have to." I felt bad about some things she said because she wrote about all the times they had together, but at the same time, it was apparent that he hadn't promised her anything—nothing like bringing her to Mexico or returning for her. It was as if they were *novios*, boyfriend and girlfriend. I still have the letters. And a picture of her. She's pretty and young. About thirty-two. She works for a life insurance company in Managua. It's obvious from the letters that she spent a lot of time with him, and he complains that I don't. But it's different when the woman has [no choice but] to work. This [particular] woman has two children; the father of the children helps her, and she has a house he gave her. She was able to spend weekends and evenings with Sergio, while I have to work on week-ends. Those are big differences. And for him it was something new. A new woman.

I used to go to lots of meetings in the evenings. I still go to some Christian base community meetings, but often I have to work and can't go. We don't have *cursillos* now because the priest, Father Augustín Toranzo, left. He's done working in the parish he belonged to, Ocotal. When the bishop told him he was done, the pueblo of Ocotal rose up and had a strike; they didn't want the priest to leave.[10] The bishop stopped the *cursillos* and won't give us permission to have them. The priest is in the agricultural school near here on the highway, like a refugee. He has no church and isn't having *cursillos* for us. They wanted to send him to the north, to Limay, and to other dangerous places. The bishop has never been in agreement with him because the priest is very revolutionary. The priest is ready to go to the border because he says that's his duty, and he has to go where they send him. But we say he shouldn't because he's always having to do what the bishop tells him. The people here don't want to let him go. They tell him not to accept it.

I haven't been to many AMNLAE meetings, either. When I returned from Mexico, I stayed in Managua and didn't belong to any group; then I came here and moved to a different barrio. I'd like to work again—with my old barrio, not my new one. I saw the person in charge of the regional defense committees. He was happy to see me and asked me why I hadn't reported. I told him I hadn't gotten settled yet, but I wanted to work again. I said I had too much work in the salon and was home only to eat and sleep, plus I had constant headaches. I don't stand watch at night. Not many people do. It's not as organized as before. People are confident and feel there's no need to do it. Nevertheless, we've had many acts of aggression in the city—the contra blew up the towers—but the muchachos in the military service are the ones who stand watch now. I don't think it should be like that, so sometimes, when I'm not tired, I watch until one [in the morning]. When the muchachos come by, I give them coffee. Maybe this barrio is just better organized, or maybe there aren't a lot of people who want to do it.

The man I owed U.S. $1500 was in jail about a month or twenty days. They investigated him and came to the conclusion that they had no proof to keep him there. They couldn't prove a crime because the people had Mexican visas, so they let him go. He was sick, too, with a spinal injury from a machinery accident in Nevada long before he took us across the border. Then he came back and got into the business of transporting people. Since he has been out of jail, he has made two more trips. He has a waiting list. I haven't paid him yet, but I still plan to. I haven't forgotten the debt. I just saw him in his van, but we haven't talked any more about it. However, he did talk with some of my relatives and told them I haven't paid.

Life in Mexico is more peaceful than life in the United States. There's more communication with people, and you can travel more easily to other places, even though it's very large. It was easier to take the bus to work. I noticed that there weren't many Nicaraguans. I think most of them go to the United States. Mexicans are more selfish than North Americans. They don't want Nicaraguans or Salvadorans to have work, but they don't want to do it either. There are a lot of people in Mexico who don't like to work but still want to live well, while Nicaraguans like to work in order to live well. Even in Nevada, the boss said that he preferred Nicaraguans because Mexicans gave him trouble, and he replaced Mexicans with Nicaraguans. There were probably ten people from Estelí working there. In Mexico, people turned Nicaraguans into Immigration, but I didn't see that in the United States. People there live their own lives. They certainly don't think about other people, but neither do they bother them. Not all Mexicans, of course, are selfish. I met noble people who helped me, people with good intentions and good hearts.

It didn't seem fair that, in the United States, some have so much while others have so little. But in a way, it's like that everywhere. It has been a problem in Nicaragua with the revolution. It's hard for us to give up what we have and say to others, "This is yours." [It'd be nice] if everyone were to think the same, but they don't; some think about what they're going to get for themselves and nothing else. It's hard to change that. Most people with money have left, but some resentful ones have stayed. Their land has been taken away to give to the campesinos, and they don't like it. Today or tomorrow, they'll leave Nicaragua.

It's with sadness that I've noticed a change in Nicaraguans. Now I see more envy, more hatred; if you can hurt others, you do it. It's not like it was before. I don't know why. I think it's because people don't know how to solve their problems. Sometimes life embitters and destroys them. They wonder why others have a little more, why others live better, and why they suffer from hunger more than others. It makes people hard. It's true that at the beginning—[when the revolution triumphed]—you didn't see so many difficulties. There were difficulties, but not like now. Inflation has made people tired. They don't have the same euphoria or the same strength as before. They've gotten weak, even though down deep they haven't wanted to. Speaking just for myself, I don't want to have to leave. It's difficult—after you've learned to love your country, after you've inte-

grated yourself deeply, after you've worked with the people and
love them—to have to leave it. I'm at a crossroads; I'm abandoning
my mother and my country. Those are two things that, for me, are
important in life. What's happening to me is happening to others.
Even though they'd like to say, "I'm going to maintain the same
strength, the same courage as before," they can't. They're disappointed, not with the government but with the situation.

Those who understand why we're in this situation and why things
have changed also understand that it's not exactly the government's
fault; it's just what happens in war. And every day it gets worse. I
don't blame people for what they're feeling now. There are those
who criticize the government and say, "They got us into this situation." But it's all the destruction that caused it. At the beginning of
the revolution, the government built cooperatives and health centers, but as many as were built were destroyed and had to be built
over again. So we didn't advance much. In the first years of the
revolution, the guardia (contra) didn't bother the people planting
the crops in the mountains. The people planted, harvested, and we
weren't so hungry as we are now. Now people working in the fields
are terrorized. They don't want to plant. The cooperatives have
been burned. And there's the aggression. No matter who you talk
with, even the most revolutionary person, they express the same
hopelessness, the same desperation as they try to figure out what to
do. Especially the families with many children. What can we as
mothers say when the children plead, "I want to eat; I'm hungry"?
Children don't understand why there's no food.

Our leaders say they have faith that they're going to triumph. I
don't think we can do that without the help of other countries. If we
get help, then we can get to the end. It's painful to see things declin-
ing after such a struggle. For example, the transportation system is
horrible. We can't get parts, things break down, and it's hard to get
mobilized [militarily]. But I admire Daniel [Ortega] and the others
because if I'd been in their situation, I would have left. I know that
what happens to them is what happens to those of us who are mothers. People keep asking them for things, as our children ask us. For
good reason, they're discouraged to see the pueblo needing so
much, and they can't respond to so many necessities. The only way
to save the pueblo from hunger is something [our leaders] aren't

going to do, and that is accept relations with the United States on Reagan's conditions.

On the other hand, people don't know that those [in government] positions do something, directly or indirectly, to deceive them. The big directors, the people government puts in positions because it has confidence in them, don't do what they should do. It's the same thing that happened to Sergio; not even the government in Estelí knows what the [central] government did with him. A little while ago I talked with a person and said, "You're the ones to blame."

It was because he said, "Where's Sergio?"

I said, "He's not here; he's out of the country."

"Ah," he said, "Sergio went because he's unstable."

"You're the first person to tell me that Sergio is unstable."

"But you're no longer with him."

"No, I'm not with him," I said. "We're separated." Then he thought I was going to say something bad about Sergio, but I continued, "He's not unstable. He's well balanced. He's a man you lost because you made him do things he didn't want to do. He never wanted to leave the country. You did to him what you shouldn't have done, what you've done to other people, and that's why you [people] are alone. Besides, you're indirectly the cause of my family being separated, of my children being separated from their father."

"You're separated for another reason."

"It's true he had a woman, but that wasn't the beginning. The beginning was when you transferred him to Managua. For you it was easy to say to him, 'Go to Managua.' You knew that life was more difficult there, and that he had his life in Estelí, so indirectly you're the cause of the family's separation."

"No," he said to me, "you're wrong."

"Maybe you don't agree," I said to him, "but what I said is true. It might not be important any more, but I'm still going to talk with a person in the Government Junta so that they take a little more care with what you do. It hurts me that educated people who intend to help the pueblo have to leave because of you and the repression against them. You demand of others what you don't do yourselves."

He didn't answer me. He just laughed.

"Sergio is a person of value wherever he is," I said, "an honest person. No one could say he stole anything, or he left the business to do other work, or he went around with women, as many do. He was a man who worked until late at night. I'm not defending him just because he's my husband. Ask the Nicaraguan Institute of Statistics and Censuses how many years Sergio worked there.[11] Ten years! Why did they make him director? It wasn't because he was any old person."

I'll never say anything against the revolution, but I'll always tell the truth. I'm not going to lie. They're taking some absurd measures. If people leave due to these problems, and then return, they're looked at with different eyes. Several people have told me that they haven't been well treated. They aren't trusted. The same thing happened to me with my license. Those who work in those positions and [treat people like that] aren't doing the government any good. When people return and ask for work, they give them a job but not a good one. It shouldn't be that way. People are afraid that when they return, they won't be given [positions] like Sergio's as the director of a business. If [the government] were to say, "We're going to get these people back, put them in good positions, give them opportunities, and recognize the errors we've committed," then, yes, many would return. But as it is, if Sergio were to return, he wouldn't find work. If he came back and talked with the people in power at the Ministry of Agrarian Reform, he wouldn't be treated well. It's not that the police would do anything to him, it's that he would be made marginal.

[Another way Sergio wasn't treated fairly was] when he was with PROAGRO: he disclosed the problem we have with lack of housing. Even so, [the government] didn't give him a house. The man who owned our house came every day to make our lives impossible. He asked me for the house, morning, noon, and evening. He always came when I was eating and said, "This is my house," saying I wanted to take it from him. He was a shameless man because he bought the house knowing that it was rented. That year in the house was especially terrible because Sergio was always at work, and I was the one who had to deal with that man. The time came when I had to make a compromise with him because he had become aggressive. With what I had and the help of my brother Raúl, I managed to buy the house across the street from my mother's, but it wasn't habitable. It was nothing more than a piece of land. PROAGRO never said to Sergio, "We're going to help you," even knowing that he was a man who gave and gave to his business. But everything was going wrong: the house, the problem with Sergio, his going to Managua. It was all out of control. That's when I made the decision to go to the United States.

They lost Sergio by not paying attention to him, as they're losing Marta right now. I know she's intelligent and she has helped AMNLAE a lot, but they don't appreciate her. The other day on our way to Managua to get medicine for our mother, we met up with Ana Fulana, a [nationally] important person in AMNLAE and in the government, and a woman, Carmela [who works for AMNLAE in Estelí] and is the one who Marta got out of trouble all the time [at work].[12] Marta did everything in AMNLAE, but Carmela took all the credit. All the while, Marta didn't even have a second outfit to wear, not enough money to buy a pair of pants or a shirt. If I had worked at AMNLAE, they would have kicked me out because I couldn't stand being as quiet as Marta has been, hiding everything and saying, "No, Carmela is busy; she has a lot of work; she hasn't gotten to it yet."

The day we ran into these women, Marta meant to talk with Ana to see if she could get a vacation at the El Velero Resort that's available for all public employees. We wanted to take our mother to spend a week at the ocean. She has never seen the ocean and could rest there. For Marta, a compañera who has been outstanding in her work, it was an opportunity to meet Ana Fulana. Carmela could have said to Ana, "I'd like you to meet Marta, an outstanding compañera who has helped me a lot in AMNLAE." Instead she treated her like any other person. If Carmela had given Marta credit, it would have been easier for Marta to talk with Ana about taking our mother to the ocean. There are mothers who've gone to the ocean with all their expenses paid—mothers whose daughters work with AMNLAE, mothers whose daughters have worked here for just a little while. AMNLAE brought in a new person from Ocotal to be next in charge after the secretary general, a job Marta could easily have done. If she didn't know so much, they wouldn't all run after her the way they do. [But they didn't offer Marta the job.] If they sent her to Hell, she wouldn't say no. She'd be ready. I've always admired her for this, but at the same time, she should be appreciated. I think we have to work, but also the workplace should value us.

I asked Marta if she'd stay with my two middle daughters. I'd take the oldest and the youngest, and Marta would manage the salon. The muchacha who works for me could continue to work, and Marta could take a wage out of what the salon earned. If I stayed or if I left, she could have a wage better than what she had with AMNLAE. It was hard for her to make the decision, but she agreed to do it. When AMNLAE was thinking about sending Marta to a place in the war zone—to Quilalí—my mother pressured her with Miguel. Marta had decided to go, leaving my mother and Miguel here, but my mother told her that if she went, my mother would no longer take care of Miguel: he wouldn't go to school because she wouldn't send him. The people at AMNLAE knew my mother was sick and living alone when they offered Marta the job far away. I was indignant. And then Marta and my mother got sick, and the people at AMNLAE didn't come to see what was wrong. When Marta left work, everyone from AMNLAE came here and said, "Marta, how's this done? How's that done?" She's the only one who knows how to do the mimeographs and the drawings and the *mantas*.[13] When they had her in the office, they didn't appreciate her, but now that they know how much they miss her, they come every day looking for her.

Even though she told me she'd learn to be a hairdresser, she still hasn't started. Instead she takes advantage of every opportunity to leave Estelí. She sneaks away to volunteer with AMNLAE, concealing it from my mother. Marta hides where she's going because my mother would be angry, but she lets me know so that I won't worry. I don't want to leave the salon in the hands of a stranger because I don't want the same thing to happen to the salon as happened when I left before. With this money, Marta could survive. It'd be only Marta, my mother, the two girls, and Miguel, and I could send them money. That is, if I decide to go, and I still haven't decided. But right now is when Marta should be learning. I know she's sick, but she never says it. She's a woman who has no aspirations. She doesn't have the spirit to fix herself up. She doesn't like to put on makeup. She has nothing that looks to me like a reason to live. She lives only because she loves her mother who needs her, as does her child, but she has no desire to improve anything.

I resent how difficult it was for me to work after I returned. I didn't think my leaving was going to cause so many problems or doubts among the people with whom I had worked before. I talked with Angelita Rugama; I had worked with her earlier in my barrio, and she has always had confidence in me, even after I returned from the United States.[14] I asked her for a letter so that I could again apply for my license; she gave it to me because she knows me well, but I know there are those who said I went to the United States because I was a reactionary.

I've had a series of problems because I always have to get involved in what I shouldn't, but as a Christian, I think I have to. And there have been consequences. Nevertheless, I'm prepared for them as a result of talks we have had with Father Toranzo, who has said that being a Christian brings consequences. For example, the other day I had a problem with a woman because I tried to help her, and she told a person who works in the army, a policeman, that I was thinking of leaving the country. Then he interrogated me to see if I was planning to leave. I told him I still wasn't sure, but I didn't think it was a crime to leave the country. I said I thought we were in a free country and I could go where I wanted to. He's the chief of police and a lawyer. He just sat there because I don't think that anyone had answered him like that before. We had this trauma before with the repression of the guardia, and we've always been afraid to tell the truth. But I'm not afraid to tell the truth to anyone. We know we shouldn't be afraid because now there's a law that no one can be mistreated by the army or the police; they can be turned in and severely punished. We have to learn to say what we feel and what we think. It doesn't matter who it is—a nobody or the sultan himself. I understand, thanks to God, that I don't have to harbor this resentment toward the revolution and toward the government.

I've usually been courageous enough, but this year, there have been moments when I couldn't find a solution to my problems. About seven months after Raúl died, the contra killed a brother of his. The contra ambushed him in the morning when he was coming from a cooperative to see his children who had been sick. He was driving a truck—he had given a ride to other people—and they shot him. The bullet entered under his ribs and exited from his back. Then the contra threw a bomb and burned the truck. He was burned up. It was hard for me; I loved him like a brother. We weren't allowed to see him afterwards because he was completely shrunken; it had made him small. When they brought him to the clinic, he was still smoking, as if he were something that had been baked.

One day I thought that the best solution was death. I talked and talked with God. I knew I wouldn't have the courage to take poison, but I thought about shooting myself. It'd be the fastest. But when I began to analyze this—I've never talked with anyone about this, and Sergio knows nothing about it—I realized [that suicide] wasn't a solution; I had to look for another way to solve the problem. I remember a Nicaraguan expression, "Nothing bad lasts forever, nor do we."[15] Either I'd die—it was the date I had to die—or my problems would get resolved. Nothing bad lasts a hundred years, and my problems weren't going to, either.

I went through this around the time that my daughters Marisa and Sofía got sick. Marisa was anemic and had to have an intravenous tube; I was afraid she'd die. At the same time, Sofía got a pain in her stomach and chest; she couldn't breathe. She was in the house in one bed and Marisa in the other with the intravenous tube when I returned from being asked by the police if I planned to leave the country. I felt bad because I had never before had to go to the police for a problem, and when I came home and found them both sick, I felt so weak. I've never been like that before. I had to take Sofía to the hospital, but I didn't know if I had the strength to do it alone.[16] I knelt down by the side of her bed. I felt so alone. It was the same day that Raúl's brother was killed. So many bad things happened at once.

Around this time, a woman showed up at the house. Marisa had a young man who was in love with her. Not exactly a boyfriend, but he had a big crush on her. This woman said she was the wife of this man and had two children. She was yelling a bunch of things. She's not really his wife, but that's what she said. And she does have his two children. I wasn't there when it happened because we were arranging the vigil for Raúl's brother. But later that night, my children told me about it. Marisa decided she wouldn't talk with that young man again. It was then that I really started to think about leaving.

I still don't have enough money to go, so I'm waiting for what Sergio can send me. A friend of Sergio's sister told me that he might have already left Mexico for the United States. There are more possibilities in the United States to get money together, but even so, it's difficult for everyone to go at once. The trip to Mexico costs U.S. $330, and the visa costs U.S. $100. They don't give a visa to everyone; the hundred dollars is a bribe [to someone in the Mexican Embassy], which is one reason I don't like Mexico as a place to live and work. You also have to show money when you enter Mexico as proof that you have it. If you go by land, which costs U.S. $100, you have to show customs U.S. $300 at the Mexican border—not as much as you have to show if you arrive by air. That means that each person has to have that much, which is why I think I'll go first. The majority of people have done it by one going first, then the other, and finally the whole family. Marisa says I should have gone when I was in Mexico with Sergio because they were fine here. They were used to being independent. They went about their normal life.

If I told Sergio I wasn't going to leave, he'd come back. He says that I do exactly what I want to do. If he says we're going to do such-and-such a thing, and I don't like that way of doing it, I do it the way I like. I've proved to him that things usually go better if we do what I want rather than what he wants. He has told me that he does what I want so that he doesn't make me angry. He never makes quick decisions. He thinks for a long time about what he's going to do. I'm not like that. If I'm going to do something, no matter if it comes out well or poorly, I do it quickly.

People always ask me how to solve their problems. Many here want to learn to be hairdressers; I have authorization from the Ministry of Education to give classes, [which I'm doing]. The students have just two months left of their six-month course. They come from eight to twelve every day, and another group comes in the afternoon. I'd like to have a large school because many students want to learn, but there are no beauty products to practice with. There are no good salons here, so people say to me, "Don't leave, Doña Leticia, because we like what you do." If I give a permanent to someone, others come and say, "I like what you did with her and want you to do the same with me." People come from far away. Most of the people who had large and luxurious salons have left, so right now, mine is one of the best. But I don't have beauty products.

Now that the children are older—Marisa is sixteen, Sofía fifteen, Chela thirteen, and Nora is six—I get up late, at seven or eight in the morning. By the time I get up, Marisa is already up and has gotten the girls off to school.[17] I wash my hands and then light the fire, but right now we have no firewood. When there is gas, I go to the heater and make coffee if I can't use firewood or coal. The custom in our family is to have coffee, and I can't start work without it.[18] The children aren't there, I'm alone in the patio, and I sit down and drink my coffee. If there are *rosquillas*, I eat those with the coffee.[19] I'm not hungry for anything heavy in the morning. After that, I bathe, dress, and leave some messages for Marisa telling her what to do in the house and what to make for meals. Sometimes she already knows what she's going to make, so I give her some money and leave, usually around ten o'clock. Marisa prefers to do the chores herself because she wants everything to be done well and gets angry if it isn't. She cleans the house in the morning and makes lunch for the other children at noon.[20] It's unusual for me to come home for lunch. I spend all day in the salon and come home at eight; if I have a permanent or something that takes a long time, it's nine or ten. The problem is that most people have jobs, so there's more work in the salon in the afternoon than in the morning. People finish work at five, and then come by the salon. I usually feel better in the salon than I do at home. Coming home makes me sad. I don't know why. It must be that in the salon I'm talking with people about one thing or another.

Once I go home, if I'm going to eat, I eat. I never watch television, but the children do. I talk with them about what happened during the day. They tell me what homework they have, or if they need money for school, or what time they have to be there, and what's going on. We talk for a while; I lie down to talk with them in bed. About nine or nine-thirty, I go to bed if no one has come by for a visit. At times people come by—women or men friends—there are always a lot of people in the house. Sometimes people come in the morning. At those times, I leave the house a little later. People know that after ten in the morning, I'm at the salon, and before that, I'm at home. I like having people around; I like it when we talk about important things, or when we talk about what we're going to do on Sunday. I usually work then, but occasionally I plan something. I have some neighbor friends about two blocks from here who'll say, "Let's get together in the afternoon so that we can talk and have some drinks." But that's unusual.

It hurt the other day when Sofía said, "I can't go to school because I don't have any shoes." I wanted Sofía to wear my shoes, but her foot is fatter, and she couldn't get them on. I told her I'd sell some shoes Marta gave me. Instead of going to school, she went to see if she could get her shoes—they are rose-colored shoes, and they have a hole in the toe—repaired. It bothers her to have her compañeras see the shoes. Now even the very poor have good shoes. I don't know how that happens, but maybe they have a business. Her friends' fathers have restaurants and stores. I remember going through the same things myself, but it didn't shame me to go barefoot to school because I was used to it. I didn't have shoes until I could buy my own; I got a neighbor to make some sandals for me for seven córdobas. But my children have been used to having shoes since they were born, so it's harder for them to go to school without shoes than it was for me to sell food in the streets.

Sofía burst into tears when I told her how I earned money when I was little, when I told her that I had to sell *elotes* and vegetables in the street to get food and help my mother, that Leonardo had to shine shoes in the park, that my mother had to send Marta, or Pedro, or Omar to the park to ask Leonardo if he had earned enough money that day so we could buy food. I tell them that even when I slept, I dreamed I was selling food. One day a sister of my mother's invited me to a movie. I must have been about seven because I was already selling in the streets. I fell asleep during the movie and dreamed that I was out selling, so I said out loud, "They're going to buy cabbage." When I said it, I woke myself up. The people around heard me, and it bothered me to have said that in my sleep. I wouldn't want my daughters to have such difficulties. I want the best for them, or at least, what's necessary. The problem is that everything is expensive.

I don't understand the politics in Nicaragua right now. They raised salaries fifty percent, but they just finished raising prices two hundred percent, so the salary increase is of no use. People feel they're drowning. Our leaders say that as long as there is the aggression, the economy is going to be this way and get even worse. Ortega is clear; he doesn't deceive anyone. But I don't know how long we can take it. After having thought about what I should do, I think I'm going to leave. What bothers me most is knowing that there's a lot to do here. I'm useful to my barrio, to my people, to my family; they need me. I'm between a rock and a hard place, as we say.[21] It's hard for me to have to leave my country and go to the very country that's doing these things to my town of Estelí, to Nicaragua. So I vacillate. I've spent my life in the revolution. Sometimes I think it was born with me. It has been a conviction of mine for so long that

I can't get rid of it. I can't say, "I'm going to take this out of my head and my heart and become something different." I'm sure that wherever I go, I'll support Nicaragua.

Marta

After we celebrated AMNLAE's ninth anniversary—it's one year older than the revolution—I was mobilized for two weeks to a settlement, an *asentamiento*, outside of Quilalí; the women there demanded that AMNLAE help them because the men didn't want to accept them as members of a cooperative. These remote places are complicated because the counter-revolution often attacks nearby; as a result, the majority of the men are mobilized, and the women have had to assume the responsibilities of the cooperatives to prevent food production from bogging down.

Later I went to an *asentamiento* that was even farther out. The contra surrounded us and tried to mortar the *asentamiento*, but our military also came—the contra and our military numbered about 250 people—for an attack that lasted three days. Afterwards we couldn't leave because the contra set ambushes in the mountains and left mines on the road. These roads are small, not like anything you would see around Estelí. A man with his beans in his ox-drawn cart passed over a mine, and everything blew up. He died, the oxen too, all blown to pieces. But the contra didn't achieve their objective, which was to destroy the *asentamiento*.

During the three days of the attack, we organized a place where the women could take care of the wounded. Some women made food for the men, but there were days when we couldn't send food out to them. We also had to keep the children sheltered from the mortars of the contra, and we talked with the women, explaining that while the men were in defense, the women had to do something with the grain. We always had to be careful so that we wouldn't be captured by the contra. There are probably five hundred to a thousand people in the *asentamiento*, men, women, and children. Most of them are women with children because in the countryside women have six, seven, eight, nineteen, twelve children. There are more children there than anywhere else.

After that I went to another *asentamiento* where there are sixteen women members of the cooperative. Then we were warned the contra was coming; we had to get ready for a night attack. The army sent the contra running, but still we were there five days without being able to leave.

The women in these places understand, in a concrete and real way, that if the men leave and the women don't produce food, there'll be no crop. In the *asentamientos* or in remote places in the countryside, they sell part of the crop in order to buy what they need; the rest they store in their homes. In some *asentamientos* there's a little store where they can buy everything that you could in a town, like soap, rice, even shoes.

People who live in the *asentamientos* are the ones who've been most exposed to the contra; they're displaced by war. They used to live in remote areas in houses separate from each other, and the contra could go from house to house, killing and kidnapping. Our government told them to make their homes closer together. The *asentamientos* don't show up on a regular map of Nicaragua. Their names are Ulises Rodríguez, Quibuto, Escambray, another [La] Estancia, another Santa Cruz. Some are four years old and established. In the beginning it was hard because people were used to having their own small parcel of land, their little house, their animals. When they were brought to the *asentamientos*, they had to leave everything. Some didn't want to come, even if the contra came and threatened them. Moving hurt these people, and it hurt us to take them away, but we didn't want them to be so exposed to the dangers.

Before they had to move, many of them joined the contra, but they don't do it after they get to the *asentamiento*. However, there's always the danger that a family member in the contra will come and convince someone to leave. It helps that those family members in the contra see that the conditions in the *asentamiento* are better [than where they used to live] and that there's something to eat, whereas before, there wasn't. A little while ago, eighty people returned from being with the contra, ready to work and be part of their families again. They joined the contra because they were deceived and returned for the same reason. If you deceive these people, they never

trust you again. The contra says to the young people, "There's communism here in Nicaragua. They're going to put you in the military
service and kill you. We don't kill; they're the ones who kill. And
they're going to take away your land. It's best to go with us because
we're going to win, and we'll give you dollars." Then they show
them dollars, but they don't give them any. "After training and your
first combat, we'll give you dollars." The only ones who have dollars
are the ones in charge, and the people never see the dollars again.
When they want to return, the contra threatens them and their families. They stay out of fear, but when they have the opportunity, they
escape.

I wish the women didn't have to go so far for water; most *asentamientos* have just one well that's used for the crops and for the house.
They have their food for the year; they eat *cuajada*, cream, and grow
avocados and fruits. They have chickens, pigs, eggs. Most *asentamientos* are near a health center and have a nurse, but not much
medicine. There are schools, and most have day-care centers that
allow the mothers to work and not worry that their children are
without food. Some of the children are so intelligent that they ask
for food to take home. At five years old, for example, they come up
and ask for another meal. I ask them, "Aren't you full?"

"Yes," they answer.

"Then who do you want this meal for?"

"For my papa and mama."

I like the people there more than the people of the city. I've worked
in the city, but I prefer to work in the countryside. The people are
sincere, affectionate, and if they love you, they love you. They don't
accept deceit; if they think you've deceived them, they never have
confidence in you again and never want to see you again. City people are different. They lie; they're egoistic, selfish. They don't share
what they have. But not in the countryside. There's love and fresh
air. Even so, if you arrive and say, "Tomorrow I'll bring a book," you
had better be sure to do it. If not, it's lying. And that's it, no more.

In the countryside they see women as housewives. For the campesino, the model woman stays in her house and takes care of the
man and children. The men say to me, "Aren't your husbands dis-
pleased with your coming out here for three days by yourselves?
Not knowing if you are doing something besides work? Maybe going
with another man?" I tell them that just because the women work in

the city, that doesn't mean less attention to the man. It just means that the women do everything. The women in the countryside don't; they take care of the children, the husband; sometimes they go outside, but only with their husbands.

The people in Quilalí asked the regional office to send me to work there permanently. I told them I loved the work, I liked being there, the work was needed, but all this time my mother had been sick. I prevailed and told them I had a letter from a doctor explaining my mother's health, and for that reason, I couldn't accept the offer to stay there. I could visit Quilalí and other places and still do my work, but I couldn't stay there. This was before Christmas, and her health was getting worse. Then I went to Jalapa, near the Honduran border, and they, too, asked me to stay. It really hurt not to be able to do it. It wasn't because I didn't want to. It was my mother's health. So I told them the same thing.

When I was in Jalapa, my mother got worse. I didn't know about it until three days later, when I returned to Estelí. When I got here, she told me she didn't feel good and I shouldn't continue working because she couldn't take it any longer. She had no strength to fight the illness.

I talked with my people [at AMNLAE], but they didn't want to accept my resignation; I did work they couldn't do, like the designing of posters, manuals, invitations, and small cartoons that carry a message. Also I did the drawings and slogans on blankets, took photos, and did interviews and transcriptions. Even though I told them I'd teach someone to do those things, they still didn't want to accept it. They gave me almost a month's vacation to take care of my mother. This was around February or January. When I saw that she was better, I went back to work again. One day she got worse; the neighbors sent for me and for a car in case I needed it, but I called a nurse to give her an injection and take her blood pressure, which at that time was high.

It's been five months now that I haven't worked permanently with AMNLAE; but as I told them I would, I work now and then. When a delegation comes that's interested in going to a cooperative that I know well, they send me to accompany it. When that happens, I do everything possible to leave my mother in the hands of Doña Luisa, a woman who lives near here. She says, "Don't worry; go without worrying." Sometimes she comes to help when I'm making tortillas or washing clothes. She helps me a lot. She worries about how we are.

In April, or maybe March, the three of us—my mother, my son, and I—were sick. My mother was very bad with her same illness. My child went crazy, talking nonsense like a war psychosis. In those days, we were expecting an attack; a plane flew near here, and they shot at it. These things affected him so much that he couldn't sleep. He was sick for two weeks, and I had a fever I couldn't control. We spent the time shut up in the house. We didn't go to the doctor because we were unable to get up. Whenever I felt halfway better, I'd make a bitter coffee or a lime drink, and each one of us drank a little. During the time the three of us were sick, the child saw that my mother was getting worse, so he cried and had a fever. When I got the fever, I shook a lot, and he thought I was going to die.

Miguel's problem was bad. He'd get up in the middle of the night and scream, "They're going to kill us! Let's get out of here! Let's get in a car!" Things that weren't true. He'd run away from me, and I had to grab him hard so that he wouldn't move and give him some alcohol. I cried because it seemed to me that my son was going to go crazy. After several days of this, he got worse late one night, and I ran to a woman across the street. She told me to take him to the doctor; the danger was that he could go permanently crazy. My mother was worried, too, because he said to her, "Don't hit me." She couldn't hit him, and neither could I. He'd say to her, "Hit Marta; hit Marta. See how she's hurting me!" So here we were.

When I recovered a little, I took him to a psychologist. They did a blood test, but he didn't have parasites, as they had thought. Instead, it was stress. The doctor gave me some pills in case he had a parasite that's hard to catch or hard to detect from the exam and for his temperature, to sleep, for his nerves, and for his head. Five kinds of pills. His problem was the tension of war. It's the biggest problem; many people suffer from it.

I had to talk with the director of his school and with his teacher. If children skip school for their own pleasure, the director will talk to the parents and ask why the children aren't there. So I showed them the medicines and the papers the doctor had given me and explained the situation. They said he could come back, but he might have trouble in the classes because he had missed a month and a half. He was afraid to go to school and told me, "I'm going to class, but only if you go with me. The other children are going to make fun of me. I'm not going to know anything." I talked with the teacher and asked her if she could talk with the children; this pressure and fear could make him sick again. I took him to school. When he returned in the afternoon, I said, "How did it go?"

"Fine," he answered.

"Is it true that the children didn't make fun of you?"

"Hugo asked me why I hadn't come. He wanted to play and said, 'Let's play.' So I did, and I was happy."

I was left weakened by the problem of the child, by my own health, and by the problem of my mother. I had such a pain in my head, just horrible. I could hardly sleep. I got frightened with every move my son made. Or I heard my mother complain, and that scared me. My nerves were shattered.

My son recovered, and so did I. The only one who hasn't is my mother.

All of this created problems for us. Not just economically but in every way; it all fits together. When I was working, I could always give Miguel something so that he could buy a popsicle, or there was a popsicle in the house. In this war situation, prices have risen, and I'm without work, so I'm not free to give him a popsicle or anything he asks me for.

But there's always one person, the muchacha called Alejandra, who's a good friend and brings some beans, a little corn, and rice. Sometimes she gives me some of the money she earns that I save to pay for the light and water.

I have to save for whatever medicine I have to buy. The doctor, who has taken care of my mother for two years, now comes to the house to see her because she can no longer leave; he told me, "The only thing I can't promise you is the medicine." When the pharmacy manages to obtain hard-to-get medicine, it corners the market and sells it expensively, sort of like the black market. It's private, and you can get more things there. It's far out, past the hill where Omar lives. Or the doctor might say to me, "Look, I'm going to give you a paper to get the medicine from a doctor in León who controls a pharmacy." But some medicines just aren't available here. The doctor has his separate clinic where he charges the others but doesn't charge me. At first I paid him from what I earned, but when he realized that I was no longer working, he said, "Don't worry; I'm not going to charge you. I know that if you were working, you'd give me what's necessary."

My grandmother, my mother's mother, got sick; I got a ride to Condega to see her. When they came to tell me early in the morning that she had died, I was afraid to tell my mother. I gave her lots of pills before I told her. She lay down, and her body shook. I asked her, "Do you think you can stay with the child while I go to Condega?" She said she could, so I went to tell my sister—it had been several days since she had come by—that our grandmother had died and asked her if she wanted to go to Condega with me. A friend of ours got a car and dropped us off in Condega. Doña Luisa came here with her husband to be with my mother until eleven or twelve at night. We left Condega about nine at night; I saw a vehicle there, went to talk with the muchacha who owned it, and asked if she was returning that night to Estelí. If so, would she give us a ride? She said yes. It would have been better to have stayed and not have moved at night because there have been ambushes, but about ten-thirty, half an hour after I got home, my mother got sick and began to vomit and cough. The cough she had wasn't a common cough; it was like cardiac asthma. I gave her all the pills. We went to bed at two in the morning but had to get up at three because she couldn't stand it. Everything ached. So much vomiting hurt her stomach, and she also had diarrhea. I definitely returned from Condega at a good time.

Starting that day, we began the treatment again. Now she's up more often, with more spirit. Her feet are still swollen, but that's the water in her body.

My mother loves me because she knows all I've done, all I've sacrificed for the two of them. An example is the refrigerator. She really wanted a new one; the old one had a bad motor, and there are no motors in Nicaragua. I sold the old one but only the outside, the box. The woman who bought it had a motor, but wouldn't sell it to me. So I sold her the outside and bought this refrigerator from Leticia for less than I sold the box.

The only thing she misses is not having her children around. She's happy if Leticia or Omar spends the day here. But those things don't happen often. It makes her sad because she feels that they want to get rid of her, that they don't love her. She's happy that—in the good times and the bad—at least I'm here. I've done everything possible to make her happy. I'd like to have the power to cure her, to make her illness only a dream, but the reality is that she's sick. The doctor said to me, "The fact is that we have to be mobilized, and we have to accept that. [We also have to accept that] your mother has a heart lesion. We know she's going to die; we just don't know when." The treatment will give her more time, but it won't cure her. So when I work, I do it all as quickly as possible so that I can return, or I don't finish everything. I ask her, "Do you feel good enough so that I can go do some things?" If she says no, I leave it for another day. Later I ask her, "Do you think . . . ?" She answers, "Yes, go." Then I leave, confident that she feels good and that she'll take her medicine. I put the bags of medicine on the walls; the hour in big letters so that she can see it and know what she should take and at what time. I have them in a row—*pa, pa, pa*—to guide her.

The tension of the war makes her nervous. There are always people coming by and chatting; they tell her someone was killed some place and someone else was burned. And the towers were blown up, and there was no water.[22] Planes come. Everything frightens her. And this year, I'm afraid, too. I'm afraid she's going to die. Her health has declined, and she's sicker. The doctor told me that she'd get sicker every day, and now every time that happens, I think she's going to die.

When you are so exposed to the war, not knowing when the contra will come and thinking you see them, that sort of tension eats at you. Some beer helps. Always, when my brother comes, he says, "Ah, I'm ready for a beer." So we have one or two beers, or a little rum. Then he goes to work again, with less tension. Well, the tension's still there, but it feels different.

I have a foreboding that I'll be more alone this year; if Leticia leaves, I'll really be alone. I can't count on my brother. If Leticia leaves, she wants me to live in her house and work in the salon. I have little, very little, desire to work there. To have a beauty salon, you have to go to Managua to get nail polish and know how to buy those things. You have to stay at the salon all the time. You don't even come home to eat. Perhaps I'll go for short periods of time—come and go. It interests me, but I don't want to be the owner. What I mean is that I like it that other people like to use beauty products, but for me, almost never. I haven't used many of those things, so I haven't paid much attention. I haven't gone out made up with stuff on my hair or on my nails. Not even well dressed. I've never done those things. I've always worked in the countryside—that's what has interested me—and you don't have to be well dressed there. These things make me a little uncomfortable. If I put on a lot of makeup and good clothes, I feel awful.[23] My friends laugh because sometimes when we go to a party, they say, "Let's go. Put on some makeup!" I say, "Oh, no! It makes me too shy." The salon requires this appearance. Leticia has this art because she likes to be well dressed and look presentable. She's used to it, but I'm not. That's how I have been. That's the only thing I don't like about the salon. But if it's necessary, I'll do it. I know I can learn.

I don't like the idea of her going [to the United States], but if she really believes that it will improve the situation, it's good that she go. But I don't like it. I don't like it. I haven't given her an opinion; if she wants to do it, she will. There's nothing more to say. We've talked very little about this; instead, she talks with me about my taking charge of the beauty salon. She also wants us to move from our house to hers. That's not right. As my mother says, "If we go to her house, and she tells us that she's coming back, and this house we have now is occupied, where will we go? No, it's better that she find a way to leave it in the hands of others and that we not move from here."

When you leave one country to take a risk in another, it's difficult. Nothing is rose-colored, even though some might tell you it is. I know you can make money in the United States if you work. If I go to the United States to make dollars, I know I will because I'll work. But to make enough dollars, I'd have to work day and night. I'm not prepared at a high cultural level, but I know I could work taking care of a child or a woman. Or wash floors. You have to work hard, but hard work isn't the problem; for me, it's being far away, alone, thinking of everyone and everything here. And I'm used to my beans; maybe they don't have them there, or they don't cook the same. I wouldn't even have time to cook the beans. Who knows where I'd live.

If she leaves the second and third daughters for me, that would worry me. I would hope that she would send for them as soon as possible. To have two young women is a big responsibility; young people think differently from how their parents think. They might fall in love and have sexual relations, and people would blame me if they didn't get married. When they go to school, I can't go follow along to watch. When they go to parties, I can't go to see what's happening. If they're your own children, you can talk to them. But even so, these things happen. Here in Nicaragua it's not unusual [to get pregnant]. Sergio is very sensitive. He'd protest and say that I'm at fault.

Last year, soon after she came back from the United States, she told me that if she returned, I should send my son. I said no. It's not because I don't like the United States or have anything against the people, but I think it'd be good if he first knew the difficulties of the people here so that he can make the decision later. If he wants to go later, then let him go. He doesn't like to be away from Estelí, maybe due to fear. He'll grow up here and develop and see things, the good and the bad. He alone will discover if he wants to go or not go. If I were to send him now, someday he'd have arguments with Leticia's daughters. And I, still being here, wouldn't know it. I know that would happen because I know her daughters, and I know my son.

If Leticia wants to go, she has to make that decision. She knows perfectly well the state my mother's in. Maybe she'll wait to see if she improves. But still, Leticia isn't very interested. I don't say these things to speak badly of her, but I like to speak the truth and not hide anything. I don't like to say that I'm going to eat chicken today when I'm going to eat beans. I'd be lying. All those days we were sick, she was in Estelí and didn't even realize we were sick. Neither Omar nor Leticia knows whether I take or don't take our mother to the doctor. Nor what medicine she takes.

We've always been alone facing the difficulties. There are days my mother is worried because it seems that we aren't going to eat, but I tell her to have patience; we're going to eat. I always have beans in the house because people give them to me. Sometimes we don't have corn and, as a result, no tortillas. My mother doesn't like beans, but my favorite meal is beans and *cuajada*. The other day friends brought us a pound of *cuajada* and said, "So that your mother has something to eat." And a friend of those people gave me some money that I used to buy butter.

Since a lot of people from Estelí sold everything and left for the United States looking for another way to live, people have the idea that they left because they didn't like the process here. If people see that Leticia's selling everything and that suddenly she's not here, they think that she's leaving because she doesn't like the system. But that's not the truth. Quite a few people, though, have left. What happens is that they don't say directly where they're going. They might say, "I'm going to Costa Rica to see family." And maybe they stay there or come back selling things. Maybe they say they are going to Honduras or Mexico. A lot have gone to Mexico; as a result, not many are able to get visas now. If Leticia leaves and doesn't return, I can only tell people that she didn't leave because she was tired of the situation.

The time when I quit work was difficult because I had worked there for many years. I've hardly ever been in my house, that is to say, doing what I'm doing now, being a homemaker. It was the opposite. There have been moments when I was dejected, when I wanted to go to work, but I didn't let myself. But I've kept up with what is going on at work so that whenever they call me, I have the information I need. I really don't know how the person who doesn't work can live. Work serves to distract you from the problems of your household and helps to connect you with people. You get to know people, their problems, and try to help them.

It still bothers me to ask people for things. I'm just not used to it. The first time, I felt terrible and cried all day. As if it were charity. Alejandra said, "Don't cry; don't be so silly. Why should you cry?"

"I don't like you to be giving me things. I like to work, to earn the money. I don't like people to give it to me."

Alejandra said, "I know that if you didn't have these problems, you'd be working." Other friends said, "Don't worry; these things happen." That helped; it gave courage, moral support. It hurts when people give me something and I haven't done any work for it. We learned very early to work, which is why it's painful to ask for things. My mother taught me to try to keep around the house the food we'll need. She says I shouldn't go about bothering people and borrowing. If I have it, we eat. If not, I don't ask to borrow because it's distressing to walk from house to house seeing if someone has something or not. Maybe you get there and they say, "No, I don't have anything." That's even harder.

If you receive a specific amount of money, you know you'll balance it through the month more or less. If you can't, you have to figure out how to do it. But health problems influence what you have for the month. I used to think that when I made money every month, I wasn't going to have health problems or any others; I'd be able to spend the money. I thought I could buy myself a blouse, but then another problem would come, so I couldn't. The next month, instead of having one problem, I had two. In all the years I've worked for AMNLAE, all I've bought for myself is a pair of pants. I've bought no other clothes, neither has my mother. I did buy some shoes for my mother and Miguel. Social Security and Welfare gave Miguel some new shoes because his father died in the war; Miguel is a war orphan. I had a pair of my pants taken apart and made into pants for him. Certainly I'd like to go out in a good pair of pants, a good blouse, and have my child be well dressed. I'd love it. And that my mother had good shoes and clothes. But right now, daily food is more important. With the clothes I have, I can get through this year and maybe even the next; but I can't tell my stomach, nor can Miguel, "Today you're not going to eat; tomorrow you can." If I bought five eggs yesterday for 500 córdobas, today I can get only two eggs for the same amount. With what I used to spend on five soda pops, today I can buy one. This sort of pressure makes things worse.

But I've survived. We've survived. We did it, even though it always caused me sorrow.[24] At the beginning, I was desperate and began selling my clothes and some things that had been given to my mother. People came and suggested that they buy things, like the television set. I had sacrificed so much for it. My mother likes to watch it; so does my son. She especially likes the stories and the news, and he likes the puppets and movies. I also wanted to keep it because Miguel had been kicked out of other homes for going there to watch television. You have to reflect on these things so you don't go too far. Several people came for the refrigerator, too. I was at the point of selling my watch, but I got the strength not to because it had been hard for me to get it in the first place and then learn to tell time.

I asked for a letter from work for Social Security and Welfare where they give food to people with limited resources.[25] If there's rice, they give you a little, or some beans. Five pounds of rice, five pounds of beans, powdered milk, and at times there's canned meat. They give you what there is. AMNLAE gave me the letter this month that has the approval of the director of Social Security. The day I went, I wanted the earth to swallow me up. I was ashamed. I was perspiring. I handed the man the letter that was proof of the work I had performed. He said to me, "I already know about you; the one in charge talked with me, so there's no problem. However we can help you, we will." But that day they had nothing, only powdered milk, so he told me to return another day.

In addition, my mother gets a monthly pension from the same Social Security, but through Managua. They give her 13,000 córdobas a month for the death of my brother. Since she's been sick, she can't go to the bank, and they won't give it to anyone else, so Social Security wrote a letter that my mother signed, and I gave it to the bank manager to get the money. This all helps me, but 13,000 córdobas are worth little [only a little more than U.S. $2.00] now.

If I have food for the whole day, I think about what I'm going to do the next day. Before the day ends, I look for a solution. For example, some friends of mine have ways of getting grains. Mostly I need corn and beans. I go and say, "Sell me . . ." because I know we're friends. He doesn't sell it to me. He just says, "Take these ten pounds and these five pounds."

Recently I had no corn, and I went to this man on the corner who has a little farm. I said, "I need five pounds of corn." I didn't have any money, but I still asked—this whole thing really pains me— "How much do they cost?"

He said, "Nothing, take these," and gave me enough for a week. We eat very little, so a pound lasts us four or five days.

I feel terrible when I know that I can go to someone, ask if they have some beans, and they'll give them to me, but they won't give them to a person they don't know. There are people more desperate than I. Doña Mila gave me some potatoes and came to see how we were. And Doña Luisa always comes and helps. She sent me over some little tortillas. Another woman said, "Take this milk for your mother. Heat it up; it will make her better." I prefer to have friends like these. When I had things or had been given things from people from other countries that I didn't need, I gave them to these people. If I had a blouse that was too small, I gave it to Doña Luisa for her daughter. Once someone sent me two pairs of shoes, one pair too big for Miguel and the other too small. I knew Doña Luisa's daughter was barefoot, so I gave them to her. If Doña Luisa asks my mother, "Sell me a bundle of firewood," and we have enough, my mother says, "Take it." Or "Sell me an egg." "Take it." You don't sell anything to anyone. When there's something and it can be used, it's used. What we really do is sow a seed in order to have a good crop. If my mother had taught us that we could eat without sharing with anyone, we would have worse difficulties. No one would take care of us or do us any favors.

There are times I feel alone, but someone comes by to chat. Doña Luisa's husband stops by and says, "Ah, Negra . . ." because that's the name he calls me.[26] "Look, Negra, don't grieve. Your mother will get better; you'll see." Talking with someone helps.

One day, I had nothing, nothing, nothing to eat, nothing. So I went about nine in the morning to Alejandra, and I said, "I have no beans; I have nothing."

"Let's go to my house," she said; "I'll give you some beans I have. I have four pounds of corn that I'll divide, two pounds for each of us." I got home about ten-thirty or eleven and quickly began to cook the beans so that we'd soon have something to eat. They weren't ready until about one, but there they were, beans, and I was happy.

I just saw David. When I knew I was going to go to Ocotal, I called him. I've been seeing him these past two months when I volunteered with AMNLAE. If we're near where he is, I let him know, and he comes by. We go along as we always have. I still haven't told him that I quit work. I don't want him to worry. He has enough responsibility in his job.

He came here to the house one day, as a friend, so my mother knows him but really knows nothing. I said, "I want you to meet a friend. He has been a good friend for I don't know how long, but he lives somewhere else." He came because he telephoned my work, and they told him that my mother was sick. He asked me why I hadn't called, and I told him it looked like my mother was improving and I was going to tell him later. My friend Alejandra in the AMNLAE office keeps me informed. She's my courier. If he calls the office and says he's coming, she tells me to tell AMNLAE that I'm coming in to do some work. I show up and do my work seriously, but I get to see him, too. It's fun, and it's happy. It's exciting, more exciting than if I were seeing him daily—I've seen him only five or six times in the last year—and I just want to keep things the way they are with him. That's my goal.

When I saw David in Ocotal, I had gone to work at a maternity house where they give lodging to pregnant women, not just from that area, but from other communities, too. Since people are building this themselves, we went to help them by bringing sand and stone. It's an important project because there are mothers who arrive at the hospital but who have their babies the next day or the following one. Or at midnight the doctor examines the woman; because there are so few hospital beds, he says, "You're going to have to return tomorrow." Or they tell them to return later that night, and the woman doesn't live in that area and has no place to stay. A delegation from Sweden sent a donation for this. I went to Managua to receive it because when the Swedes came, I had to interview them and take some photos to send back to their solidarity committee. The maternity house is almost built, but we still need beds and a volunteer nurse to take care of the women. Next to the maternity house is a day-care center; we thought women would come with their small children; they can play there while their mother is having another. These aren't women of the city who can go to the hospital at midnight or whatever hour the pain starts; these women have to walk part of the way or come in a car. We, men and women, see this as important and have formed brigades to build it. Others have lent trucks to haul sand, and our government has helped with part of the money. I tell my mother that I do it because then I can ask AMNLAE for help. But really, I do it because I like the work, and it gives me the opportunity to see David. We talked with another friend, and she said she goes there every month. She's going to try to have me go with her. I'd work there, but also that would give me two days every month to see him.

I know I said that if one of us had someone else, we'd tell each other and finish this relationship as friends. Right now I think he has another woman, but he says he doesn't. I don't believe him. I mentioned it to him and he said, "Don't pay attention; they're lies." I laughed. I understand him. He really can't be without a woman all the time, but he's afraid to tell me.

So I said, "Tell me, what does she look like?"

He said, "Who? I don't have anyone."

"Her name is . . . ," and I invented names. And more names.

Then, "No, I don't even know them."

"They tell me that she works . . ." And I invented names again.

I'm sure about this. I have a friend who didn't know about my relationship with him, so I went to her and said, "And David, how's it going with the woman he has?"

"Fine, but he doesn't live with her; they just see each other weekly or every three days."

"Oh yes, he told me that," I said to her. "He told me that they had been fighting, but that things were better."

"Yes, it seems it was nothing serious."

The woman I talked with is a friend of mine; I helped her solve a problem with the help of a lawyer from AMNLAE. She's thankful, loves me a lot, but when she found out about David, she said, "And I [was the one who] told you!"

I felt bad when I found out, really sad. But I remembered that we had an agreement. But he says no, no. He's afraid, I think, that if I know, everything will end. But I said to him, "Look, I understand you." Suppose that I can't be with him for three months; I understand that he needs another woman.

He said, "No!"

I said, "If that's true, if you have no one else, why don't you take me to dance? Why don't you take me out to eat?" He asked me if I wanted to go. I said yes, so we went.

I think the other woman knows that he has a commitment but doesn't know my name. She knows nothing about me, but she knows I'm there. She's a brown-skinned muchacha and sort of pretty. She lives farther out from where David lives, in a remote place. I met her through the friend who told me about her. I went to this place, walked around with her, and got to know her. We talked about work. (She didn't know who I was.) I went out of curiosity. I momentarily felt jealous, but afterwards, I didn't. He doesn't see her constantly; certainly I wouldn't agree if it were a permanent relationship. Each of us has a cultural backwardness, and inside it isn't easy to get rid of this backwardness. It isn't easy to learn to share, for example.

It bothered me the day [I found out about her], but I began to think that it would have been worse if I had another man. He wouldn't be taking this the way I am. He wouldn't accept that I had someone else. That's why I don't think about anyone else. And also, I love him. To have one here and another there isn't correct for me. It wouldn't seem right. And if there were complaints, arguments, well, I can't stand those things. If I've done something to be criticized for, that's one thing, but to have it caused by jealousy, I wouldn't be able to take it.

Very few people have ever seen me cry. My mother and, at times, my friends at work. But very few people. Generally I put up with things so that people don't know my problems. It seems to me that if I cry in front of someone, I'm showing that I can't solve my problems. It's a display of weakness. If I cry and don't do anything, the problem remains; if you find a solution and don't cry, it's more effective. If the problem has a solution, it will solve itself; if it has no solution, even though you cry and cry, it won't solve it.

I've seen David cry.

What I do, instead of crying, is get sick.

If he knew I had quit, it'd cause a problem in that he'd be here more often instead of my being there. It's as if we are playing chess. It's also that I don't want him to worry. And I don't want my mother to know about him. I can only imagine what would happen if she knew, and it scares me. If she knew, she'd say, "Aren't you going to work? Aha!" Every day there would be scoldings. It's better to avoid it.

When I hear the song on the radio, the one where the first line is, "I'm afraid, I'm afraid, afraid of losing you, my love," I feel—I don't know, exactly—but I feel frightened. When I'm alone I cry. The song is true. I'm afraid of losing David. I'm just getting myself used to the idea of not seeing him anymore, and it hits me like fear. It takes two or three days to get to where he is, and I'm not confident that if I leave AMNLAE, I'll continue seeing him.

I like David's humility, his simplicity, his humble way of being. For me, "humble" means a person who talks in a simple way, someone who's hard-working and has had to work hard to be what he is. By that I mean that if I have a responsible job, it's because I've worked hard and have earned it. And I don't brag about it. I don't like that person who says, "*I* can . . ." I don't like that in a man. I like a man to tell me things about his life, if he's a hard worker, if his parents sacrificed for him to survive. But mostly I like sexual relations with him. He's a tolerant man who understands me, who isn't jealous; he knows my work is important and doesn't think I'll go with someone else. He has confidence in a woman, and I like that.

I dislike men who got where they are by luck or by *amiguismo* instead of working hard for it.[27] And I don't like it if, in their job, they don't behave toward people the way they should. If I hadn't been a woman who worked hard, a woman with difficulties and misery, I wouldn't understand women. If I grew up somewhere else, it might not be important to me that women suffered, that they advanced or not. And I don't like a man to be like that. David isn't that way. I like everything about him. Everything. The other things happened with other men: jealousy, no confidence, thinking I wasn't with them because I was with someone else.[28] I don't like that. Jealousy is not a symbol of love. It doesn't consolidate a relationship but pulls it apart.

There's a man who says he has been waiting three years for me. I met him about five years ago through another friend. He came to the house and to work, asking me questions, but I didn't think he was interested. Later he told me he wanted to marry me. I told him no; the fact is that I don't intend to get married. So he said, "Let's not get married, then; come live with me."

I said, "Not that either. Look, give me time to think about it. I'll let you know. But for the moment, no."

He asked me if I had another man, and I said I did. He asked me if my mother knew. I said no. Then he said that he didn't believe it because I lived in my house, and this was proof that I had no one else. He told me I was astute, intelligent, and said, "I'll wait for you." I told him that we were just friends, but he said he wouldn't give up, and he'd fight. He started visiting my mother. He got her affection; he tried to get along well with her so that she'd help him by convincing me. He told her he loved me, but I didn't love him. My mother asked me why I didn't accept. I told her I didn't love him, but she thinks I'd have a better future with him [than I would alone], and after her death, I'd be protected. What would happen to me is what happened to her. Not exactly what happened to her because she was forced to get married; her parents made her marry a man she didn't love. She's not making me do it; she just tells me to accept. I tell her, "It's not that I don't want to be married, just not now." I don't want to annoy him or upset her. I don't want to have trouble with anyone, only friendships. I don't want anyone to be hurt or unhappy.

One of the men who came by yesterday likes me, even though I just met him. If I thought I'd like to make love with him, I wouldn't say it. But if that man knows that I want to, then he can tell me, and maybe I'll accept. But, in general, if we women in Nicaragua like someone, we never tell the man. It has always been the man who says it to the woman. No doubt, it's a little *machista*. There are times when you want to make love with someone, so you look for someone who'll tell the other person. It facilitates the situation. And you don't have to say anything directly to him. I did it once. [Laughter]

Men make the mistake of thinking that women want to have something to do with them if women dance and laugh with them. We all like to have fun when we're with thousands of men, which is how it is when we're mobilized. There are men who like you without any other interest, but there are others who think that if you smile, it's because you want them. You have to clear these things up. When it begins, they say to you, "When are we going to go out?" At that moment, you say, "Look, the fact that I've danced with you does not mean I'm interested in you." That way you avoid misunderstandings that can take place. Let's suppose that there's a man who's falling in love with me at a party, but all I want to do is dance, nothing more. If I laugh or dance with him, he thinks I want to be with him. Other people look at me—not everyone, but one or two—and think that, yes, it could be. When I see that, it hurts so I clear it up and tell him and the other people. Directly. I tell them that I have a man I love. I explain, "So far, it hasn't occurred to me to have another man, but when it does, I'll look you up." We end up friends, everything peaceful.

I don't know why it happens that when I have friendships with women, most of them tell me their problems, even the sexual relations they have with their husbands. Sometimes I don't even want to know, but they tell me anyhow. It distresses me when they do because I can't tell anyone else. But I'm not going to tell them mine; that would bother me. I ask them why they tell me, and they say, "Because I trust you." Or, "You help me see reality." Or, "You help me see if I'm making a mistake."

The majority of the men in Nicaragua have what we call a *querida*, another woman. I ask the man, "Why you do have another woman?"

He says, "Because I feel good with the other one. With the one in the house, I feel good, too, but I respect her."

Then I ask, "But why do you do it with that woman, the *querida*, and not with her? If you think about it and talk with your wife . . ."

But he says no and backs down. These are men in whom I have confidence, and I talk well with them about it. They say they'd be afraid. But afraid of what? Of whom? That's why he has another woman. The one in the house he sees with more respect. The man and wife don't talk together about their intimate life. For me it's fundamental to have the confidence to say, "How do you feel? How do you like this way?"

I've never thought of getting married. When you're married, there's no longer any excitement in seeing each other. It seems to me now—I didn't have these ideas before—that if you have a husband in the house, you have to say, "I'm going to the movies." And he says, "No, don't go," because he wants you to stay at home. Or he likes to go to the movies, and you don't. Things like that. My mother has understood my work and that I have to go, so it'd be difficult for me to begin living such a rigid life. It's boring to be stuck together like that. It frightens me. I see it as hard, difficult.

If I ever did get married, either in the church or by the state, it'd be a big commitment. The church ceremony is done for society so that people know you're married, and there are no divorces. It's a commitment that ties you down. The priest says that [even though] bodies or people separate, this separation doesn't exist before God. But for me, the civil ceremony is worth more. After a civil ceremony, you can get a divorce by mutual agreement, without giving explanations to people. In Nicaragua, the cultural conceptions are a little backwards: a woman shouldn't get a divorce, should tolerate whatever the man wants to do, all those things. But I don't think anyone should put up with whatever a man wants to do. I prefer that people settle things by mutual agreement; if they don't understand each other and the situation is difficult, they separate, get a divorce.

Women as well as men can have lovers, but generally, the man does that more than the woman does. It's because men have the idea that they can have many women and that the woman shouldn't have other men, none. Only if the couple is separated can a woman have another man. So in general, here in Nicaragua, you don't find many married women who have lovers. Married women have told me that when they had lovers, they felt bad. To tell their husbands, or not tell them? There was this nervous tension, and it seemed he was going to find out, and then they'd lose their marriage. However, the other woman, the *querida*, is usually a single woman, not a married woman. It's not that the woman accepts [the man having another woman], but there's nothing else to do; you separate or stay in the situation. Sometimes the woman stays because they love each other, or

she still loves him. Or it might not be a long-lasting thing; he doesn't
see the *querida* daily. It isn't as if the wife is seeing the other woman
with her own eyes; in some ways, it doesn't bother her. When a man
wants to conquer a woman, he says, "I live with so-and-so because I
haven't found another, but I don't want to stay with her. With you
it's going to be different." These things. A man has his way of convincing the woman.

Things have changed. Women used to feel that they couldn't talk
at a meeting or even go to one. The man always talked in the name
of everyone, and she sat there quietly. We explained to the men that
women had the right to speak and the right, not just to discuss, but
to demand things. For example, there are women who lost their jobs
in the business district because they were pregnant. When we saw
this, we began to talk with the women and men, saying, "She has a
right to a pre- and post-natal leave"—forty days before and forty
days afterwards—and not be kicked out of a job. Instead, she'll receive pay but be at home. So the women started waking up, talking,
and demanding. Another example is that women used to think that
they were incapable of driving a tractor, but they had never tried;
they didn't even want to learn because their husbands would get
jealous. So we started with a single woman, not a married one.
Afterwards we asked, "Can a woman drive a tractor?" They couldn't
say no because they could see the muchacha driving the tractor.
Eventually there were twenty women here driving tractors and fifteen somewhere else. We explained it to the men: "We want to learn
to do these things because if you have to defend the country in this
war, the land will still need to be worked." For example, the contra
tried to destroy the town of Jalapa. All the men, along with some
women who had the courage to be armed, had to defend the town.
The women who had a lot of children preferred to stay and do the
work that the men usually did. It went on for months like that. We
see that as a clear example that women can do those things.

At the beginning there were lots of separations. The woman had
to be very determined to advance. Sometimes she'd back down,
preferring to stay with her husband, but then she saw other women
learning things they hadn't done before. There were seminars and
talks that woke her up. Sometimes the man was afraid and jealous
that the woman would learn more than he. For that reason, we did
things equally; the preparation we gave to the woman, we also gave
to the man so that they could advance together. Nonetheless, there

were separations. Married by the church or by the state, they separated.

Now I'm a homemaker. I don't really like it. I get up at five-thirty
in the morning, start the fire, make coffee, and get Miguel's clothes
ready. When there's bread, I buy it. If the chicken lays an egg, I
prepare it for Miguel. He eats it and goes to school at 6:40. If there's
corn for tortillas, I wash it before I go to the mill to grind it. I return
and get the fire going well. Before I make the tortillas, I boil the
beans, if there are beans to boil. When they are done, I put the
comal, an earthenware dish used to prepare and then bake the tortillas, on the fire. Then I wash clothes. There aren't many, but they're
very dirty. I eat at eleven or ten-thirty. If there's rice, I make a little to
eat with the beans. Then I clean the house, sweep and mop the floor.
I might buy a *chiltomá*. Miguel comes home at twelve-thirty to eat. If
I have time, sometimes I lie down for a while.

Throughout all this, I make sure that my mother takes her medicine and has an *atol*[29] or a little milk or a raw egg. It gives her
strength and also helps her stomach after all those pills. If there are
limes, I make a lime drink for her, or give her just a little bit of lime
when everything else repulses her. At four in the afternoon, I begin
again in the kitchen. If there are things to wash, I wash. I light the
fire again, fry some beans, and heat the tortillas. If there are only
beans, we eat them with the tortillas; if the chicken in the house lays
an egg, we eat it. My mother barely eats anything because she isn't
hungry. All she has is milk or *atol*. That's about five o'clock. I'm not
busy at six so I say to her, "Let's sit down for a little bit." We sit until
about six-thirty. If we don't start to chat and tell jokes, we sit and
watch stories on television and then the news. If there's a movie that
Miguel wants to watch, I sit with him, and she goes to bed. At nine-
thirty or ten, we turn off the television and go to bed. If I have to go
somewhere with the compañeras of AMNLAE, I have to get up at
four in the morning, and sometimes I leave the coffee already made,
beans prepared, and powdered milk mixed up for her to have during the day. Some days she's happy and gets up before I do. "Get
up," she says to me, and I get up quickly, lightly. While I wash
clothes, she makes the tortillas. Then we decide what each one of us
will do. But there are other days when she doesn't get up. Doña
Luisa says my mother is like the flower that wakes up happy in the
morning but wilts by the afternoon.

There are people who understand why we're in the situation, but at the same time, there are people who think that this is something our government is doing in order to subject us to other things. Things are difficult, for some more than others. We're having terrible troubles, but in fact, it's not the fault of the government. The government doesn't want the people to have trouble; they'd prefer that we have an abundance of food. The crisis is a matter of grains: corn, beans, rice. We produce it, but in some places, principally in Quilalí and San Juan, the counter-revolutionaries burn the place where all the grains are collected. If one cooperative produces basic grains, but another is attacked by the contra, the first cooperative has to give grains to the other one so that they can eat. And they have to keep some to sell. So what we think is going to produce, doesn't produce.

We produce coffee here to export and obtain dollars; with that money, we buy medicines and things we don't produce. What happens is that other countries buy our products cheaply. If they pay a good price for coffee somewhere else, they come to Nicaragua and say, "I'll buy it but at a [lower] price." So we have to sell it cheaply and lose. With this small amount of dollars we can't buy enough medicine and tools.

There are Nicaraguans who buy things cheaply and sell them for a lot of money. People from Managua and especially from here in Region One buy corn, beans, and rice in large amounts at twice what the government pays. They return to Managua and sell at an even higher price. There's free trade. People can sell to whomever they want. In Managua right now, a pound of beans is worth 2000 córdobas on the black market. Here in Estelí, you can buy them for 150 or 200 córdobas a pound. When that happens, the government has to say that nothing leaves this area so that we're not left without food. Free trade is stopped; the people who were selling at a high price in Managua have to bring it back to sell at a lower price. People who live by this business say, "[The government] doesn't let us work." Of course not. Those people are exploiting other people. How can you begin to think of 2000 córdobas for a pound of beans!

Many feel disappointed because they believed that with the triumph, things were going to be better. Or at least there would be no war. And without war, there wouldn't be so many difficulties. My mother, for example, never thought the war would continue and

people would still die. As the economy gets worse, people are disappointed even in our leaders. These people haven't understood
the situation. A leader isn't to blame for what the counter-revolution
is doing to us; instead, a leader explains these things to us. I know
that a lot of people—even some who still have enough to eat—are
disappointed. Out where there are more problems, they feel even
more disappointed. People say, "I fought so hard, but not for this."
We agree, but we hadn't had a war like this before nor a counter-
revolution. We're sorry about it, but I have confidence that the situation is going to change. While it changes, I know there'll be hard
days. Some people will give up, others will resist, and others who
are able to leave will go.

But I, for example, how could I say that I'll leave? With what? Or
how will other poor people, with more problems than I have, be
able to go? Where would they go? And how? That requires money
and knowledge of other things. People can do that if they have
family outside the country who can send for them. Even if I felt
hopeless, what could I do? What would I do, without money or
training, in another country? Be pitied? Other countries expect you
to have training or an education. Here people know me, and I can
go anywhere I want to work. If I went alone and left my family here,
I'd eat, but would my family? So, no. We'll stay here and try to solve
the problem. But to go somewhere else, I think not.

I can't even imagine what will happen to the people who feel so
hopeless. I hope this year the crops are good and there'll be enough
food. If people have food, they're happy. That's the way it is everywhere. But without food, it's difficult. Shoes wait because you can
walk barefoot. Clothes wait. The stomach doesn't. There have been
moments after I quit work that I lost faith. There were days when I
didn't leave, when I felt that hopelessness, and I couldn't get enough
air. And there were nights when I thought that my problems were
suffocating me, days when I'd say to myself, "The child is going to
ask me for food," and I didn't know what I'd do. In those moments,
I lost hope.

Going to the cooperatives refreshed me. If I walk around and see
how the crop is, it gives me courage. I say to myself, "There will be
[food]!" Those moments are so wonderful, so good. It's marvelous
to see the corn, the beans. They are beautiful.

We have hope in our brothers and sisters in North America who have seen what's happening. I know there are people there who think it's our government's fault that we're in this situation, but that's because they don't understand that the contra is doing these things. Let them come and visit, talk with the people, see the burned trucks, the burned cooperatives, and the children who are missing an arm, mutilated by war. They'd understand that when the homes of the campesinos are destroyed, the government, instead of building houses for people in the city, needs to build them for the campesino who produces food. I have confidence in the North American people because I know they've come often. I hope that their objective is to understand the situation and pressure Congress not to give support to the contra. If the contra forces didn't have the guns that were given them, they'd have disappeared years ago. It frightens them to confront our army; that's why they burn cooperatives, blow up towers, set ambushes.

The future of Nicaragua depends on whether or not the government of the United States gives help to the counter-revolution. If they don't help, the cooperatives will produce more and there'll be fewer deaths. The hospitals won't have as many wounded people and will be kept up better. More attention will be given to the people in the countryside; there'll be more housing. If we produce enough, everyone will have food. Costs will go down. But if the war continues, each day we'll have more problems because the economy will worsen. More people will leave. We'll have fewer professionals and more limitations.

The hardest thing this year for me was making the decision to leave work. I thought I'd die of hunger, not just me, but my whole family. But I also knew my friends would help me. When I made the decision to quit, I talked with my mother's doctor; he told me that leaving work was the best thing I could do because what bothered her the most was when I went to the war zone. She knew I was out there, but I could never tell her exactly where I was. I always lied to her. If I was going to be a week in a place, I told her, "I'm only in La Trinidad." Maybe I was far away, having problems with the contra, but she didn't know. I was in San Juan, Jícaro, Jalapa, Ocotal, Somoto, Limay, Condega, the whole region, but on different days or different weeks, and always in the war zone on unpaved roads and in the mountains, places where the counter-revolutionaries hide and ambush people. We know that when we go to the war zone, no one knows if we'll return. It hurts to leave, and I always think, "Will I return, or won't I?" I tell Maricruz and Alejandra, "If something happens to me, I don't want my mother to be hungry. Take care of them. If she dies, ask my son who he wants to go with." It helps to go knowing that.

I know I have David, but I don't have him for sure, as if you have something in your hand that's yours. Everything in life comes to an end. I do know, though, that I could call him any time, and he'd talk with me. I know he'd come, too, if he had the time. If he couldn't, he'd say, "Today I can't, but I can on such-and-such a day." Certainly, seeing him after not seeing him for a month or two weeks is happiness. He makes me forget, momentarily, the problems of the household.

I used to insist that Omar get a vehicle to take our mother to the ocean. She has never seen it, and I want to take her there before she dies. They give people in the military the opportunity to go with their families without it costing a cent. If he'd just talk with the people who give the orders, I know he could get it. I talked with Omar, and he says he'll talk with them. I always repeat it, but we're still here. I intend to go to Managua to talk with someone—I don't know who—so that they can get it for me. I think they'll tell me, yes, we can go one way, but there would have to be a vehicle to bring her back after five days at the ocean. AMNLAE told me they'd help, but they have only two vehicles; one's busy most of the time, and the other doesn't run well; it's been in the shop for eight months and can't be fixed because there are no parts. I know how to drive, but I don't have a license; they were going to give me a car with a driver who'd let us off and return to pick us up, but the vehicle broke down. If I could just get a car to leave on a Sunday at 4:00 in the morning and return in the afternoon, it'd be enough because she'd have seen the ocean. And I'd be satisfied because I'd succeeded in getting her there.

I don't know if we're a united family. It's not that we're disunited, but at times some forget their responsibility and leave. When they remember, they return. If I asked them to come, they would. But they shouldn't be detached; they should be involved. The unity exists, but it comes and goes. There are times when they come, and we joke, sing, and all sleep together. My mother is happy at that moment. She loves to see us talking and laughing together. But when they stay away, she cries because she says that they've forgotten her.

I still think I'll die first. I don't know where I get that idea. Really, it's not a divinely-inspired thought. It just seems so to me, even though I wouldn't like it.

Omar

We've had numerous and serious family problems this year with my mother's sickness and the death of my sister. All this has affected the family. And all Nicaraguans have had money problems. The government has to take certain measures because of the war, and we Nicaraguans have to endure it. At no time do we blame the government; the blame belongs to those who are financing the war against Nicaragua. We all suffer together: the president, the National Directorate, the government, all of us.[30] The government looks for ways to resolve this economic situation; they travel, asking for support for the Nicaraguan people. Some people say it's the government's fault that sometimes we can't find food, but it isn't the government; it's the war imposed upon us by the United States. Most of the campesinos have had to leave their land because the counter-revolution has attacked their cooperatives. People have had to stop producing food in order to defend themselves. And while they're defending themselves, their homes are burned and their grains are stolen. This affects all the pueblo. Then those of us in the military have to leave our families to go to the war front and fight. When we come back, we find that there's no oil, no rice. That's how the year has gone.

This matter will end; we'll finish this war. I look forward to my children going to school without fear of the war, to my wife being in our house and taking care of the children, to my not leaving for the mountain where I could die and leave my children as orphans.

The children are always sick, even though we have medicine. Sometimes there isn't enough medicine, though, or it isn't good—I don't know, but it doesn't help. The doctors say that Isabel's asthma will disappear as she gets older, but she has had it for six years. Winter bothers them most; in the summer they're better.[31]

Things are better with Irene. We haven't been separated this year, but she's sick, too. Her blood pressure rises, and she feels like she's drowning, so she isn't working. When she does work, that helps. Her work is hard. She has to leave for work early in the morning and leave the children alone. That's when they get sick because they don't take care of themselves, so Irene has to leave work to take care of them. Sometimes they don't go to school when they're alone. If she leaves food already made, they eat it before lunch time. There's no control, and you can't have that. But when Irene doesn't work, I have to buy everything—shoes, dresses—and ends don't meet. The government doesn't have enough money to pay more. When I stay home from work, that makes the economic situation even worse.

It doesn't matter whether one makes more money or not because the government—or the economy—evens it all out [so that you never get ahead]. If you make more money, things cost more. [No matter what happens], it's not enough for the month. I have to borrow from the next month's pay. If I buy shoes for one child, I can't buy them for the other. If I buy a dress for one, I can't buy the material to build a house. So that's why we still live in the same one.

There's enough food [in Nicaragua]. The problem is bureaucracy. Some people hoard rice, coffee, and corn; then the *expendio* doesn't have enough food for two weeks or a month. Sometimes there's no [cooking] oil, but it isn't because there isn't any; we produce it here, as we do rice and sugar. The shortage is caused by people who load themselves up first; only after they do that [do they think about] the pueblo. Even though the government takes measures against these people, it's always the same. Sometimes donations [of food] come from other countries and are stored; then they spoil on the pretext that there's no transportation and a bunch of reasons for not taking things out of storage. The problem is bureaucracy. There's more of it than before, in spite of steps taken by the government.

For example, last year there was no free trade in grains. Now there is. People can buy what they want in *quintales* of corn and beans.[32] Last year the government took steps against the speculators because many people bought corn during the harvest, and when the poor couldn't find corn or beans, these people sold it at high prices. They were punished. Later, the government saw that production increased, so they opened it up again, allowing people to buy anything they wanted. But there are those who take advantage of the situation in order to play with the hunger of the people by selling them things for too much money.[33]

There's a new boutique in Estelí where the government sells expensive things to people who have farms, who have stocks and bonds, who like to dress luxuriously in the latest style.[34] You can pay in dollars or in Nicaraguan bills. There are foreign liquors, whiskey, everything, from all over. As a result of our past, there are people who can buy there. They acquired land by exploiting the campesino. Let's say that a campesino borrowed some money from a *patrón*, and when the campesino couldn't pay back the money, the *patrón* took away his land.[35] The *patrón's* hacienda got bigger and bigger that way. Sometimes the *patrón* lent money to the campesino to buy medicine, but the campesino had to give his cows as collateral. When the campesino couldn't pay, the *patrón* took away his herd. The government leaves the *patrón* alone, even though it knows the cattle were stolen, and the *patrón* gives the impression that he worked for the cattle.

In Estelí there is an association of stockbreeders, a group of the richest ones.[36] The government buys livestock from them in dollars; in addition, the stockbreeders obtain dollars through the livestock they sell for export. Since they have dollars, it's easier for them to buy parts or send away for them.

I've conquered the psychosis myself. I consciously decided that it no longer existed, that everything I imagined was nothing but a lie. I'd tell myself that before taking a bath or when I had an hour to rest. I'd meditate and tell myself that I wasn't sick, that I was well. I haven't been sick once all year. I no longer have those dreams. I sleep without pills. And I'm hungry. Still thin, though; that's just how my body is. I was sick with the psychosis for eight years, starting from before the triumph.

The past year I still had a problem with liquor, but not this year. With the psychosis, I felt more courageous when I drank, but now I don't need it. It's not like before when a week would pass, and I'd spend the whole time drinking. For example, [now I drink] one day a month for just a little while, and that's all.

The journalists say that Nicaragua is a traumatized country, but really, it isn't. The last time the *Pájaro Negro*—the spy plane of the United States—flew over, no one got frightened.[37] We laughed this time. We won't be afraid again of a plane so powerful as the *Pájaro Negro*. The pueblo has gotten rid of this war psychosis. Now we live for each moment. It no longer bothers us to hear shots at night; now it's natural in Nicaragua to hear shots. It's not like it was at the beginning when the people got frightened upon hearing an explosion. Now you hear them everyday, and the fear of the sound of war, of shots, of explosions has disappeared.

In May and June, it was dangerous in Estelí. There were ambushes on the highways and in the cooperatives. The army mounted an operation called Pride, and we fought the guardia (contra) around Estelí. They fled once again to Honduras and left behind piles of dead. The people are more confident now. It's not necessary to stand watch at night because the Ministry of Defense has informed us that the guardia is in Honduras. Life has returned to normal. Those who stand watch are sleeping.

Irene and my mother get along well now. Irene visits her often, and my children go [to my mother's house] on Sundays to watch television. My mother's sickness has caused us to be more concerned.[38]

Marta and I don't have serious arguments, but sometimes there are misunderstandings—temporary ones. She might have something I need, so I ask her to lend it to me, and then comes the argument. Let's say I don't have a bed for a child to lie down on, and Marta does. I ask her to lend it to me, and we argue. If I had the means, I wouldn't bother anyone, but there's no one else to ask. I have no other family. So we argue. She gets angry over this, and I try to make her see that individualism and selfishness shouldn't exist.

I've been with Irene eleven years. I don't have another woman. She's the only one who has put up with me and, as we Nicaraguans say, all the misfortune. Problems or no problems, she tolerates me. I have to love her because she has my two children, and I love them a lot, too. Irene and I get along well now. Sometimes I think about Dora, the one I married on the mountain, but what I felt before has ended. You can't think about one woman when you have another, even though at times I use Dora as an example of a woman who sacrificed herself, who died for the revolution. It's the example, nothing more, that I remember.[39] And Irene accepts the memory as an example. I'd never compare them and say who was better, who was prettier, who was fatter, who was skinnier.

I have a greater responsibility at work now. I don't go to the mountain as often as I did before when I used to stay there for two weeks or a month at a time. Now I go home every day in the middle of the day, which helps me see the situation there. I spend more time sitting and writing than going to the mountain. I prefer this year's situation. I work twenty-four hours and rest twenty-four. I don't have a rank, but I have more responsibility. I'm chief of personnel, the head of forty people. Before, I was chief of patrol for the mountain.

At work, the first thing in the morning is formation. After that, I record what people are doing and the military movements of the enemy. I check the offices to see that they're clean and send everyone to work. At twelve we have lunch and at two we start work again. I make sure that people are working, not sleeping, and summarize the work accomplished during the day. I finish that around one or two in the morning, when I inform the chief of everything that occurred, like a terrorist action against a cooperative, how many counter-revolutionaries entered such-and-such a place. After the report, I sleep. At five in the morning, I get all the personnel up to do their morning exercises and send them to the dining room. I hand in the report and come home. When I get home, I usually do nothing but sleep. I don't sleep much at work because I'm always being told what's happening.

Before, someone sent me to do the work, but now I'm the one who sends the person. I don't really like to give orders because I remember that I didn't like it when someone ordered me. I give orders to people who have ranks. Even though they might be a lieutenant or sergeant or chief of a detachment, they still have to ask for my consent to do certain work. The ones with rank are more educated than I am, but they have confidence in me because I have more experience in the military command as well as in the guerrilla. I know more things about war than the new people do.

I take political classes on the history of the struggle of the Frente Sandinista. I learn how to make the revolution strong, what its achievements have been, its errors, its importance, how it began, and how the struggle of Sandino compares to the struggle the Frente has right now. Based on the books and writings of Sandino, we compare the historical legacy with the present situation; we study whether the Sandinista government fulfills what Sandino said about turning over the land and becoming anti-imperialists and whether the new commanders are complying with the struggle that started in 1961 when the Frente was formed. We see that in a certain way they are, because one of the first matters for Sandino was that the land would be for whomever worked it. Sometimes every two weeks, the government turns over land. And it provides housing for people displaced by war.

I don't want to be a commander, like Omar Cabezas, even though I think I've earned it, but I'd like to be like Omar Cabezas the person. He's jovial, happy, friendly, and he relates to the masses. As we Nicaraguans say, "he's an earthy guy."[40] Cabezas speaks the same language as the pueblo, as the campesino. Instead of calling a chair *la silla* or *el asiento* as the aristocrats do, we say *taburete* ["stool"] or *banca* ["bench"] or *pata de gallina*.[41] We don't go to a hotel to eat, we go to a *comedería* in the market to eat with the people. That's Omar Cabezas.

Rank, as Commander Tomás Borge says, isn't for those who want it so that they can ride in a vehicle, or give orders to people, or feel better than other people. Many military people, when they get a rank, change their personality. They become more serious, sometimes as a result of being in the military, where you have to be serious when they tell you to be serious and happy when they tell you to be happy.

I've had a lot of friends in the military: chiefs of staff, chiefs of the army, and guerrillero commanders who are friends of mine. There's Commander Pichardo, whose pseudonym was Isauro. We were together on the mountain, and he still knows me, even though he's the regional chief of the Ministry. He hasn't changed at all. Neither has Alvaro Baltodano.[42] But the new ones who didn't participate in the struggle against Somoza and who became commanders as a result of their academic preparation are the ones who feel big when they get a rank. They feel untouchable and think everyone has to respect them. They haven't acquired the consciousness that rank means a responsibility not to humiliate anyone. Their ambition is the rank, the power. The government has noticed these people and removed them. Sometimes, instead of dismissing them, they form a study circle where they explain to them the character a soldier needs. For example, if your brother is a prisoner, you can't get him out with the help of your rank. It would be like the Somocistas who used their rank to obtain profit. In the days of Somoza, everything confiscated at customs went to the chief of customs; no one could say anything because he was the chief. He had a vehicle, a house, television sets, recorders. Today the government removes people like that from their posts, demotes them to a lower category, or kicks them out of the army. Just last week, the government took measures against a business official who was selling parts secretly to his friends. The sale of the parts hadn't been authorized by the Ministry of Transportation, so he was sent to the Prosecutor's Office to be punished.[43] The government is even more rigid with the military. If we need a spoon, for example, and take it without the consent of the chief, they punish us because it begins with a spoon and continues until we take a television set for our house or a car.

Sometimes young people are anxious to complete their military service; they admire others who've returned with their medals of valor, with the title of *cachorro*, or combatant. The young want to go to the mountain to fight and return in two years with all the pueblo happily waiting for them in a plaza.

Those who evade the military service leave the country. It isn't their fault. Sometimes it's the fault of mothers who love their children too much. A mother isn't going to send her children to die. When the time comes, they hide their children or send them to Honduras, or the United States, or Costa Rica. If they send them to Honduras, they are recruited in the Nicaraguan Democratic Front, become counter-revolutionaries, die there, and the mother doesn't know what happened to them.[44]

I saw in the paper that the majority of those who went into the military from 1986 to 1987 went voluntarily. The government policy is that if they leave work to join the military, they're assured of getting their jobs back when they've completed their service. Sometimes the government facilitates their integration into cooperatives. For example, the government is able to start bus cooperatives, where they might give a hundred *cachorros* some buses to drive, like a business. Others get land to work. Some are sent outside the country to study medicine. The government facilitates all this, but not for the one who evades the military service or doesn't show up. Many compañeros have health problems, and they don't have to go. If he's the only son in the family, or if he's the only one who supports the household, they leave him.[45] But the matter of military service would exist even if the country weren't under attack. In all countries—in

Honduras, in the United States—the draft exists, but with more reason in Nicaragua. Since it's a law of the State, the government penalizes those who don't fulfill their military service. They can finish their sentence and then complete their service. While they're being penalized, the government makes them see the necessity of fulfilling their duty and that whether they do it or not, we all die in the end. When they've finished the two- or three-month penalty and acquired that consciousness, all they need to do is show up for their service. There's no resentment; well, maybe a resentment on the part of the family because they love their son.

I've had my happy times this year and my sad ones, but there's nothing that made me jump for joy. The new job is normal—without happiness—just a duty to fulfill. It's not easy to go from one job to another. For me it isn't happiness to sit in an office with a telephone. And I haven't had any sadness. I'm sad when my family is sick, like my mother or my daughters, or [when someone dies], like my sister and my grandmother. But I look at those feelings as normal. We're humans, and we have to feel it. I was surprised by the death of my grandmother, even though she was old.[46] But the rest has been normal. I just go from my house to work and from work to my house.

The man who my mother told me was my father said if the world were to fall on top of him, he'd step to one side. That's how I take things. One must take things calmly and know how to measure them. I don't rush into things that I'm not curious about in the first place. I don't give much importance to certain things, and that way I've avoided many problems. Sometimes the one who's curious gets involved in problems. If someone sees a box on the highway, for example, and goes to look at it, and it turns out to be something serious, the first thing said is, "The one who was here is so-and-so over there." So I avoid those problems.

Two weeks ago, just down the hill from my house, a [man's] body showed up. He had died of liquor. He turned up dead, about twenty-five yards from the house.[47] At first no one paid any attention to him. They thought he was just a drunk who was lying down; they didn't know he was dead. Finally curious people came to look, and later the police picked up those same curious people and investigated them. So I'm not a lover of looking at curiosities. Maybe because of that I've survived. Many have died due to that same curiosity. People didn't come to check on the drunk's health; instead they came to see how his face looked. To see if he was skinny, what shape he was in. Pure curiosity, nothing more. They didn't come because they valued that person; they came to see his face in death. I can't go along with that.

Nicaraguans use the phrase, "I'm very sorry," but I don't think they are. The one who's sorry is the family. Saying they're sorry is just a custom, a tradition of the pueblo. I don't say it because I'm not sorry. It's not possible to tell the dead man, "I'm sorry for you because you died, and I'm alive." Nicaraguans go to the vigil and funeral out of commitment but also because [the family] gives you coffee and bread. If there's liquor, the drunks go. I go only if it's a very good friend. If it's a neighbor with whom I have little contact, I don't go. I don't visit people on my block. I have friends, but I don't visit them; they visit me. The neighbors say, "Why don't you visit me? Why don't you like to visit?" Sometimes people visit you [out of curiosity]: to see what kind of bed you have, what you sleep in, how you have the folding screen, whether you eat or not.[48] A lot of people visit just to see how you look.

Even though we're living in a situation that isn't favorable for the pueblo, my years on the mountain were worth it. I don't think it was in vain. I'd do it again. And we keep on doing it because we have the same enemy that supported the Somoza dictatorship. It's the same struggle, and we continue fighting it every day in Nicaragua. If we were invaded, it wouldn't matter. We'd fight again as we did before, even better.

Epilogue

DOÑA MARÍA López never did get to the ocean. The family managed to arrange for a car but couldn't find enough gasoline. They found her unconscious due to a cerebral hemorrhage the morning of December 21, 1987, and she died that evening at the hospital with Leticia at her side. Two hours later, Leticia called me. Her mother's death had freed her, and she immediately began looking for ways to leave Nicaragua. Inflation continued, and early in 1988, when the Nicaraguan córdoba hit the level of 25,000 córdobas (50,000 on the black market) to U.S. $1.00, the Sandinista government devalued the currency and attempted to take control of the economy.[1] The contras and Sandinistas signed a truce that began April 1, 1988. Four days later, Leticia arrived alone in Mexico City. She left behind her four daughters, who moved in with Marta and Miguel. She sold half her beauty products to make the trip, moved the salon into Marta's house, where her oldest daughter cut hair, and boarded up her own house. On April 21, Leticia called me from Brownsville, Texas; she had once more managed to enter the United States illegally. She was on her way to Miami where she hoped to be reunited with her husband, who had earlier arrived there from Mexico City.

On June 5, Marta called from Estelí. She had been sick and hospitalized with kidney and nervous problems and called for help because she had nothing, or as she said, "Nada, nada, nada." The price of the beans she loved so much had risen drastically—when you could find them. She also wanted more birth control bills—she was still seeing David—and Miguel needed shoes. It was the first time that Marta had ever called to ask me for anything.

On June 20, 1988, Leticia called from Miami. She and Sergio had spent a lot of time talking and were trying to get along. He worked at a bicycle factory, and she worked at a bakery, cut hair, and sold

273

cosmetics. They lived with a brother of Sergio's but hadn't managed to save any money because they had bought a car. Sergio said, according to Leticia, that without a telephone and a car, you can't make any money in Miami. Cuban employers in Miami preferred to hire Nicaraguans because they worked so hard. For that, Leticia was grateful. On the other hand, the Cubans often hired illegals and therefore paid whatever amount they wished. Sergio's brother told them that there were more jobs at higher salaries in Los Angeles; maybe they would go there. She had not learned any English but was hoping to get her beautician's license; she could do that in Spanish. She still planned to bring the oldest and youngest daughters to the United States first, and then the middle two. She thought that eventually even Marta would come. When she last talked with Omar, he was dispirited and hoped to quit the military in September to take a job he was offered planting potatoes. Leticia worried most about her children. They weren't eating much or well in Nicaragua, and every time Leticia ate in Miami, she thought about that.

On August 11, Leticia's friend Carlos called me from Los Angeles and then put her on the phone. A Nicaraguan hairdresser whom she had known in Estelí called Miami to ask Leticia to work in her Los Angeles salon and stay at her home. Leticia and Sergio drove across the country and had arrived a few days before she called me. They had been poorly paid in Miami, and the Nicaraguan woman in Los Angeles needed someone in the salon she could trust. Sergio had a work visa and hoped to deliver pizzas. Leticia had a statement of voluntary departure status, meaning that she wasn't illegal anymore but had to leave by July 1989. She was going to have to learn English because many "gringos" came to the salon, and her friend was going to help her get a license. Carlos had just returned from a trip to Nicaragua with photos and news of the children. To Leticia, the girls all looked so big in the photographs. Carlos reported that Marisa had dropped out of school and seemed quiet and withdrawn. The rest of the children were fine. Marta was sad, lonely, and—much to his surprise—burst into tears when she saw him. She rarely left the house, but on Sundays she went to her mother's grave to pull weeds that sprouted up among the flowers she had planted. She seemed to get along well with Leticia's four daughters, all of whom were responsible for certain household chores, but Carlos thought that Miguel got lost in the shuffle. They had no refrigerator, but they still had their television set, and that kept their house the center of the neighborhood for little children.[2] Omar came over some evenings to watch television with his children.

Miami had been difficult. Leticia hadn't been able to look for the *señor* on the beach, but she had managed to spend part of a day with the elderly woman she had befriended. Sergio seemed to be always irritated; although it was hard for Leticia to feel anything for him, for the sake of the children, she had to put up with it and control her feelings. During the drive from Miami to Los Angeles, she saw many beautiful places where she wouldn't mind living some day. Miami was just too large, especially in comparison with Estelí. What she would most like to do is return to Nicaragua to buy a little farm; however, she knew that was impossible and still hoped to bring her children to the United States. Nonetheless, the extreme difference she saw between rich and poor bothered her, as did the fact that no one paid any attention to it. Just that morning, she had seen an old black woman who reminded her of her mother.[3] The woman had slept all night in a doorway, and her face was swollen from crying. People walked by her, but Leticia stopped to see if she could take the woman to the hospital. She wondered why others hadn't done the same.

Even before a hurricane hit Nicaragua late in October 1988, the economy had collapsed. According to Leticia, a *quintal* (100 pounds) of beans now sold for U.S. $50; the bean growers weren't accepting payment in *córdobas*. Sergio's brother in Mexico said that for a total cost of U.S. $1500, he could bring Marta and the five children to the United States. Marta had finally decided that she, too, had to leave. Omar also wanted to go.

Acronyms
Notes
Glossary

ACRONYMS

AMNLAE	Asociación de Mujeres Nicaragüenses Luisa Amanda Espinoza; Luisa Amanda Espinoza Association of Nicaraguan Women.
ARDE	Alianza Revolucionaria Democrática; Democratic Revolutionary Alliance.
BLI	Batallones de Lucha Irregular; Irregular Fighting Battalions.
CDS	Comité de Defensa Sandinista; Sandinista Defense Committee.
CIA	Central Intelligence Agency
CMA	Civilian-Military Assistance.
EPS	Ejército Popular Sandinista; Sandinista Popular Army.
FDN	Fuerza Democrática Nicaragüense; Nicaraguan Democratic Force.
FSLN	Frente Sandinista de Liberación Nacional; Sandinista National Liberation Front.
GPP	Guerra Popular Prolongada; Prolonged Popular War.
INCINE	Instituto Nicaragüense de Cine; Nicaraguan Film Institute.
INEC	Instituto Nacional de Estadísticas y Censos; National Institute of Statistics and Censuses.
INRA	Instituto Nicaragüense de Reforma Agraria; Nicaraguan Institute of Agrarian Reform.
INSSBI	Instituto Nicaragüense de Seguridad Social y Bienestar; Ministry of Social Security and Social Welfare.
MICOIN	Ministerio de Comercio Interior Nicaragüense; Ministry of Internal Commerce.
MIDA	Ministerio de Desarrollo Agropecuario; Ministry of Agricultural Development.

MIDINRA	Ministerio de Desarrollo (Agropecuario) y Instituto Nicaragüense de Reforma Agraria; Ministry of (Agricultural) Development and Agrarian Reform Institute.
PROAGRO	Productos Agropecuarios; Agricultural Products.
PROLACSA	Productos Lácteos; Dairy Products.
UNAN	Universidad Nacional Autónoma de Nicaragua; National Autonomous University of Nicaragua.
TP	Tendencia Proletaria; Proletarian Tendency; Prole.

NOTES

1 Introduction: The Family and Their City

1. AMNLAE is the national women's association that was created a year before the revolution triumphed. The acronym stands for Asociación de Mujeres Nicaragüenses Luisa Amanda Espinoza; in English, it is the Luisa Amanda Espinoza Association of Nicaraguan Women.

2. "CIA Plane Used by Nicaraguan Rebels," *Gazette-Times*, Corvallis, Oreg., 7 October 1983, 3A.

3. Doña—in this case, Doña María—is a title of respect used in front of a woman's first name.

4. An article, "A Nicaraguan Family," published in *minnesota review* 25 (Fall 1985): 19–35, and a book chapter, "Leticia: A Nicaraguan Woman's Struggle," was published in *The Human Tradition in Latin America: The Twentieth Century*, ed. William Beezley and Judith Ewell (Wilmington, Del.: Scholarly Resources, 1987), 259–73.

5. *Va, pues* is a shortened form of *Vaya con Dios, pues*. In English, it means "Go with God."

6. Elena Poniatowska, "The Earthquake," *Oral History Review*, 16, no. 1 (Oral History Association, Spring 1988): 16.

7. Leticia is the one I know in the Christian base communities.

8. Carlos is a pseudonym for a friend of Leticia's and mine.

9. An organization, in this context, refers either to a grassroots special-interest organization or to an official group organized by the government.

10. The sentence is better in Spanish with the play on the words *dólares* and *dolores*: "*Los dólares son los dolores de cabeza.*"

11. Edward Sheehan, *Agony in the Garden: A Stranger in the Garden*, (Boston: Houghton Mifflin, 1989), 145.

12. Poniatowska, "Earthquake," 15.

13. Based on a 1971 census, there were 19,800 people, with a projection of 54,800 by 1990. *Análisis Demográfico de Nicaragua*, Parte II, Boletín Demográfico No. 5, (Managua, Nicaragua: Oficina Ejecutiva de Encuestas y Censos, December 1978), 113.

14. Penny Lernoux in *Cry of the People*, (New York: Doubleday, 1980), 98.

15. As quoted in Claribel Alegría and D.F. Flakoll's *Nicaragua: La revolución sandinista* (Mexico, D.F.: Ediciones Era, 1982), 357.

16. According to David Nolan's chapter, "Chronology of the Nicaraguan Revolution" in *The Ideology of the Sandinistas and the Nicaraguan Revolution* (Coral Gables, Fla.: Institute of Interamerican Studies, University of Miami Press, 1984), 155–89, Estelí was the site of the following events:

- 3000 people rioted in Estelí in May 1978.

- 9 September 1978: the Sandinistas attacked the guardia in Estelí, among other cities, and large numbers of semi-armed civilians joined the revolt besieging guardia garrisons, which held out while elite guardia troops and firepower retook the cities one at a time.

- 17 September: Estelí was surrounded by 1200 guardia and subjected to heavy bombardment.

- 20 September 1978: the guardia retook Estelí. "At least 1500 and as many as 5000 (Red Cross estimate) died in the course of the September uprising with Estelí being the hardest hit."

- 8–13 April 1979: Estelí was bombarded. One thousand guardia isolated the city on 11 September and began major attacks on the 12th.

- 16 July 1979: the guardia garrison in Estelí fell.

17. Leticia describes *crackling* as follows: "Crackling, which is called either *charrasca* or *chicharrón*, is made after you prepare a pig. You take off the hair and toast the underneath layer in pork fat."

18. The *nancites* is a tropical fruit that grows in Nicaragua between July and August.

19. An *elote* is an ear of green corn; the leaves are taken off, and the ear is cooked in water with salt.

20. *El pipián* is a vegetable similar to a squash.

21. The *chiltomá* is a sweet green pepper.

22. Most of Nicaragua's blacks live on the Caribbean coast, an area that was colonized by the British and where the people speak English.

23. Even though the counter-revolutionaries are the ones who attacked nearby La Trinidad in 1985, Leticia categorizes them as Somoza's guardia because they are backed by the United States (as were Somoza's guardia) and many of the contra leadership came from Somoza's old National Guard.

24. Leonel Rugama was a poet and student revolutionary from Estelí who was killed by the guardia. His mother and aunt have a bookstore in Estelí. Rufo Marín fought with Sandino. According to Omar, Enrique Lorente and René Barrante died around 1974 or 1975.

25. "At the end of 1983, when a draft law was implemented for the first time in Nicaraguan history, Irregular Fighting Battalions (BLI) began to be formed. Some were drafted, some were volunteers, but the '*cachorros* (cubs) of Sandino,' as the young draftees of the BLI are called, changed the course of the war by the end of 1985." *Envío* (Managua, Nicaragua: Instituto Histórico Centroamericano, August 1988), 9–10.

26. It is better in Spanish with the use of the verb *joder*: "*El que ha sufrido más la guerra, lo vienen jodiendo, como dicen, a cada rato.*"

2 The Years before the Revolution

1. That would put the year of her birth around 1919.

2. The fact is that Sandino was a Liberal. I recommend *The End and the Beginning: The Nicaraguan Revolution* by John A. Booth (Boulder, Colo.: Westview Press, 1985) for more complete information.

3. There are many definitions for *turco*, but the family had the impression that this *turco* actually came from Turkey.

4. The children say that Leticia, Norma, and Leonardo are children of the same father; however, that is not the way Doña María told the story.

5. According to many historians, but not all, René Schick was a puppet for Luis Somoza Debayle. See Booth, *The End and the Beginning* or Thomas Walker, *Nicaragua: The Land of Sandino* (Boulder, Colo.: Westview Press, 1981).

6. *Tamales* are minced meat and pepper wrapped in corn husks or banana leaves.

7. Their father was not Leticia's father. That the oldest children were brought up by their father contradicts their mother's testimony.

8. The *Barricada* is the official newspaper of the Sandinista government. *La Prensa* opposed the Somoza government before the triumph and has since opposed the Sandinista government.

9. *Cuajada* is a salty, white cheese that tastes a little like Greek feta cheese.

10. Nicaraguans say that when one gets married in the church, there is no possibility of divorce. However, divorce is possible if one marries in a civil ceremony.

11. The university goes by the acronym UNAN, which stands for Universidad Nacional Autónoma de Nicaragua and translates into English as the National Autonomous University of Nicaragua.

12. Leticia adds, "The doctors in those days were interested only in making money however they could. For example, my last child was born three years ago in 1981 in the Jinotega hospital. It was complicated because I was very nervous about the war. A private clinic in Matagalpa would have charged me 10,000 córdobas that we did not have. A Cuban did a cesarean and also another operation on me so that I would not have any more children—it was all free."

13. La Trinidad, in this case, means a hospital that was run by the Seventh-Day Adventists in the small town of La Trinidad, a few miles south of Estelí.

14. According to Leticia in a 1985 interview, the hospital is now run by Nicaraguans. When her first daughter was born, "some Nicaraguans worked

there, but they also had to be Adventists. But little by little [after 1979], they left. Some of the Nicaraguans went back to the coast, and the North American doctors left. They left because they wanted to leave. Maybe they didn't like the system, maybe they didn't feel good here—I don't know—but they left. When the insurrection took place, the hospital passed into the hands of the people. It was a hospital for the pueblo. Some of the Adventists stayed, and even though they didn't take up arms, they worked within the process. There are still some here, and they are building some houses next to the hospital."

15. Dr. Bolaños, according to Leticia, was later killed by the Somoza guardia. They took him from the hospital while he was operating on a patient and killed him in the street. The patient also died. Leticia describes both the Estelí poet Leonel Rugama and her boyfriend Oscar Benavides as disciples of Bolaños. An article in *Barricada* (July 1, 1985) reported that Alejandro Dávila Bolaños and Eduardo Selva were operating in Estelí during Holy Week 1979 when the guardia took them outside and killed them.

16. *Gusanos* (worms) are Cubans who left their country after the 1959 revolution.

17. The acronym for Sandinista Defense Committees (Comités de Defensa Sandinista) is CDS. Originally, they were called Comités de Defensa Civil.

18. A centavo is to the córdoba what a penny or cent is to the dollar.

19. Many Nicaraguan men still have their shoes shined even though the economic situation in Nicaragua is difficult. It is thought that the custom originated in Spain, where you could tell a gentleman by his clean shoes, a sign that he rode a horse and did not walk in the dusty roads.

20. Omar said, "José Benito Escobar, the one who first got me involved, came to Estelí on the fifteenth of July, 1978. That was the last time I saw him. He told me he had come to do a job in a barrio that used to be called Bella Vista but now is called Barrio José Benito Escobar in his memory. He was on his way there when the guardia saw him on the street, fired at him from a vehicle, and killed him. When we realized what the guardia had done, we tried to find José Benito's body, but the guardia had taken him to the [military] barracks here in Estelí. We demonstrated in the street to get his body, but the guardia, instead of burying him in a cemetery, buried him on the river bank. Later a group of us dug him up and put him in a coffin—the guardia had put him in a bag—and we buried him. Then we went out again to demonstrate in the streets. A neighbor was shot and killed by the guardia while we were demonstrating. The same night we burned several houses that belonged to some Cubans from Miami."

21. Most people claim that Estelí had three insurrections (September

1978 and April and July 1979), but Omar describes one as being earlier, in October 1977.

22. I have rarely heard anyone in Nicaragua say that someone became a guerrillero or joined the guerrilla. Instead, they usually say, "*El se va para la montaña*" (He's leaving for the mountain). When used in this context, the word for *mountain—montaña—*is usually in the singular and represents commitment, revolution, growing up, and courage.

23. Omar said, "At the training school, there were many kinds of guns, and we learned about them, but the first time I shot was when the guardia entered a camp where we were. I began with a Garand, then had an Enfield, and later they gave me an *FAL* machine gun."

24. Irene is the woman Omar married in a church wedding after the triumph of the revolution.

25. In Spanish, the Prolonged Popular War is the Guerra Popular Prolongada; the acronym is GPP. According to David Nolan, "the GPP was the ultimate romanticization of the guerilla." See his *The Ideology of the Sandinistas and the Nicaraguan Revolution* (Coral Gables, Fla.: Institute of Interamerican Studies, University of Miami Press, 1984), 42.

According to Walter LaFeber, there were three groups: "the Proletarian Tendency, which urged warfare; the Prolonged Popular War (PPW), which argued for mobilizing campesinos to fight a long-term conflict; and the Third-World Tendency (Terceristas), which was the most open and pluralistic (although it did oppose the Communist party), and advocated war in both the cities and villages." See his *Inevitable Revolutions: The United States in Central America* (New York; W. W. Norton, 1983), 229.

The Prole were the Proletariam Tendency/Tendencia Proletaria/TP.

26. In this context and many others, I have translated "*Sigo adelante,*" an oft-heard expression in Nicaragua, as "I will keep going," even though the English doesn't quite accurately express the determination conveyed in Spanish. Other translations could be, "I will go on," "I will carry on," or "I will go forward."

27. The *jocote* is a Spanish plum.

28. The *guineo* is similar to a banana.

29. Black and red (*rojo y negro*) are the colors of the Sandinista flag.

30. The actual word is *junco*; it's a rush, a reed, or a vine.

31. *Atol* is a drink made from corn flour.

32. *Compa* is a shortened version of *compañero* or *compañera*.

33. *Ocote* is a species of pine.

34. "Che" is Ernesto "Che" Guevara, a doctor from Argentina who joined liberation groups in Guatemala in 1954, in Cuba in 1959, and later in Bolivia, where he was killed by the Bolivian military with the assistance of

the United States Central Intelligence Agency in 1967. He is still a hero to many Latin Americans and to revolutionaries throughout the world, and many still read his diary.

35. The pseudonym César Augusto Salinas bears a certain resemblance to the name of Nicaragua's hero, Augusto César Sandino.

36. There are only two seasons, winter and summer, a wet one and a dry one. If it is cold all the time, as it is in the mountains, it is winter all the time.

37. A *quintal* is 100 pounds.

38. When Omar speaks of a camp, he means the particular group of people, not the location.

39. When weapons were in short supply, the inexperienced people had the smallest armaments.

40. The scientific name for mountain leprosy is *leishmaniasis*. According to *LINKS*, "Leishmaniasis is a protozoal disease common in mountainous areas where sandflies, the disease vector, live." See "The Scars of Mountain Leprosy," *LINKS*: Central America Health Report (The National Central America Health Rights Network, Spring 1986), 6.

41. Pomares was one of the Sandinistas' most effective commanders; he was killed in early 1979. See Gary Ruchwarger, *People in Power* (South Hadley, Mass.: Bergin & Garvey Publishers, 1987), 31.

3 Insurrections and the Time of the Triumph

1. According to the family in Estelí, there were three insurrections—times when the Nicaraguan people rose up to mount a strong fight against the Somoza government—and the dates are September 1978, April 1979, and the final one in July 1979.

2. Scratches, beards, muddy clothes all signified to Somoza's guardia that the scratched, bearded, or muddied person was involved in the fight to overthrow the government.

3. Leticia and Pedro had different fathers. He went to the home of her father.

4. *Oreja* literally means "ear."

5. As a result of the Somoza-Agüero pact of 1971, this election was held in 1974, and Somoza was elected. According to the dates that Leticia gave me, she would have been married at this time. I suspect that she was referring to an earlier election.

6. This was the same Dr. Selva who was later killed by the Somoza guardia; see note 15 in Chapter 2.

7. Fighters against Somoza's guardia pulled up the paving stones from

Nicaragua's streets and used them to build barricades to protect themselves.

8. Carlos Fonseca was one of the founders of the Frente Sandinista and the ideological intellectual of the organization. The guardia killed him in 1976.

9. "Juro ante la Patria y ante la memoria de Carlos Fonseca y Sandino seguir adelante sin flaquear. No hago un paso atrás, y si yo incumplo este juramento, la sangre de nuestros héroes y mártires caerá sobre mí y la justicia de los guerrilleros será mi muerte."

10. *Tiqui* is Spanish onomatopoeia for the sound made by the fox.

11. The pro-Sandinistas captured the town center of Rivas, a town in southern Nicaragua; in response, 1000 guardia circled Rivas, and Somoza's air force bombed it (Ruchwarger, *People in Power,* 34).

12. "On June 4, the FSLN Joint National Leadership called for a general strike, effective June 5, and announced the beginning of the final offensive. This paralyzed the country." Ricardo E. Chavarria, "The Nicaraguan Insurrection: An Appraisal of its Originality," in *Nicaragua in Revolution,* ed. Thomas Walker (New York: Praeger, 1982), 35.

13. Before he was killed in battle, Oscar Pérez Cassar was "the political leader of the Terceristas' Internal Front . . ." See Shirley Christian, *Nicaragua: Revolution in the Family* (New York: Random House, 1985), 60.

14. The woman was Glenda Monterrey, who eventually became the National Secretary of AMNLAE.

15. George Black is quoted in Gary Ruchwarger's book as saying that the Sandinistas withdrew the night of June 21. The next morning, when the guardia attacked them as usual, they were shot at by soldiers left to cover the retreat. "Under the cover of night three columns—containing 6,000 people instead of the 1,500 originally planned—had left Managua in single file." They got lost in the darkness, and the trip took thirty hours, but they did it with six dead and sixteen wounded (Ruchwarger, *People in Power,* 33).

In an interview with Arqueles Morales, Commander Walter Ferreti remembers that the reason behind the withdrawal was that the guardia could not penetrate the Sandinista territory, so to confront the guardia, the Sandinistas had to leave their area, putting them at a distinct disadvantage. The controversial decision was made to turn the situation around, weaken their physical lines of defense, and allow the guardia to penetrate. This gave the Sandinistas, with their low caliber arms, the advantage. See Morales, *"En la insurreción de Managua, lo más duro fue replegarnos"* (*Barricada,* 4 July 1985, Managua, Nicaragua).

16. At six in the afternoon, it is already dark in Nicaragua.

17. Omar said that this plane was made in the United States, had an

engine in the front and back (Marta disagrees; she said there is only one engine), and was fast. I don't know exactly what kind of plane it is. Nicaraguans say that it was used by Somoza: cans of gasoline and bombs were dropped from the "push-and-pulls," and machine guns were fired from the plane. Later in the oral history—after the establishment of the U.S.-backed contras—Marta mentions the use of the planes by the contras.

18. While I have not been able to document the existence of Israeli mercenaries in Nicaragua, documentation of Israeli arms abounds. One example is Penny Lernoux, who writes in *Cry of the People* that "after international opinion belatedly forced the U.S. Government to suspend arms shipments to Somoza, Israel rushed in to fill the gap with antiaircraft missiles, surface-to-surface missiles, and other armaments. Though the State Department claimed it was none of its business, Israeli manufacturers, most of whom work under U.S. licenses, could not have supplied the National Guard without Washington's consent" (100–101).

Another example is Shirley Christian, who reports that "even before the official termination of U.S. supplies, Somoza had turned to Israel, which was filling the gap" (*Nicaragua: Revolution in the Family,*) 91.

Other sources include an article, "Israel Is Said to Seek Nicaraguan Diplomatic Ties," in *The New York Times* by Henry Kamm, that claims that the fall of the Somoza dynasty deprived Israel of an important arms customer (12 Dec. 1966), 15.

19. "It was vital to take the communications building. A few minutes after the attack began, Rolando Orozco penetrated the building from the north and fell in combat. There was a lot of consternation and rage among us because he was a much loved compañero" (Walter Ferreti in an interview with Arqueles Morales, "La Pérez Cassar en la liberación de Jinotepe," *Barricada*, Managua, Nicaragua, 5 July 1985).

20. At the end of combat, the Pérez Cassar Squad had taken 142 prisoners, killed 18 Somocistas, and wounded many others (Walter Ferreti, ibid).

4 The Postrevolutionary Years: 1979–1984

1. In the 1984 November elections, Daniel Ortega was elected president of Nicaragua. Most international observers, including a task force from the Latin American Studies Association, declared the election to be a free and open one. The U.S. government, however, claimed that the elections were fraudulent.

2. The López family frequently used the term *aggression* to refer to the low-intensity war the United States waged in their country. Although it might seem to be an inappropriate word choice in English, the Spanish

word, *agresión*, means "an unprovoked attack." I decided to leave the word as "aggression" rather than repeating "unprovoked attack."

3. I assume that she meant that the government might take away the house, but I don't really know.

4. The acronym is MIDINRA, Ministry of (Agricultural) Development and Agrarian Reform Institute [Ministerio de Desarrollo (Agropecuario) y Instituto Nicaragüense de Reforma Agraria] as a result of a 1980 merger of INRA (Nicaraguan Institute of Agrarian Reform) and MIDA (Ministry of Agricultural Development). See David Kaimowitz and Joseph R. Thome, "Nicaragua's Agrarian Reform: The First Year," in *Nicaragua in Revolution*, ed. Thomas Walker (New York: Praeger Publishers, 1982), 228.

According to Leticia, MIDINRA is an institution of the State where they work on matters concerning rural areas, as does PROAGRO (where Sergio worked), but PROAGRO depends on the Ministry of Agrarian Reform. Kaimowitz (229) reports that PROAGRO is another department of INRA that controls the distribution of seeds, fertilizers, and pesticides. According to Leticia, the acronym stands for Productos Agropecuarios which means Agricultural Products in English; when she refers to it, she means PROAGRO del Norte (Northern PROAGRO).

5. She meant she would have to have a cesarean section.

6. Leticia defines herself as a Sandinista, but both Marta and Omar earned their *militancia*, an honor given to those who have been outstanding in their participation.

7. The purpose of rationing was to prevent the rich from hoarding, as they had done in the past, and to provide everyone equal access to basic foodstuffs.

8. Leticia and I discussed this point for hours. It always turned out that the State paid more for crops than they sold them for, but one time the campesino found it more acceptable than they had at another time.

9. When I first met the family in the summer of 1985, Sergio was in Cuba.

10. Leticia later describes the *cursillos* and the Christian base communities as similar groups that meet to discuss how the Bible is reflected in their lives and to take actions to help the needy within their community. Some people belong to a *cursillo*, some to a base community, and Leticia belongs to both. Christian base communities are groups of Christians who get together and discuss how the Bible applies to their daily lives.

11. Homes made of wood are considered to be inferior to homes made of brick. Omar, for example, just had a small amount of brick on the front of his house. The other three sides of the exterior were made of wood.

12. A year later, in 1985, Leticia said the following about Yamara: "The

young girl I helped last year learned to be a hairdresser. Afterwards she worked in Matagalpa, but then I lost track of her. By coincidence, I saw her six months ago in Estelí. She had married a muchacho from Corinto. He had lived in the United States for several years, so she went back there with him and worked in a beauty salon. I hardly recognized her because she had become a woman. She said to me, 'I thought you weren't going to recognize me, but you did when you got close.' We talked about many things and wanted to see each other again, but it wasn't possible."

13. Obando y Bravo is the Catholic Church's cardinal in Managua. He opposes the Sandinistas.

14. A vigil is similar to a wake.

15. As recently as 1986, there was at least one Cuban doctor in Estelí. When my husband commented that he had trouble understanding the Cuban's Spanish, he was told not to worry because the Nicaraguans couldn't understand him either. Nonetheless, the Cuban was considered a fine physician by foreigners and Nicaraguans alike. The physicians all worked together: the Nicaraguans, Cubans, and North Americans.

16. At this point, Doña María added, "And he would want you to know it."

17. There were about 28 córdobas to the dollar at that time.

18. In the early years after the triumph of the revolution, the Ministry of Housing built a number of homes for low-income families. Construction has stopped as a result of the increasing expense of the war against the contras.

19. The Sandinista Popular Army is the EPS, Ejército Popular Sandinista.

20. The dead men were Dana Parker and James Powell. They belonged to a group called Civilian-Military Assistance (CMA), which claims 1000 members in northern Alabama and southern Tennessee. They went to Honduras in late August and "were still there on Sept. 1, when small contra warplanes attacked a military training school in north-central Nicaragua. Calling the school a hotbed of Cubans and Libyans, Reagan administration officials said the raiders had killed four Cuban military advisers. Nicaraguans denied it, saying the body count had run to a woman and three children." See Russell Watson, "The Friends of Tommy Posey," 17 September 1984, 55. In 1989, I asked Marta if there had been Libyans there. She burst into laughter, said absolutely not, and added that she had never seen or met a Libyan in her life.

21. Miskitos are Indians who live on Nicaragua's east coast.

22. Again, there are approximately 28 córdobas to one dollar at this point.

23. Omar views the guardia of Somoza's time and the U.S.-backed contras as one and the same.

24. Marta was present when the children in Santa Clara were killed. In Ayapal a helicopter crashed as it was taking children out of the war zone.

25. Omar Cabezas was a university student who became a revolutionary hero in the struggle to overthrow Somoza. He wrote *La montaña es algo más que una inmensa estepa verde*. The English version is called *Fire from the Mountain*. The "Omar" of this story was very pleased that I had chosen "Omar" as his pseudonym.

26. The acronym is ARDE, for Alianza Revolucionaria Democrática, a counter-revolutionary force led by Edén Pastora and based in southern Nicaragua and northern Costa Rica.

27. Omar means "former guardia" who probably belong to the counter-revolution now.

5 A Threatened Family and City: 1984–1985

1. She seems to mean that drunks have to steal things in order to have something to sell. She is afraid that they will steal from her, and that is why she closes her door while she naps.

2. *Chorizo* is a sausage seasoned with red peppers.

3. Mothers of the Heroes and Martyrs is an organization set up to help the mothers and families of those who fought and died in Nicaragua's wars. The membership consists of the mothers.

4. Miguelito is a diminutive and affectionate use of the name Miguel, and Mamita is the diminutive for Mama. Miguel refers to his grandmother as Mama and his mother as Marta.

5. In this context, Leticia means the fundamentalist Christian churches in the area.

6. *Expendios de comida* are government stores where people can use their ration cards to buy rice, beans, and so forth.

7. Sergio's mother lives in Matagalpa.

8. There's school five hours a day, five days a week, from February until the first days of December. They have two months of vacation in December and January.

9. *Chicha rosada* is rose-colored corn liquor.

10. Father Miguel D'Escoto is a Maryknoll priest and the Minister of Foreign Affairs. He fasted for several weeks in 1985.

11. In the Catholic Church, the Way of the Cross is a devotion in which the faithful accompany the Lord, in spirit, on His journey to Calvary and meditate on His sufferings and death, according to the *Saint Joseph Daily Missal* (New York: Catholic Book Publishing Company, 1957), 1325.

12. Son of a bitch and cuckold.

13. A *ventecita* in this case is a table that displays vegetables that are for sale.

14. Raúl and Leticia have the same father, but different mothers.

15. *Asentamientos* are places where people have resettled. In Nicaragua, it usually means a small community where the government has built houses for people who have been displaced by the war between the Nicaraguan government and the U.S.-backed contras.

16. According to Leticia, she did not receive an *aguinaldo* because she had a private salon. Her husband did receive one because he worked for the government. In private businesses, the employees receive their *aguinaldo* from the owner of the business.

17. *La Purísima* is the Catholic Feast of the Immaculate Conception.

18. Webster's defines a novena as the recitation of prayers and the practicing of devotions during a nine-day period, usually for some special religious purpose.

The *gritería*, according to Nicaraguan scholar Xiomara Pérez Flores, is a celebration during which the people go through the streets from six in the evening until two in the morning calling out, *"¿Ouién causa tanta alegría?"* ("Who causes so much happiness?"), and the owner of each house responds, *"La concepción de María"* ("Mary's conception" [of Jesus]).

19. Webster's dictionary describes a scapular as two small pieces of cloth joined by strings, worn on the chest and back, under the clothes, by some Roman Catholics as a token of religious devotion.

20. La Trinidad is a small town a few miles south of Estelí. There is a hospital there, too, so at times people are just referring to the hospital instead of the town. In this case, however, the reference is to the town.

21. "Over the next two days, on the outskirts of the northwestern city of Estelí (pop. 75,000), they damaged two bridges on Nicaragua's main artery, part of the north-south Pan-American Highway." See Jill Smolowe, "The Contra's Revived Challenge," *Time*, 12 August 1985, 28–29. "By Thursday the government declared a state of alert for the 50,000-odd residents of Estelí." See David Newell, "A Bold Assault by the Contras," *Newsweek*, 12 August 1985, 48.

22. "A Sandinista official said, 'our people have been through a lot and don't get scared easily' " (Newell, ibid., 48).

23. The contra, "in a daylight raid, stormed La Trinidad, a town of 8,000 people located 40 miles south of the Honduran border. Residents said the rebels swarmed over the surrounding hills, overwhelming the badly outgunned militia" (Newell, ibid., 48).

"Shortly after daybreak, several hundred insurgents swarmed into La Trinidad, a small town near Estelí. For three hours they shelled a military barracks and battled government troops; at least 33 contra and eight militiamen were killed. Before withdrawing, the rebels set fire to government grain silos and food-storage sheds" (Smolowe, "Contra's Revived Challenge," 28–29).

24. "On Thursday the air around Estelí reverberated with the sounds of ordnance from Mi-8 helicopters and rocket-equipped Cessnas firing into the hills where the contra were believed to be hiding" (Newell, "Bold Assault," 48).

25. "In a war where exaggerated claims have become routine, the real significance of the battle last week was that the contra had won an important psychological victory" (ibid., 48).

26. Marta says, "It's illegal to have an abortion here because we're believers. There are contraceptives in the health centers. There are talks for the man as well as for the woman. In Nicaragua the women have at least seven, ten, twelve children, especially in the countryside. No one had ever talked with them about it before. Now we go in and explain it to them."

27. In this case, the *pensión* is similar to an outpatient clinic.

28. With Omar's use of the feminine pronoun, I assumed he meant his wife, Irene.

29. Omar took pills before he came to his mother's house for this interview.

30. Four of the children belonged to Irene's mother who died; two more are from Irene's first marriage, and the two youngest are Irene and Omar's.

31. One of the things that increased Omar's terror was the proximity of the war. He lives in hills that are close to the ones strafed by Sandinista helicopters in their attempt to stem any thought of a contra attack. If the contra had been able to enter Estelí, they would have come through these very hills.

32. At that point I slipped him 4000 córdobas under the table. He thanked me and then said, "I'm perspiring." The reason that I secretly gave him money was that his sisters had told me that his wife took all the money from him and that it was better that any money be given in such a way that his family benefited from it rather than it being squandered by his wife. After listening to his story, though, everything looked a little different to me. No matter how it looked to whomever, we are not talking about a lot of money.

33. During the interview, a North American medical student I knew entered the house, and I introduced the student and Omar to each other. Doña María said, by way of explanation, to the student, "He's sick from the war. The war penetrated his head, and at the least expected moment, he relives the war and becomes uncontrollable." Omar looked at the floor all through her explanation, and we soon continued the interview.

34. I assumed that the "they" meant the military leaders.

35. Omar is referring to people he trained in guerrilla warfare in Masaya

just before the triumph of the revolution. The training took place near a cemetery; therefore, those he trained are called *people from the cemetery*.

36. Omar added, "But just talking has helped me a lot. I've really enjoyed this! It already seems that I'm getting better. I don't feel the same as before." It was another one of those moments when I knew that my interviews affected their lives.

37. Joe Garfunkel, a psychologist at the Corvallis Clinic, Corvallis, Oregon, read Omar's interview and said his symptoms were consistent with the symptoms of Post-traumatic Stress Disorder. In Dr. Garfunkel's report, he said that "the paper clearly presents an accurate and compelling portrait of an individual's response to war and trauma. As Omar requests more treatment time, he is acknowledging the depths of his despair. Medication is highly valuable, but essentially helps manage symptoms and may prevent further deterioration. But tranquilizers do not deal with the underlying trauma, guilt, and feelings of futility. The 'story' stands on its own as a psychological and behavioral portrait, without any need for reference to colder, technical criteria."

Dr. Garfunkel referred to the *DSM III Diagnostic and Statistical Manual of Mental Disorders* (Washington, D.C.: American Psychiatric Association, 1980), 236, as follows: "Commonly the individual has recurrent painful, intrusive recollections of the event or recurrent dreams or nightmares during which the event is reexperienced. In rare instances there are dissociativelike states, lasting from a few minutes to several hours or even days, during which components of the event are relived and the individual behaves as though experiencing the event at that moment. Such states have been reported in combat veterans. Diminished responsiveness to the external world, referred to as 'psychic numbing' or 'emotional anesthesia,' usually begins soon after the traumatic event. A person may complain of feeling detached or estranged from other people, that he or she has lost the ability to become interested in previously enjoyed significant activities, or that the ability to feel emotions of any type, especially those associated with intimacy, tenderness, and sexuality, is markedly decreased."

Garfunkel also referred to page 237: "Symptoms characteristic of Post-traumatic Stress Disorder are often intensified when the individual is exposed to situations or activities that resemble or symbolize the original trauma."

6 Leticia in the United States: February 1986

1. Under a pseudonym, Leticia addressed several Spanish classes at Oregon State University and one at Crescent Valley High School. The *Daily Barometer*, OSU's newspaper, interviewed her and published an article on

her views of Nicaragua. I didn't know until she arrived in Corvallis that she had entered the United States illegally. To protect her, we kept the speaking commitments to the ones I had made ahead of time and we also made sure that she did not have to publicly address the question of how she got into the United States.

2. I found a one-way ticket from Reno to Miami that I could buy for $100. After much discussion, it was determined that Leticia could probably find work and not be noticed in Miami. There she could make enough money in order to buy airfare for herself and her daughter from Miami to Managua. So I bought two one-way tickets, and about two weeks later, they were in Miami.

3. The land cost 200,000 córdobas.

4. El Rosario is dangerous because it is located in the foothills surrounding Estelí. Any contra ground offensive would have to come through these small, poor barrios.

5. Both Leticia and Marta use the phrase "to have relations" to refer to sex. This may seem formal in English, but the translation is true to the words they used.

6. Managua does seem far from the war, even though food is scarce, prices are higher than they are in the countryside, the crowded buses are miserable, housing is in short supply, and there is a shortage of electricity and water. As difficult as life is in Managua, the danger of war is much lower than it is elsewhere in Nicaragua.

7 A Family Growing Apart: 1985–1986

1. Monterrey, who was referred to in Omar's account of the years before 1979, is again probably Glenda Monterrey, at that time in charge of AMNLAE.

2. Leticia was still in Miami. Her mother's birthday is celebrated on Mother's Day because her actual birth date is unknown.

3. According to the family, Adela died of a cerebral hemorrhage.

4. María Elena was a young relative who was killed by the contra. Marta explains it more thoroughly in her interview.

5. The seventh anniversary celebration of the Nicaraguan revolutionary triumph was celebrated in Estelí. For whatever reasons, maybe the contra attack of the previous year, the Sandinistas expected trouble during the celebration. The people of Estelí were greatly relieved and proud that the celebration took place with no difficulties.

6. The first day that Leticia worked for Avon, she sold $300 worth of products. She could keep half that amount, $150. In Nicaragua, it took Sergio three months to make that amount of money.

7. In 1980, boats full of Cubans from El Mariel port in Cuba entered the

United States. About 125,000 Marielitos were granted permanent residency. See John S. Lang, "Castro's Crime Bomb inside U.S.," *U.S. News and World Report*, 16 January 1984, 27–30.

8. Omar and Marta weren't there because they had to work.

9. Leticia and I worried about this part of the trip. She had entered the United States illegally, so she had no papers. If you have no papers, how do you leave? I tried to find answers discreetly but with no success. We didn't know if there would be trouble on the U.S. side or the Nicaraguan end. I waited by the phone all day in case she had to call me, although I had no idea exactly what I would say. As it was, she left without any trouble, arrived in Nicaragua with fourteen boxes, and cleared Immigration and Customs with no difficulty (getting things out of customs a few days later is usual), all of which she credits to the Lord.

10. I had seen Sergio earlier, and he told me that he quit his job and was going to Mexico because his salary was not enough to support his family and he hoped to find something better there. His salary in Nicaragua was the maximum salary for the government employee (the equivalent to a little over U.S. $50).

11. The acronym is MICOIN, which stands for Ministerio de Comercio Interior Nicaragüense in Spanish; in English it is the Ministry of Domestic Commerce.

12. The children's school vacation begins just before Christmas.

13. On 9 April 1984, Nicaragua filed suit before the International Court of Justice in The Hague, the Netherlands, charging the United States with illegally mining its harbors. On 27 June 1986, the International Court found the United States in violation of international law, thus condemning its aggressive actions in Nicaragua. See *Envío* (Managua, Nicaragua: Instituto Histórico Centroamericano), July 1986, 22.

14. When Marta uses the word *mercenaries* she is referring to the contra. The implication is that they work for pay, in this case, dollars.

15. Leticia told me that one of the people on the van managed to escape, hid in the woods, and witnessed what happened. The torso of a headless and legless woman is often seen in Nicaragua. It is often made of alabaster, and I have seen such a figure given to a woman by AMNLAE in gratitude for work done. It represents the fact that although women have been tortured and killed by the contra, they will not give up.

16. Marta's family still does not know about David, and probably never will; however, Marta gave me permission to use the information about him in the book.

17. Since a meal in a modest restaurant would cost Marta's entire month's salary, one saw mostly foreigners in Nicaraguan restaurants, especially as inflation increased. At the end of this trip, my husband and I each had a

drink, something like a Mai-Tai, in a Managua hotel bar; then we realized that we had just spent the same amount on two drinks as Marta made each month.

18. According to *Envío*, the *asentamientos* are populated by three groups: "1) people who have been displaced by the war; 2) people who lived in the general region and have come because of the services offered (including the security of a larger community); and 3) people who have left agriculturally poor areas (for example, the so-called 'zonas secas': vast deforested, arid zones in Regions I and V). Some 250,000 people have been displaced by the war, some leaving their homes on their own and others moved by the government." See *Envío* (Managua, Nicaragua: Instituto Histórico Centroamericano), July 1988, 20–21.

8 Survival: 1986–1987

1. She sits outside so that people will say, "*Adiós,*" an expression used in leave-taking and in passing. When I walked down the street to their house, the children on the street often called out, "*Adiós.*"

2. A large house at the end of the block belonged to the government, and Sandinista commanders used it as a place to stay when they were in the area. It was called *la casa de protocolo*, the protocol house. I have been interviewing the family when commanders came to that house. It caused great excitement in the neighborhood, and we all went out to look.

3. At this point, Leticia told me that Dōna María's physician used to work in the hospital but was now on his own.

4. During this conversation, she blamed the Ministry of Commerce and the Ministry of Housing. In her mind, either one or both of them is at fault.

5. Marta had been in two car accidents while working with AMNLAE. The first one was in 1984 on the Cuesta de Cucamonga, which is well known, according to Marta, for being a dangerous road with many curves. That particular time, it had rained a lot. Visibility was limited, and the driver lost control. The car turned over three times. Two compañeras were unconscious, the other with four broken ribs, and Marta was hospitalized with a broken collar bone. The other accident was when she was taking a group of people from INCINE (Nicaraguan Film Institute) who were making a film that she called *Mujeres de la frontera*. The film was to be made at an *asentamiento*, and Marta was going to introduce the campesinos to the filmmakers. The roads were narrow and unpaved. A tire blew out, and the car ended up in the river. Her leg was hurt, and she had trouble walking. Coincidentally, David came along and helped. They were not lovers at that time.

6. Irene came by and gave Dōna María 10,000 córdobas. I watched as Dōna María wordlessly put her head down and cried. That year, instead of

giving the family's money to Leticia as they had requested, I gave Omar his $20 separately. Only I knew at that time that he already had his money, which is why he had enough money to give his mother 10,000 córdobas. Needless to add, I did not say anything about that to Dõna María nor to anyone else.

7. The acronym is INSSBI, which stands for Instituto Nicaragüense de Seguridad Social y Bienestar.

8. La Renta and La Junta de Reconstrucción Nacional.

9. The people who asked her to bring things back also helped pay for her return airplane ticket because she didn't have enough money herself. In addition, there were many problems in El Salvador at that time, and with her packages, it would have been difficult to change buses during the trip. The other people also paid the taxes to get their boxes out of customs, but hers are still there.

10. The head of the diocese, the bishop, was in Estelí.

11. The acronym INEC, which she used, stands for the Instituto Nicaragüense de Estadísticas y Censos.

12. I've changed the names of the two women in this anecdote. Marta's life would not be in danger, but she definitely would not be in anyone's favor if the two women were to read this. The women will know who they are, even though I have omitted some important details, but the rest of the world will not know.

13. *Mantas* are a type of fabric that Marta drew revolutionary slogans on with marking pens.

14. She is the sister of the late Estelí poet Leonel Rugama. I wrote her a letter in 1986 to help facilitate Leticia's return to Estelí by testifying that Leticia had given talks to students at Oregon State University and at Crescent Valley High School. Leticia was worried that when she returned to Nicaragua, she would be considered a reactionary.

15. *No hay mal que dure cien años, ni un cuerpo que lo resista,* which can be translated many ways.

16. Leticia did not tell me that she actually took Sofía to the hospital, but certainly my assumption throughout this interview was that she did.

17. Leticia talked about early education in Nicaragua: "Nora is in the first grade. Now with the new government, before children start the first grade, they have to go to preschool to learn things that aren't taught in first grade, like colors and getting along with other people, so that when they get to the first grade, it isn't that difficult. They have to go to preschool for three years, but it wasn't difficult for the little one, so she was there only a year. It seems that she's quite intelligent. When I took her to school to enroll her in the first grade, the teacher asked me for her grades from preschool. I told her

I didn't have them, but I wanted them to test her to see if she was ready. They said she did it perfectly."

18. At this point, Marisa came to ask her for money because the muchacha in the salon needed some curlers. A little carton with sixteen curlers cost 23,000 córdobas, or around U.S. $4.00.

19. A doughnut, or type of bun, made with corn flour.

20. Leticia told me that Marisa's anemia prevented her from attending school.

21. Actually, she said that she was between "*la espada y la pared,*" which is between "the sword and the wall."

22. Marta says, "The contra attacked the electrical plant. People near here worked with the contra and received dollars for information. They kept track of all movement, the number of people who watched the electrical tower, how they did it. That day, there was a change of the watch, and the contra realized how many people were going to be there. Really, there weren't a lot of people taking care of the tower. The contra came with a sort of dynamite, the kind used by the CIA, with a plastic thing, and they stuck it on the tower. It was powerful because it blew it up. We spent two days without water and light. The compañeros who worked in electricity spent day and night working to re-establish the energy. That day, the State Security caught the ones who did it with more things in their bags to blow up more towers. Now they are prisoners. They gave information on the length of time they had been with the contra and what work they did. I think it happened two months ago."

23. Later Marta and I went out; she wore a dress and put some blush on her cheeks, neither of which I had ever seen her do before. A friend stopped to talk with her and said, "You've got something on your face." Marta immediately wiped off the blush.

24. Later, we took a break. Leticia, Marta, their mother, and I were standing outside by the front door. A young man started down the street, and Marta slapped me on the arm and said, "Diana, you want to know how I survive? Watch!" The man was carrying a paper bag and was going in the direction of his house, directly across the street from Marta's. She called to him and asked him what he had in the bag. He just laughed. She then turned around, ran into her *solar,* and came out with a small bowl. Before he could get into the safety of his house, she was at his side, laughing all the while, as were we. She came back with six limes in the bowl and said, "And that is how I do it." It was a wonderful moment, and we all enjoyed it.

25. Marta: "When I was working, they recommended that we give an allotment to Social Security and Welfare from our salary to help others. For example, when people have no money and a child or a family member dies,

Social Security buys the coffin for them. Or they buy bread or sugar so they can have the vigil and funeral. It doesn't cost the family anything. When I was working, I gave this allotment. Now that I'm not working, the allotment has come to serve me. It's not permanent."

26. *Negra* is a term of endearment and affection used with a child, between relatives, friends, boyfriends and girlfriends, and spouses. However, Marta said she would not use it with someone older, like her mother, and that its meaning depends on one's tone of voice.

27. *Amiguismo* is the term for getting promoted or helped by using friendships.

28. In a letter dated May 1988, Marta said that there have been three men in her life, but only two were important: Antonio, who was Miguel's father, and David.

29. *Atol* is a drink made from corn flour.

30. The National Directorate of the Sandinista National Liberation Front is considered to be Nicaragua's main governing body. It is composed of nine members, with three members from each of the three main political groups involved in overthrowing Somoza: the Proletarians, the Terceristas, and the Prolonged Popular War. See Department of the Army, Foreign Area Studies, *Nicaragua: A Country Study* (Washington, D.C.: U.S. Government Printing, 1982).

31. Winter and summer are relative. When the family complains about the cold, I think the weather is pleasant.

32. According to Omar, a *quintal* has four *arrobas*; therefore, each *arroba* is 25 pounds.

33. Omar gave an example: "In Quilalí, the cooperatives sell a *quintal* (100 pounds) of corn, which is four *arrobas* (twenty-five pounds), for 25,000 to 28,000 córdobas (about U.S. $4.50). But when it's sold in Estelí, just one *arroba* sells for 25,000 córdobas, which is what a whole *quintal* costs in the cooperatives. The seller makes 75,000 córdobas (about U.S. $13.00) a *quintal*. The people in Estelí have to buy it at that price because there's no cropland near here, only far away. The rich go there to buy the corn and come here to sell it to the poor. The government sometimes penalizes the people who do that, but it continues just the same."

34. During the summer of 1987, I noticed a new store in Estelí. It was a boutique that sold expensive clothes, shoes, liquors; its window displays and inventory looked out of place in Nicaragua. I went in there with Marta. There was nothing in the store that didn't cost many times the family's monthly salaries.

35. *Patrón* doesn't translate well. According to the dictionary, in English it can be "patron," "landlord," "master," or "boss," but it is larger than all those words.

36. On 11 July 1988, U.S. Ambassador Richard Melton and six other embassy employees were expelled from Nicaragua. In turn, the United States expelled Nicaraguan Ambassador Carlos Tunnerman and six employees. In both the *Barricada Internacional* (14 July 1988) of Nicaragua and *El País Internacional* (18 July 1988) of Spain there is mention of Melton's meeting with opposition employers in Estelí on 3 July as one of the catalysts leading to his expulsion. I don't know if the Estelí stockbreeders were part of the opposition employers, but they certainly could have been.

37. *Pájaro Negro* (Black Bird) is the name the Nicaraguans have given to the supersonic spy plane that belongs to the United States and flies over Nicaragua. It breaks the sound barrier and causes a sonic boom. When it first happened, terrified Nicaraguans thought an attack was underway on the part of the United States.

38. At this point, Omar updated me on Irene's three sisters, who lived with Omar and Irene for many years. In 1987, one was working in the army. Another had received her degree from the university in León, had two children, and was in Quilalí with her husband. The third one had left Omar's home about four years ago at the age of fourteen or fifteen to go to Managua with her married uncle who was thirty-two, or as Omar said, twice her age. The uncle, the uncle's wife, and Irene's sister all live in the same house. The wife takes care of the children and Irene's sister sleeps with the husband—her uncle. They live normally, according to Omar, and have no disagreements, but Omar still thinks it was foolish. He said it was shameless and showed a lack of self-respect, a lack of respect for women in general, and in particular, a lack of respect for the dead woman who was the mother of the girl and the sister of the uncle. According to Omar, Irene has another sister whose daughter was raped by her own father. He was put in jail for his crime.

39. Omar's youngest daughter has the same name as his first wife (Dora).

40. The Spanish is better: "*Es un tipo jodido vulgar.*"

41. According to Nicaraguan sources, *pata de gallina* is a three-legged stool, like the foot of a chicken, which is the literal meaning of the expression.

42. Alvaro Baltodano Cantarero is the "son of wealthy businessman Emilio Baltodano Pallais. Joined FSLN with Luis Carrión and Joaquín Cuadra through the Christian MCR in 1973. Trained by Oscar Turcios. A leader of the Tercerista attack on Masaya in October 1977. Involved in the State Security shooting of Jorge Salazar in November 1980. Serves as an EPS Commander on the northern frontier." See David Nolan, *The Ideology of the Sandinistas and the Nicaraguan Revolution* (Coral Gables, Fla.: Institute of Interamerican Studies, University of Miami Press, 1984), 138.

43. Fiscalía del Estado.

44. The acronym is FDN, which stands for Fuerza Democrática Nicaragüense (Nicaraguan Democratic Force), commonly called the *contras*.

45. It is difficult to know if Omar means "only son" or "only child": "*Si es el único hijo de la familia, lo deja.*"

46. The grandmother's daughter, Omar's mother, was close to seventy.

47. Literally, "*Amaneció muerto.*" It could be translated as "He turned up dead," or "He woke up dead."

48. A folding screen might be used to create a room or provide privacy around a bed.

Epilogue

1. In June 1988 the government made another adjustment in the exchange rate. On August 30, the government "decreed wage increases of 140 percent for government workers and [declared] a 125 percent devaluation of the córdoba . . . the third major adjustment of economic variables this year." The córdoba stabilized at 400 to the dollar on the black market, and the official rate was 180 to the dollar, according to David R. Dye in the article "For the Sandinistas, the 'Year of Stabilization' Could Be the Year of Living Dangerously," *In These Times,* 21-27 Sept. 1988, 9. Those figures were corroborated by *Barricada Internacional,* the official Sandinista newspaper, in an article by Richard Stahler of the Centro Regional de Investigaciones Económicas y Sociales (CRIES), "La economía sobre el tapete," 8 September 1988, 6-7.

2. To buy a refrigerator in 1988, they would have had to buy it in Costa Rica and with dollars.

3. Leticia described the woman as "an old black woman who was very brown."

GLOSSARY

abuela   Grandmother.

aguinaldo   Christmas bonus.

aindiada   Indianlike.

aldea   Little village; hamlet.

amaneció muerto   Idiomatic expression meaning "He turned up dead" or, literally, "He woke up dead."

amiguismo   The term for a person's getting promoted or helped by using friendships.

arroba   A quarter of a *quintal*, or twenty-five pounds.

asentamiento   Settlement, usually in the countryside, built for those displaced by war.

asiento   Chair.

atol   A drink made from corn flour.

Barricada   Official Sandinista newspaper.

cabrón   Cuckold.

cachorro   The young people who compose a special fighting battalion and actively continue to fight the contras are called *cachorros*; literally, "cubs."

casa de novio   A place to buy wedding clothes.

casa de protocolo   Protocol house.

centavo   A penny (¹/₁₀₀th of a córdoba).

Centro de Belleza   Beauty Center.

Centro Dermatológico   Dermatological Center.

charrasca   Pork crackling.

chayote or *chaya*   A small pear-shaped squash.

chicha   Corn liquor.

chicha rosada   Rose-colored corn liquor.

chicharrón   Pork crackling.

chiltomá   A sweet green pepper.

chorizo   A sausage seasoned with peppers.

comal   Earthenware dish used to make and bake tortillas, similar to a griddle.

comedería   Inexpensive eatery, usually located in an open-air market.

comunidad   A community of few homes that are spaced farther apart than in the usual village.

córdoba   Unit of Nicaraguan currency.

cuajada   A salty, white, curdled cheese.

cursillo   Religious group that discusses how the Bible is reflected in the members' lives. The members take actions to help the needy in the community.

doña   A title of respect used before a woman's first name.

elote   Ear of green corn.

entre la espada y la pared   Part of a Spanish expression for "between a rock and a hard place." It would literally translate as "between the sword and the wall."

Es un tipo jodido vulgar   He is an earthy guy.

Escuela de Belleza   Beauty school.

Esteliano   Person from Estelí.

expendio   Short form of *expendio de comida*.

expendio de comida   Government-controlled store where people can use their ration cards to buy rice, beans, and so forth.

Frente   Front (Sandinista).

Frente Sandinista   Sandinista Front.

galerón   A building similar to a carport in this context.

gallo pinto   A Central American dish made of rice and beans.

gritería   A celebration during which Nicaraguans go from house to house proclaiming the Immaculate Conception of the Virgin.

guaro   Liquor.

guineo   Similar to a banana.

gusano   Worm; used here to describe people who left Cuba after 1959 revolution.

hielera   Place where ice is made.

hijo de puta   Son of a bitch.

insurrección   Uprising.

jícaro   Calabash tree.

jocote   A Spanish plum.

joder   To screw (and similar words).

jornada One day's work, often done to harvest a certain crop or raise money for a specific cause.

junco A vine, rush, or reed.

La Prensa Newspaper that opposed Somoza and now opposes the Sandinistas.

La Purísima Feast of the Immaculate Conception.

La Trinidad Can mean the town a few miles south of Estelí or the hospital in the town.

machismo An exaggerated sense of masculinity stressing such attributes as courage, virility, and domination of women.

machista Adjective implying that one has a macho attitude.

manta a banner, thinner than a blanket and thicker than a sheet.

mestiza Of both Indian and white ancestry.

militancia An honor in the Frente Sandinista earned by outstanding participation.

mondongo Soup made of tripe. Popular on Mondays to ease hangovers.

nancites A tropical fruit that grows between July and August.

negra Term of affection widely used in Latin America, especially in Caribbean countries.

No hay mal que dure cien años ni cuerpo que lo resista Latin American expression that translates as: "*No evil lasts 100 years, nor a body to bear it.*" (Many other translations are possible.)

novenario Novenary.

novio or novia Boyfriend or girlfriend.

ocote Species of pine.

oficialia Taking turns standing watch in the business district.

oreja Literally, "ear," but in Nicaragua it means "spy."

Pájaro Negro "Black Bird" literally, but it refers to a U.S. spy plane.

pata de gallina A three-legged stool, like the foot of a chicken.

patrón Can mean boss, landlord, master.

pensión Place that provides board and lodging, similar to a boarding house.

piñata Container full of sweets which is broken with sticks on the first Sunday of Lent.

pipián Squash.

pitaya or pitahaya Cactus or a small, round, yellow fruit from the cactus plant.

planillero   The person who has control over workers, their pay, and their schedule.

portón   A big door.

posta   A cheap cut of meat.

querida   The other woman, sweetheart.

quintal   100 pounds.

quiquisque   A smooth, colored yucca.

rojo y negro   Red and black, the Sandinista colors. Also a term used by Marta to refer to the Sundays when she and other women volunteered to plant or pull up beans or work in the tobacco fields.

rosquillas   A doughnut made with corn flour; sometimes has honey in the center.

Sandinista   Adjective or noun. *See* Sandino.

Sandino, Augusto César   The man from whom the Sandinistas take their name and their spirit.

sarta   Threading of tobacco leaves.

Segoviano   Person from Segovia, the region where Estelí is located.

señor   Man, but said with a little more respect.

silla   Chair.

solar   An indoor-outdoor room that serves as a kitchen, garden, and chicken coop.

Somocista   Adjective or noun based on the Somoza name.

tabacalera   Tobacco factory or company.

taburete   Stool.

tamal   Minced meat and red peppers wrapped in cornhusks or banana leaves.

tapesco   A rough bed made of wood.

testimonio vivo   Live or living testimony.

tijera   A canvas bed on poles that can be folded.

tiqui   Spanish onomatopoeia for the sound made by a baby fox as it walks in the mountains; also the sound used to call chickens or small animals.

ventecita   A little place where small items are sold. Could be nothing more than vegetables on a table.

vigorón   Typical dish made of pork crackling, yucca, and salad.

zancudo   Mosquito or sand fly.